The Complete Idiot's Guide to Baking
Reference Card

Common Equivalent Measures

Dash/Pinch	2 or 3 drops (liquid) or less than $\frac{1}{8}$ teaspoon (dry)
1 tablespoon	3 teaspoons or $\frac{1}{2}$ ounce
2 tablespoons	1 fluid ounce or $\frac{1}{8}$ cup
$\frac{1}{4}$ cup	4 tablespoons or 2 fluid ounces
$\frac{1}{3}$ cup	5 tablespoons plus 1 teaspoon
$\frac{1}{2}$ cup	8 tablespoons or 4 fluid ounces
$\frac{3}{4}$ cup	12 tablespoons or 6 fluid ounces
1 cup	16 tablespoons or 8 fluid ounces
1 pint	2 cups or 16 fluid ounces
1 quart	4 cups or 2 pints or 32 fluid ounces
1 gallon	4 quarts or 8 pints or 16 cups or 64 fluid ounces
1 pound	16 ounces

Substitutions

Instead of:	Use:
1 cup cake flour	1 cup minus 2 tablespoons all-purpose flour.
1 cup all-purpose flour	1 cup plus 2 tablespoons cake flour.
1 cup self-rising flour	1 cup all-purpose flour plus $\frac{1}{2}$ teaspoon baking powder and $\frac{1}{2}$ teaspoon salt.
1 cup granulated sugar	1 cup brown sugar or 2 cups confectioners' sugar.
$\frac{1}{2}$ cup brown sugar	$\frac{1}{2}$ cup granulated sugar plus 2 tablespoons molasses.
1 package active dry yeast	1 cake compressed fresh yeast.
1 square unsweetened chocolate	3 tablespoons unsweetened cocoa powder plus 1 tablespoon vegetable oil or butter.
1 cup buttermilk	1 cup whole milk plus 1 tablespoon white vinegar or lemon juice. Stir and let stand two minutes. Or, use 1 cup plain yogurt or sour cream.
1 cup plain yogurt	1 cup sour cream.
1 cup whole milk	$\frac{1}{2}$ cup evaporated milk plus $\frac{1}{2}$ cup water. Or, use dry milk and follow the package instructions to reconstitute the amount you need.
1 cup raisins	1 cup currants or other dried fruits such as cranberries, blueberries, or cherries.
1 tablespoon cornstarch	2 tablespoons flour (for thickening purposes).
1 cup corn syrup	1 cup sugar plus $\frac{1}{4}$ cup water.
1 cup honey	$1\frac{1}{4}$ cup granulated sugar + $\frac{1}{4}$ cup liquid.
1 tablespoon fresh lemon juice	1 tablespoon bottled lemon juice or 1 tablespoon distilled vinegar (do not use the vinegar if you want the lemon flavor, but it's good for making water acidic or souring milk).

tear here

alpha books

Common Food Equivalents

Almonds	1 pound	3 cups whole, 4 cups slivered
Apples	1 pound	3 medium, 2¾ cups sliced
Apricots, dried	1 pound	2¾ cups, 5½ cups cooked
Bananas, fresh	1 pound	3 to 4; 1¾ cups mashed, 2 cups sliced
Blueberries, fresh	1 pint	2 cups
Blueberries, frozen	10 ounces	1½ cups
Butter	1 pound	2 cups
Butter	1 stick	8 tablespoons, ½ cup
Cherries, fresh	1 pound	2½ to 3 cups pitted
Chocolate wafers	18 wafers	1 cup crumbs
Chocolate chips	6 ounces	1 cup
Cranberries	1 pound	3 cups
Cream (sour, half-and-half, light)	½ pint	1 cup
Cream (heavy)	½ pint	2 cups whipped
Flour, all-purpose	1 pound	3 cups sifted
Flour, cake	1 pound	4½ to 5 cups sifted
Graham crackers	15	1 cup crumbs
Lemons	1 medium	3 tablespoons juice, 2 to 3 teaspoons zest
Maple syrup	16 fluid ounces	2 cups
Milk, whole	1 quart	4 cups
Oats, rolled	1 pound	5 cups
Oil	1 quart	5 cups
Peaches, fresh	1 pound	4 medium, 2½ cups chopped
Peaches, frozen	10 ounces	1⅛ cups slices and juice
Pumpkin, fresh	1 pound	1 cup cooked and mashed
Raspberries	1 pint	scant 1½ cups
Shortening	1 pound	2 cups
Strawberries	1 pint	2½ cups sliced
Sugar, brown	1 pound	2¼ cups packed
Sugar, confectioners'	1 pound	3½ to 4 cups
Sugar, granulated	1 pound	2 cups
Vanilla wafers	22 wafers	1 cup crumbs
Walnuts	1 pound	3¾ cups halves, 3½ cups chopped
Yeast	¼-ounce package	1 scant tablespoon

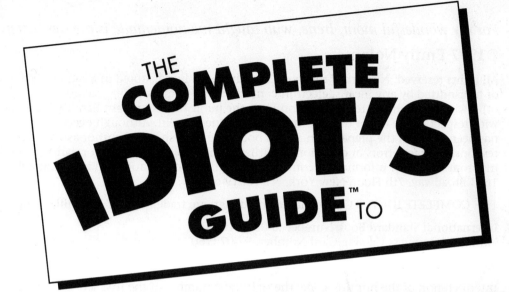

THE COMPLETE IDIOT'S GUIDE TO

Baking

by Emily Nolan

alpha books

A Division of Macmillan General Reference
A Simon & Schuster Macmillan Company
1633 Broadway, New York, NY 10019

For my wonderful mom, Irene, who taught me homemade is always better.

©1997 Emily Nolan

THE COMPLETE IDIOT'S GUIDE name and design are trademarks of Macmillan, Inc.

International Standard Book Number: 0-02-861954-4
Library of Congress Catalog Card Number: 97-073160

99 98 97   8 7 6 5 4 3 2 1

Interpretation of the printing code: the rightmost number of the first series of numbers is the year of the book's printing; the rightmost number of the second series of numbers is the number of the book's printing. For example, a printing code of 97-1 shows that the first printing occurred in 1997.

Printed in the United States of America

Brand Manager
Kathy Nebenhaus

Executive Director
Gary M. Krebs

Managing Editor
Bob Shuman

Senior Editor
Nancy Mikhail

Development Editor
Gretchen Henderson

Production/Copy Editor
Lynn Northrup

Editorial Assistant
Maureen Horn

Cover Designer
Michael Freeland

Cartoonist
Judd Winick

Illustrator
Krissy Krygiel

Designer
Glenn Larsen

Indexer
Nadia Ibrahim

Production Team
Angela Calvert, Cindy Fields, Tricia Flodder, Laure Robinson

Contents at a Glance

Contents

25 Quick Breads and Muffins 275

26 Yeast Breads 287

Foreword

Welcome to the delicious world of baking! When I began learning about baking, as I certainly wasn't born with a silver whisk in my hand, I was spurred on by my sweet tooth to figure out the whys and wherefores that made everything turn out magically. As a beginning home baker, I learned through trial and error how to make all sorts of baked goods better and better.

Of course, baking is not really magic—a few rules and reactions make up the craft. I understand how intimidating baking can seem, since it is a science as well as an art. A chicken essentially looks the same before and after it's cooked. The baker, however, begins with flour, eggs, sugar, and other ingredients that get mixed together to produce many different results.

I recommend starting with the simplest recipes. This helps you learn why certain methods or ingredients produce the results they do, and how each recipe comes together to form the luscious whole. I began with lemon bars, for instance. I used the freshest possible ingredients—pure, just-squeezed lemon juice, unsalted butter, flour, sugar, and eggs, and followed the recipe word for word. I always recommend doing exactly what a recipe states at least once; when you make it again, you can then vary one step or ingredient, but only one at a time.

Don't rush yourself, but set aside some time as you begin to bake. Measure carefully, check the oven's temperature, and use the equipment called for in the recipe. Don't get caught up in worrying about fancy mixers, machines, or gadgets. Remember that bakers worked for hundreds of years without those items, and you can too. Bake what intrigues you, so that you'll be excited, and expand your sweet horizons. The best thing to remember is that you can always eat your mistakes.

The recipes in this book are geared toward successful baking. Build on your successes, and you'll gain the confidence to try other recipes. Many baked goods that you can buy commercially taste better when home baked, if only because they are fresher and infused with the pride of you, the baker. It's a grand feeling of accomplishment to learn how to do something you have not done before. Baking is an exciting, satisfying activity, and the more you learn and do, the better you'll become. I am always happy to introduce newcomers to the kitchen, and I know that you'll be happy baking scrumptious cookies, breads, pies, and muffins for family and friends.

Flo Braker
Author of *The Simple Art of Perfect Baking* and *Sweet Miniatures,* and past president of IACP

Introduction

The purpose of this book is to teach you how to become a proficient and independent baker. You may feel like you know nothing now, but when you finish reading this book, you'll be competent in the kitchen and you'll know that baking skills are something you can easily learn. *The Complete Idiot's Guide to Baking* will acquaint you with familiar, as well as unfamiliar, ingredients, and also teach you things you may not know, such as the secret to flaky pastry crusts and how to zest a lemon. From organizing your kitchen to be an efficient workspace to storing your baked goods properly, you'll have the tools you need to become a successful baker.

But you mustn't forget the most important ingredient when you go into the kitchen to exercise your talents, and that is to be sure to bake with love. Whether the inspiration for baking is remembering a birthday, making a sweet treat for the family, bringing dessert for a dinner party, or welcoming a new neighbor or co-worker, you can certainly taste the difference when it's baked with love—you're saying the person is important enough to you that you take the time to do something special!

Before You Get Started

Prior to getting up to your elbows in batter, I recommend you read *The Complete Idiot's Guide to Baking* from cover to cover. From getting started to putting the finishing touches on your baked item, there's a lot you'll learn and you should be aware of the different steps involved. Be honest when you look around your kitchen and assess what you and your workspace are capable of doing. Remember, practice makes perfect, so the more familiar you become with baking and handling your ingredients, the more proficient you'll become as a baker. Don't go overboard the first couple of times you try baking. Start off with easier recipes involving just a couple of ingredients and build from there. Rome was not built in a day, and neither will your baking skills be.

Before you get started, it's important to acquaint yourself with the hows and whys of baking. What are the roles of each of your ingredients? By understanding each individual ingredient, you'll be able to understand *how to bake* instead of *how to follow a recipe* (there's a big difference). When you understand how to bake and learn the various techniques to make you successful, you'll gain confidence in the kitchen and become a proficient baker.

Technique is not just how flawless a frosted cake looks or how beautiful a pie crust appears, but how to measure and mix ingredients. *The Complete Idiot's Guide to Baking* explains to you the various techniques for all kinds of baking situations. And with good technique, the sky's the limit. So, roll up your sleeves, clean off the countertop, and get ready to start baking!

What You'll Find in this Book

Part 1, "Baking Basics," discusses the pros of baking homemade goodies. You'll learn how to get organized in the kitchen by preparing a pantry list, how to store what you have, what to keep in the refrigerator, and what you can keep on hand in the freezer. You'll also get a complete rundown of the pots, pans, and appliances most commonly used in baking.

Part 2, "The Lingo," familiarizes you with the most common baking terms and techniques. It gives you the vocabulary to feel comfortable with reading recipes and instructions. I also review many of the kitchen gadgets you can use and explain their roles. You'll also find a complete breakdown of basic ingredients used in baking and learn how they work together.

Part 3, "Getting Down to the Nitty-Gritty," gets into the mechanics of baking. I review the role of the oven, how it works, and what to look out for. I also give advice on what to look for when you're reading a recipe and tips on what to look for to avoid any problems, as well as tips on how to measure various ingredients. There's also a chapter that explains basic techniques you'll need to know for some of these recipes, such as separating eggs and whipping egg whites.

Part 4, "Now You're Baking!" breaks down the different types of baked goods you can create, from cakes and cookies to pies and yeast breads. It explains in detail what makes each different, gives tips on how to get the most out of what you want to bake, and explains the various roles of common ingredients in each different category. You'll obtain a well-rounded understanding of each category of baked items in this section.

Part 5, "Um, I Have a Question," discusses many common occurrences while you are in the process of baking. There's a chapter about the most common problems encountered in the kitchen and what to do in case you meet them. There are also many suggestions for what to prepare for special occasions and how to present your baked goods. You'll find serving suggestions, tips on flavorful creams, and even how to make great teas and coffees to serve with your treats. There are storage suggestions for when you have a few leftovers you want to keep fresh. You'll also find a whole chapter full of helpful tips, such as advice on stains, first aid in the kitchen, food safety advice, and high-altitude adjustments.

Part 6, "The Recipes," is a collection of basic recipes (you'll find many favorites here) that have been kitchen-tested and family-approved. They all have prep and bake times, so you'll have an idea of how much time it will take you to make something, plus there's a level given to each recipe. The "easy" recipes require little technique and are mostly a matter of mixing ingredients and baking. "Intermediate" recipes add a new technique or two or might use unusual ingredients. "Challenging" recipes encourage you to try a new technique, but the recipes are still fairly basic.

By the time you finish reading the book, you should have a good foundation on the principles of baking and, with practice, will become a successful baker.

Extras

You'll notice the following sidebars throughout this book. They highlight certain points I want to be sure you catch.

Kitchen Utensil
These boxes lend a little extra advice that will make baking a bit easier.

Kitchen Informant
Check these boxes for definitions of important terms.

Bakers Beware!
Look in these boxes for warnings of what not to do or things to watch out for to prevent mistakes from happening.

Information Station
These boxes give you some extra information or little-known facts.

Special Thanks from the Publisher to the Technical Editor

The Complete Idiot's Guide to Baking was reviewed by an expert who not only checked the technical accuracy of what you'll learn in this book, but also provided invaluable insight and suggestions. Our special thanks are extended to Deborah Callan.

Deborah Callan has turned a life-long passion for home-cooked foods and a culinary history into a multifaceted career. Where once graphic, apparel, and textile design were her creative outlets, she now develops and tests recipes and freelances as a private chef and caterer. Ms. Callan fondly recounts time spent as a cooking school assistant with professional and celebrity chefs, observing the depth and range of technique, style, and personality within the kitchen.

Acknowledgments

A very big round of applause goes to the following people for making this book happen: Nancy Mikhail, Senior Editor, for her time and support. Gretchen Henderson, Development Editor, for all of her time, patience, and help getting and keeping me organized. Lynn Northrup, Production/Copy Editor, for her hard work, good questions and suggestions, and keeping me well on track. Krissy Krygiel, the illustrator, who drew like a mad woman under a tight schedule for this project and continues to inspire the masses to draw slotted spoons and spatulas. Agnes Nolan, my grandmother, who passed on her many wonderful family recipes for me to use (I love you!). Kathleen Nolan, my sister, who was another great source for family recipes and recipe testing, plus all that sisterly support. Kevin (for your tech support) and Carol Nolan, Jesse Dengate, Carrie Schoen, Anita Dickhuth, and Martha McCoy who also shared with me their family recipes when I cried "I need easy recipes!" and for testing them out, too. And to Jeff Baker, whose kind words of encouragement, never-ending patience, and willingness to do all the weekend chores for about three months, enabled me to get all my work done. I could not have done it without you.

Trademarks

Part 1
Baking Basics

There comes a time in many people's lives when the mystery of baking unfolds. The desire to create becomes stronger than the desire to pick up a pack of cookies at the store, and you think: Hey, I'm a smart person, I can do this! And you can. But before you get up to your elbows in batter, there are some fundamentals you should know. This section covers the very basics in baking, discussing what to keep in the pantry and the gear you'll need when you step into the kitchen to create.

A well-laid foundation makes it easy for bakers to build their skills, so you'll also learn all about ingredients and how to store them properly so you'll be assured that your ingredients will have a good shelf life and be fresh when you want to use them.

Successful Baking

So, you've decided you want to learn how to bake? Congratulations! Perhaps you have tinkered in the kitchen but feel uncertain about what you're doing, or maybe your attempts at creating something in the oven have not been very successful. Or perhaps you just have some general questions about baking. Reading this book is a good start for answering the fundamental questions that arise when you want to bake. Soon you'll be well on your way to becoming a better baker!

Answering Your Call to Bake

Baking really is a lot of fun when you feel comfortable in the kitchen and at ease with what you are making. Unfortunately, baking can also be a source of great anxiety and frustration when you're not sure what you're doing or feel like the ingredients are staging a rebellion against you. But it's time to calm the troops. You've chosen the right book to get started!

Baking differs dramatically from other forms of cooking. It involves a kind of magic. From mixing up batters to working bread doughs firmly but gently to watching your dough rise, baking brings a spectacular feeling. Other forms of cooking are more about sustenance—feeding hunger. But baking is something special. It's both an art and a science. And the science really does count—instructions and ingredients work together to create delicious results. Wondrous aromas will waft from your kitchen, filling your home with flavors and sweet memories to come.

Baking is rewarding in many ways. First and most basic, it allows you to feed yourself and provides you with the ability to choose what you eat. You can give up the ammonium alginate, disodium guanylate, and guar gum you find in cake mixes. Your breads will no longer be preserved with sodium propionate. And your pies will be heptylparaben-free. Welcome to the world of butter, sugar, flour, and vanilla.

There's also something deeply satisfying about taking those basic ingredients and turning them into something everyone loves, like cakes and cookies. Freshly baked treats say to the people you share them with: "You are special to me." And the recipient feels special because you took the time to create something for them. Welcome a new neighbor with fresh bread, surprise your office workers with a crumbcake for coffee break, or treat your children to homemade cookies.

Baking is a way to enjoy the simple pleasures of life. An afternoon spent in the kitchen baking bread or making cookies to pack in lunches for the rest of the week is a nice gift to give yourself or your family. Mixing up a batch of cookies with your children, room-mates, or loved ones is a great activity that doesn't cost a lot of money and that will give you lasting memories.

If baking is so great, then why does it seem like it's so hard? Did you ever get a chance to learn the basics? How many bad experiences have you had in the kitchen with burnt cookies or dry cakes? Now is the time to forget all that you don't know (and perhaps your past kitchen disasters) and look toward a new horizon. You are about to equip yourself with the knowledge of how to bake.

Where to Get Started

Sometimes it's hard to know where to get started when it comes to learning something new. This book is a good start. Take the time now to read it from cover to cover. If you just skip and skim chapters, you might be leaving yourself with big gaps in your culinary education, which might lead to harder times in the future. It's important not only to familiarize yourself with *what* you are baking, but also *how* to bake. Knowing how to bake is not just knowing how to read a recipe and follow the instructions. Learn how ingredients interact with one another. Have an idea of what will happen when you combine certain things. Be familiar with the variety of ingredients available. When you equip yourself with this knowledge, you will discover how easy and fun baking can be!

Preparing Your Kitchen for Use

One of the best things to do when you're getting ready to begin baking is to look around your kitchen, because that's where all your baking will be taking place. If you don't spend a lot of time there, take stock of the equipment you have. Take a peek in the oven. Does it need to be cleaned? When was the last time you used your oven for baking? (I know a woman who lived in her apartment for six years and never once used the oven.)

Look around your kitchen. Do you have a lot of counter space or just a little? Do you have a lot of cabinet space? I have very little counter and cabinet space in my kitchen, so I have organized things to hang on the walls just about everywhere I can. A utensil or pot or pan is within reach from almost anywhere I stand in the kitchen, and that simplifies my baking time immensely. Think about what you use, and as you read through this book, keep in mind what you might need to make your kitchen efficient and bring it up to speed.

Counter space is the hottest real estate in the kitchen. If you have a lot of things cluttering up your counter (spice racks, napkin holders, paper-towel holders, appliances, etc.) it might be time to reorganize. Take a good look around your kitchen and decide what you can put away and what you want to leave out. If you only make coffee on the weekends, then tuck your coffee maker in a cabinet for more counter space during the week. If you seem to always be searching for utensils, think about organizing your most frequently used utensils in a can or small crock that you can keep on the counter.

Bakers Beware!
Never store your knives with any other utensils. If you reach for a spoon, you could easily cut yourself on the knife's sharp blade.

Take a look in your cabinets. Do you have a lot of half-used bags of flour? Half-used boxes of brown sugar that are now rock-hard? Store-bought cookies you forgot about? You should clean out your cabinets at least twice a year, once in the spring and once in the fall, to get rid of forgotten treasures and to prevent any sort of insect infestation.

Take the time now to organize things so later you will not be looking for all the parts of the food processor or the bottom plate to your springform pan. Feeling comfortable in your own kitchen is a huge help in feeling comfortable with baking.

Kitchen Utensil
Three-tiered hanging baskets are a huge space saver in the kitchen. They are inexpensive and have literally hundreds of uses, not all of them food-related. Use them to store plastic container lids, spice jars, scraps of paper, loose pens and pencils, recipes, and so on.

Thoughts and Ideas for Recipe Selection

To become better at baking, the best advice I can give you is to practice, practice, practice. If you're unfamiliar with baking, choose a recipe that's labeled "Easy" and that doesn't have a lot of ingredients. (Check out the recipes labeled "Easy" in Part 6 of this book.) Practice beating butter and cream together. Get used to mixing, measuring, scooping, and timing. Once you master that, try recipes that have a longer list of ingredients. Then move on to the intermediate recipes, which might include a slightly more difficult technique, such as whipping egg whites. When you feel comfortable with these techniques, move on to the most challenging recipes, like baking bread (which really is not that hard) or making homemade double-crust pies. (Chapter 12 gives you the lowdown on the different crusts you can make.) There's is a lot you can do with baking, and now is the time to get started.

> **Information Station**
>
> The kitchen can be a dangerous place for papers, recipes, and even books. A cookbook can get into a lot of trouble on a kitchen countertop. Place your cookbook in a convenient place, but not in direct line of fire of ingredients, especially liquids, and *never* place books or paper near stovetops where they could catch on fire. Read the recipe several times before you start, then place the book a few steps away from where the action is. Recipe notecards can be taped onto cabinets, at eye level, so they'll always be in view but not in harm's way.

The Least You Need to Know

➤ The best way to get comfortable with baking is with practice, practice, and more practice.

➤ Take time now to get your kitchen organized so you feel comfortable in it.

➤ Don't overchallenge yourself when you first set out to bake. Choose easy recipes with few ingredients.

➤ Move on to more complicated recipes with techniques that are unfamiliar to you when you feel confident at your present level.

A Well-Stocked Pantry

A well-stocked pantry really makes a difference when it comes to baking. It's a huge time-saver because it eliminates repeat trips to the grocery store, it allows you to create delicious treats whenever the mood strikes, and if you happen to run out of one ingredient, you're more likely to have a substitute on hand. In this chapter you will discover the ingredients for a well-stocked pantry and how to store your ingredients so they will have the longest shelf life possible.

A Look in the Larder

You don't need a lot of room to have a good pantry, but you do need to be organized and store your ingredients well to maximize space and the shelf life of your ingredients. The following sections list the staples you should have on hand when you begin baking. Of course, you don't have to purchase everything all at once, but you might be surprised at how quickly you will build your pantry and how much easier baking will be when you have a well-stocked kitchen.

Bakers Beware!
Be smart when you shop. Price clubs and other huge retail discount stores may seem like a great bargain at the time, but if you buy too much and it spoils before you use it up, then it's no bargain at all. Remember, spices and baking powder will loose their oomph after a while, so you are better off purchasing smaller quantities of these to be sure to use them up.

Kitchen Utensil
Baking soda is great for removing coffee stains from metal pots or ceramic mugs. Just sprinkle a tablespoon or two inside the pot, rub with a dishcloth, and watch the stain disappear. It's also essential for destroying odors and keeping your refrigerator and freezer fresh. Keep a box near the stove in case of grease fires. I like to have a box in the bathroom to add to my bath after a day of baking in the kitchen—it softens my skin and keeps me smelling fresh!

Be a smart shopper when you're stocking up. Look for items on sale at the local grocery store. If space is not an issue, buy two or three of a popular item (my theory is you can never have enough baking soda). Also, take a look in discount stores and those ever-popular dollar stores. Recently, I found nonstick cooking spray at the dollar store—a great deal since it can cost double or triple that amount in my local grocery store. You might be surprised at how inexpensively you can stock your pantry when you shop around.

Stocking up on Pantry (Dry Goods) Staples

Your dry pantry can be in cabinets, on shelves, in a cupboard, or in a designated pantry/closet. Make sure you keep the floor clean and remove everything and wipe down the shelves at least twice a year (spring and fall). And, of course, clean up right away if you spill anything to avoid any sort of animal or insect infestation.

Baking Powder

Baking powder usually comes in small, round, sturdy containers with airtight lids. It's essential for cakes, cookies, muffins, and quick breads, where it acts as the leavening agent. Choose double-acting baking powder, which is the most readily available. Baking powder can be stored in its own container, but if your baking powder has been sitting around for several months, be sure to test for its potency. Dissolve 1 teaspoon in $1/4$ cup of hot water. If it does not foam within a few seconds, it's time to get a new container.

Baking Soda

Baking soda, when mixed with an acidic ingredient such as sour milk, buttermilk, yogurt, or citrus, acts as a leavening agent for cookies, cakes, and muffins. But baking soda also has many other uses in and around the kitchen, so it's always a good idea to keep a couple of boxes on hand.

Storing baking soda in its box is okay. If it gets moist, it will harden, making it difficult to use (it will clump up and you will have to dissolve the whole clump). You can also transfer the baking soda to an airtight container (be sure to label it!) if you rarely use it, but since it has so many wonderful uses, this is probably not necessary.

Chocolate

Baking chocolate usually comes in individually wrapped 1-ounce squares (usually in 8-ounce boxes). There are many varieties of chocolate available: unsweetened, semisweet, and sweet (German, dark, or milk). Always use the variety called for in a recipe. Do not substitute one type of chocolate for another. Also, each brand of chocolate tastes a little bit different from the others, so experiment to find a brand you like. Stay away from artificial or imitation chocolate. White chocolate (or vanilla chocolate) is not true chocolate because it does not have chocolate liquor in it.

Store chocolate in a cool, dark place (do not refrigerate). When chocolate is exposed to air for a long period of time or the temperature fluctuates a lot, chocolate will "bloom," meaning it will have a whitish haze or may become crumbly. This is not an indication that it has spoiled, but only that the cocoa butter has separated out, and it still can be successfully used in baking. Chocolate has a long shelf life when stored properly—up to one year.

Cocoa Powder

Cocoa powder is ground unsweetened chocolate (not to be confused with the cocoa you mix with hot water or milk to drink, which has sugar and milk solids added) and is used often in baking cakes, cookies, and brownies. Cocoa powder comes in tins with fitted lids. If you run out of unsweetened chocolate, you can mix 3 tablespoons of cocoa powder with 1 tablespoon of vegetable oil or shortening to equal 1 ounce unsweetened chocolate.

Coconut

Sweetened or unsweetened coconut is great for decorating cakes and cookies and is the essential ingredient for coconut-cream pies and meringue cookies. You can usually find coconut in 12-ounce bags with other baking supplies in the grocery store. Store it in an airtight container or sealable bag. You can refrigerate or freeze coconut if you don't use it very often. Make sure you read the package carefully when buying coconut; both sweetened and unsweetened are available and you want to be sure you are buying the right one for the recipe.

Cornmeal

I am a huge fan of cornbreads and spoonbread. Cornmeal is also great for keeping pizza crusts from sticking to the baking sheet, so I always keep some on hand. Cornmeal can be white, yellow, and even blue—the availability and your preference will probably depend on where you live. Always store cornmeal as you would flour: in an airtight container in a cool, dark place.

Cornstarch

Sometimes cornstarch is used in baking to thicken the juices in pies. It's also used to thicken gravies and sauces. Cornstarch will keep forever; just make sure you store it in an airtight container in a cool, dry place.

Cream of Tartar

Cream of tartar is sold with all the other spices in the supermarket. Use it in baking to stabilize egg whites. It's also good to have on hand to mix with baking soda, in case you run out of baking powder.

Decorative Frostings

Tubes of different colors of decorative gels or frostings make it easy to add spur-of-the-moment decorations to cakes and cookies. They keep forever and are always ready to turn the ordinary into something extra-ordinary.

Dried Beans

Dried beans may seem like a strange thing to keep in the kitchen for baking, but they act as inexpensive pie weights when you are baking a pie crust without a filling. Store the dried beans in a glass jar with a tight-fitting lid and mark them as pie weights. Once beans are used as pie weights, you cannot cook them because the heat of the oven will dry them out too much. However, you can re-use them many times as pie weights. When they start breaking apart because they become so dry, you might want to think about using new beans.

Evaporated Milk and Dry Milk

These are great to have on hand in case you ever run out of fresh milk. Just dilute 50/50 evaporated milk and water and you can substitute it for fresh. For example, if you need a cup of milk, mix together $1/2$ cup evaporated milk and $1/2$ cup water and use in place of the milk. Once you open a can of evaporated milk, it's a good idea to transfer it to a glass or plastic container with a lid. It will keep in the refrigerator for about a week. Dry milk is also an economical choice that can be stored indefinitely. It is homogenized milk with all the liquid taken out. It can be reconstituted with water or another liquid for baking purposes.

Flour

There are several different kinds of flour available for baking; all-purpose, cake, bread, self-rising, and whole-wheat are just a few. Don't store any of your flours in the paper bags you buy them in. Instead, transfer them to airtight canisters and store them in a cool, dry place to make sure your flour will not absorb any odors or off-flavors. Be sure to label and date the containers so that you can remember the different varieties and when you bought them (they tend to look the same out of the bags). If you want, you can also double-bag your flour and store it in the freezer for up to a year. Again, just be sure to label everything. A trick my grandmother uses is to tear off a piece of the bag with the name of the product on it and drop it in the jar. You have to avoid this piece of paper when scooping out flour (not too taxing a chore), but you will never be left wondering what type of flour you have stored, because sometimes homemade labels wear or wash off.

For more about the varieties of flour, see Chapter 5.

Information Station

Flour seems to be the perfect nest for weevils—a moth-like insect that will hatch in your flour and flutter around your kitchen. You can tell if your flour has weevils by just looking at it. If it seems to move, that is the flour shifting into the places where the weevils have been. Placing a few whole bay leaves in the flour will keep weevils from making a home there—apparently they hate the smell of bay leaves. Storing your flour in the freezer will prevent weevil infestation. Proper storage of flour and purchasing your flour from a store that has high turnover (so you know the flour has not been sitting around) will greatly reduce your chances of hatching your own batch of weevils.

Food Coloring

This is great to keep on hand for tinting coconut or frostings and for making colored hard-boiled eggs. Be careful when using food colors—they can stain!

Herbs, Spices, and Extracts

Herbs, spices, and extracts lend a wonderful flavor accent to all baked goods. They should never overwhelm a dish and should be as fresh-tasting as possible. You should buy small amounts of spices to ensure a high turnover in your own cupboard. Be sure you replace your spices once the flavor has dissipated (after about a year). If you buy your spices in bulk (at gourmet shops, baking-supply stores, natural-food stores, and spice shops), this is not a costly thing to do. I always avoid purchasing my spices from the supermarket and discount stores because I find them to be too costly and don't know how long they have been around. Store all your herbs and spices in airtight jars, label them, and keep them in a cool, dry place.

Extracts are the essential oils of foods or plants, unless they are artificially made. They are concentrated flavors, usually in an alcohol base. Choose pure extracts over artificially flavored extracts, even though the pure is more costly. It will make a difference in your final product. Some flavors will only come as imitation, so that's okay; but when it comes to vanilla, always choose pure. Store extracts in a cool, dry place and make sure their caps are screwed on tightly, and they will keep indefinitely.

Kitchen Utensil
If your honey hardens or crystallizes, you can make it liquid again by placing the jar of honey in a pan of hot water for 10 to 20 minutes. You can also try microwaving it in 30-second intervals to liquify it. It will re-crystallize once it cools down again.

Honey

Honey is used in many recipes, especially in breads and muffins. There are many varieties of honey, depending on the flower source of the bees that make it, the most popular being clover, orange blossom, and sage.

Liqueurs and Alcohol

Liqueurs and alcohol (bourbon, rum, brandy, etc.) add a nice flavor to many cakes, pies, and cookies. The alcohol evaporates during cooking, so unless a cake is soaked in the liqueur or it is uncooked, there's not much chance of overindulging. Always choose a good-quality alcohol when baking—the quality will be passed on to your finished product.

Kitchen Utensil
To keep your molasses jar from sticking shut, try rubbing the threads of your jar (the part where the lid screws on to the glass jar) with vegetable oil.

Molasses

Molasses is a strong-flavored syrup that comes from what is left over after granulated sugar has been extracted from sugar cane. It comes in light or dark varieties and is used to make gingerbread and to flavor cakes and muffins. Molasses will keep for a long time and should be stored in tightly closed jars in a cool place.

Nonstick Cooking Spray

I love nonstick cooking spray for one-shot, super-easy greasing action. It's especially great for greasing bundt pans because the molded design makes them difficult to grease by hand. There is also a product called Baker's Joy, which "greases and flours" your baking pans for you.

Oil

Mild-flavored vegetable oils such as corn, canola, or peanut are often called for in quick bread, muffin, and some cake recipes. Oil can also be used to grease baking sheets or pans. You don't have to refrigerate vegetable oils; they will keep indefinitely. The exception is extra-virgin olive oil, which is not generally used for baking. Extra-virgin olive oil should be refrigerated to preserve its delicate flavor. It will also go rancid faster than other more refined oils.

Peanut Butter

Great for peanut butter cookies and peanut butter pie, among other things, peanut butter will store for many months in the cabinet. If you purchase an all-natural brand, you should store it in the refrigerator for a longer life since no preservatives are added to keep it fresher longer. Don't be alarmed if the oil separates from the ground peanuts. This is normal for unprocessed peanut butter—just mix it up and use as normal.

Raisins

Raisins are an essential ingredient for many breads, cookies, quick breads, and muffins. I love to have them on hand to just throw into something that might need a touch of sweetness. There is a baking raisin on the market that doesn't dry out during baking. However, you don't have to buy these baking raisins to have moist raisins. Simply soak the raisins in hot water (try adding a splash of vanilla extract or rum for added flavor) for 30 minutes or so to plump them up. This trick always results in moist, chewy raisins. Raisins are usually sold in boxes or in containers with sealable lids. It's safe to store the raisins in either container. However, if you find your raisins are drying out too much, transfer them to an airtight container.

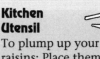

Kitchen Utensil
To plump up your raisins: Place them in a small bowl and add hot water to cover (you can flavor the water with coffee, rum, brandy, or bourbon, if you like). Let the raisins soak for 30 minutes or up to two hours. Drain the raisins and use as directed in the recipe.

Rolled Oats

Rolled oats are essential for oatmeal cookies and any sort of streusel or crumbly pie or cake topping. I also like to make oatmeal bread.

Quick oats generally come in a large cardboard container with a tight-fitting lid, which is fine to keep them in for storage. You can also find oats in the bulk section of many supermarkets. If oats are sold in a plastic bag, do not store them that way; instead, transfer the oats to an airtight container. If you don't use your oats more than a couple times a year, store them in the freezer.

There is a difference between quick-cooking oats and old-fashioned rolled oats. Old-fashioned oats come from oat groats (which are cleaned and hulled whole oats) which have been steamed and rolled flat. They take about 15 minutes to cook on top of the stove. Quick-cooking oats are rolled oats that have been cut into several pieces and generally rolled thinner than old-fashioned oats. When it comes to baking, old-fashioned and quick-cooking oats are interchangeable. However, instant oats are precooked and cannot be used to replace old-fashioned rolled or quick-cooking oats in a recipe.

> ### Information Station
>
> If you have a bulk section in your supermarket or natural-foods store, purchasing ingredients from there is an economical choice. However, you should never store your items in the plastic bags for more than a week. Instead, save your jars and containers! Washed, clean jars or containers from spaghetti sauce, salsa, yogurt, peanut butter, and applesauce make great containers to hold any items you purchase in bulk. Baby-food jars recycle into great spice jars. Don't forget to mark your jars with masking tape and permanent marker (don't use non-permanent marker; it can rub off and you will be left wondering what you put in your jars).

Salt

Salt is invaluable in the kitchen. It not only adds its own flavor, but helps bring out the flavor of other ingredients. When used in baking, it's important to follow the precise amount called for in the recipe. There are three types of salt available for baking: table salt (by far the most popular), kosher salt (has less of a salty taste than table salt), and sea salt (which has a fresher taste and is usually used for salt grinders). All of these salts can be used measure for measure in baking.

Most table salt has an anti-caking agent added to help prevent it from clumping. However, on humid days (especially during the summertime) salt still tends to stick or clump. To prevent this, add about a teaspoon of rice to your salt shaker. The rice will absorb the moisture and keep your salt free-flowing. You never want to add the rice to anything you bake. If you must get the rice out of your salt, sift the salt through a fine-mesh strainer.

Shortening

Solid vegetable shortening comes in cans or in premeasured sticks, can be stored indefinitely, and has a multitude of uses. It has no flavor, making it ideal for greasing cookie sheets or cake pans, and can be used measure for measure for butter in most baking recipes. It is also the secret ingredient for flaky pie crusts; however, butter is often added to the recipe for flavor. Butter-flavored shortenings are also available, which are fine to use in baking and give a small flavor boost, but certainly are not a replacement for real butter. Try them out and see if you like the results.

Sugar

The three varieties of sugar to have on hand are granulated, confectioners', and brown (light or dark). Granulated sugar is the most common sugar called for in baking. Confectioners' sugar (also called powdered sugar) is also used in baking for uncooked frostings and for dusting cakes and cookies. Brown sugar comes in two varieties: light or dark. Light brown sugar is the most common type used in baking, but the more assertively flavored dark brown sugar is also used. Recipes will specify which brown sugar to use when it makes a difference; otherwise you can use whichever you have on hand.

Store all your sugars in an airtight containers in a cool, dry place. For more about sugar, see Chapter 5.

Vinegar

It's always a good idea to have distilled white vinegar on hand in case you have to sour milk—1 tablespoon added to a cup of milk will make 1 cup of buttermilk. Vinegar has many uses for cooking, too.

Kitchen Utensil
Make a list of ingredients you use up while baking. Keep a piece of paper attached to the refrigerator, or if you have a chalkboard or notepad nearby, use it to write them down. Then you can add those ingredients to your next shopping list and lower the risk of being caught short the next time you want to bake.

Refrigerator (Perishables) Staples: Keep 'Em Cool

Unlike the products you find in your pantry, staples that you keep in the refrigerator are far more perishable. Be sure everything you use is fresh and has not picked up any refrigerator odors. If in doubt, always throw it away and buy new ingredients.

Butter/Margarine Sticks

There is nothing like butter, which imparts its own fresh, creamy flavor to baking. Stick margarine can always be substituted in recipes where butter is called for, unless otherwise stated. Always store butter in the refrigerator away from strong odors, and make sure it is well wrapped. When butter goes bad it becomes rancid, which is indicated by a bad odor and taste.

Bakers Beware!
Tub margarines or any "lite" butter or margarine with less than 65 percent fat are not suitable for baking.

Butter will stay fresh in the refrigerator for a few weeks. Butter always freezes well, so you can stock up when it's on sale and freeze it for several months. Remember, butter can be a sponge for odors, so make sure you wrap any butter you will be keeping in the freezer. Think about storing your butter near an open box of baking soda, too.

Eggs

Always buy large, fresh eggs that do not have any cracks. Check the expiration date printed on the carton to make sure your eggs will keep. Also, open the carton you intend to buy and wiggle each egg gently in the container to make sure they are not stuck in the carton. DO NOT store your eggs in the refrigerator door. This is the warmest part of the refrigerator and you want your eggs to be cold. Keep the eggs in the carton or place them in a bowl and store them in the refrigerator. Keep them away from any strong odors. For more about eggs, see Chapter 5.

Jellies and Jams

Jellies and jams make great fillings for cakes and cookies. And what's better spread on a piece of fresh bread? Unopened, you can store all your jams in the pantry. Once opened, keep your jellies refrigerated for up to six months.

Lemons and Oranges

Keep lemons on hand for freshly grated zest (the colored skin, not the white pith underneath) and for their juice. These bright cheery fruits will keep for several weeks in the vegetable crisper. To maximize the amount of juice you can extract from them, roll the whole (uncut) lemon on the counter, pressing down hard on it as you roll, before you cut into it and juice it. If your recipe calls for lemon zest and juice, remember to zest the lemon before you cut it and juice it.

Kitchen Utensil
Believe it or not, it takes quite a bit of syrup to impart maple flavor to baked goods, even frosting, so pick up some maple extract and try that before using your precious syrup, which I like to drizzle over cakes, cookies, and breads.

Maple Syrup

Maple syrup is the boiled sap from the tree. I always use pure maple syrup, but it is quite expensive (unless you live in Maine or Vermont; then it's much cheaper—if you travel or live there, look for it in the grocery stores for the most reasonable price). Keep your maple syrup in the refrigerator after you have opened it. Trust me when I say this—I once lost a whole gallon of pure maple syrup to mold because I did not refrigerate it. It might turn darker in the refrigerator, but it will not affect the flavor.

Milk and Cream

Milk comes as whole, low-fat, and skim. Unless the recipe specifically states it, you can use any variety of milk when baking. Milk will keep in the refrigerator for about a week. Be sure to look for the expiration date printed on the carton when you buy milk. You can always freeze milk if you don't think you'll use it before it expires. One sniff, and you will be able to tell if your milk has soured or not.

Here's a breakdown of the types of cream available:

➤ *Light cream.* Some recipes call for light cream. It is much richer than milk and can substituted for it in many recipes. It is also tasty in coffee. Light cream will not whip up, though.

➤ *Heavy (whipping) cream.* Heavy cream is the richest of all the creams. It is used to make whipped cream and for some cooked frostings. Ultra-pasteurized heavy cream has been sterilized and will keep for several weeks in the refrigerator. Regular heavy cream will keep up to one week.

➤ *Half-and-half.* Half-and-half is just what the name says, half cream and half whole milk. In general, half-and-half can be used in recipes that call for cream. However, half-and-half will not whip up like heavy cream will.

Kitchen Utensil

To whip heavy cream, use a whisk or a hand-held or electric mixer. Pour the chilled cream into a chilled metal bowl and whip until it thickens and just forms soft peaks (do not overbeat). Add 2 tablespoons of granulated sugar or 4 tablespoons of confectioners' sugar and 1 teaspoon of vanilla when the cream begins to thicken but before it forms soft peaks. But be very careful not to overwhip heavy cream, or else it will turn into butter.

Yeast

Yeast is the leavening agent for breads and rolls. I like to store active, dry yeast in the refrigerator to ensure its freshness, although you don't have to. However, you must store compressed cake yeast in the refrigerator or freezer, because it is highly perishable. Be sure to check the expiration date on all yeast packages before using. You can also "proof" your yeast to make sure it's still alive. For more about yeast and proofing yeast, see Chapters 5 and 14.

Yogurt

Plain yogurt is often used in quick bread and muffin recipes. Its tangy flavor and richness adds a nice component to baked goods. You can substitute yogurt for sour cream in many recipes. Check the expiration date on your yogurt container to make sure it is fresh and use it up within one week of opening it.

Freezer Staples

Just about anything can be frozen and it will turn out okay. Items in the freezer will usually keep up to a year without any damage to their structural integrity, so I freeze everything: soups, homemade broth, summertime berries and fruits, breads, butter, and fruit juices, among many other things. If you have the space, you can even freeze milk and some cheeses! Keep a box of baking soda in there too, to keep the freezer fresh-smelling.

Frozen Fruit

During the summertime, I love to go to pick-your-own farms and stock up on all kinds of fresh fruits. I like to freeze my harvest for winter months when a fresh blueberry pie perks up my spirits. You can also keep frozen berries and fruits on hand (you can pick them up at the supermarket, if you like) for muffins, pancakes, and for pies and other desserts. Freeze strawberries and raspberries in a single layer on a baking sheet, then put them, frozen, into a container.

Frozen Dough

Pie crusts, well wrapped, will keep for up to a year in the freezer. Just defrost the dough before rolling it out. You can also keep puff pastry and bread doughs on hand.

Nuts

Because most nuts have a high oil content, they can go rancid quickly, so I store all of my nuts in the freezer to make sure they stay fresh. You can still chop and grind them without any defrost time, so there really isn't any reason not to freeze them.

Substitutions: What to Do in a Pinch

Despite your well-laid plans, sometimes you'll find that your pantry is missing a crucial ingredient when you're in the middle of baking. Although it's always best to have the ingredient called for, there are substitutions that can be made when you're in a pinch. The following table is a list of substitutions that will provide satisfactory results.

Instead of:	Use:
1 cup cake flour	1 cup minus 2 tablespoons all-purpose flour.
1 cup all-purpose flour	1 cup plus 2 tablespoons cake flour.
1 cup self-rising flour	1 cup all-purpose flour plus $\frac{1}{2}$ teaspoon baking powder and $\frac{1}{2}$ teaspoon salt.
1 cup granulated sugar	1 cup brown sugar *or* 2 cups confectioners' sugar.
$\frac{1}{2}$ cup brown sugar	$\frac{1}{2}$ cup granulated sugar plus 2 tablespoons molasses.
1 package active dry yeast	1 cake compressed fresh yeast.
1 square unsweetened chocolate	3 tablespoons unsweetened cocoa powder plus 1 tablespoon vegetable oil or butter.

Instead of:	Use:
1 cup buttermilk	1 cup whole milk plus 1 tablespoon white vinegar or lemon juice. Stir and let stand two minutes. *Or,* use 1 cup plain yogurt or sour cream.
1 cup plain yogurt	1 cup sour cream.
1 cup whole milk	$1/2$ cup evaporated milk plus $1/2$ cup water. *Or,* use dry milk and follow the package instructions to reconstitute the amount you need.
1 cup raisins	1 cup currants or other dried fruits such as cranberries, blueberries, or cherries.
1 tablespoon cornstarch	2 tablespoons flour (for thickening purposes).
1 cup corn syrup	1 cup sugar plus $1/4$ cup water.
1 cup honey	$1 1/4$ cup granulated sugar plus $1/4$ cup liquid.
1 tablespoon fresh lemon juice	1 tablespoon bottled lemon juice or 1 tablespoon distilled vinegar (do not use the vinegar if you want the lemon flavor, but it's good for making water acidic or souring milk).

The Least You Need to Know

➤ A well-stocked pantry gives you confidence in the kitchen and cuts down on extra trips to the grocery store.

➤ To keep your pantry updated, keep a shopping list on the refrigerator or some other convenient spot so you can always write down what ingredients you have used up.

➤ It's best to use the ingredients called for in the recipe, but if you're in a pinch, there are substitutions that can be made.

Chapter 3

Going Over the Gear

In This Chapter

➤ A comprehensive list of the equipment you will need

➤ A breakdown of gadgets that will add pleasure and ease to baking

➤ Finding the right tool for the right job

One reason that baking is a good activity is that there is relatively little start-up cost. If you have a bowl, a mixing spoon, and some baking sheets, you don't need much more to make cookies or even bread. I am a huge fan of kitchen gadgets, but I live in a tiny apartment, and I have to streamline what I buy in the interest of having walking-around room. In this chapter, I have put together the very basics of what you'll need in order to use this book.

Are You Equipped?

If you are starting from scratch, I recommend looking for bakeware and appliances on sale. Department stores usually have a good sale every few weeks in their housewares section, so keep your eye out for quality products at a reasonable price. Outlet malls are also a good place to find discounted stuff for the kitchen. Also, garage sales, flea markets, and your parents' kitchen are inexpensive places to pick up baking supplies (just make sure Mom and Dad know what you want to take!).

Kitchen Utensil
If you're not fully committed to the idea of baking, you can always find heavy-duty aluminum foil baking pans in just about every shape and size at the grocery store. You can usually only use the pans once, so they're not an economical choice, but they are perfect if you don't bake often or are bringing a baked good to a friend's house. This way, you don't have to worry about getting the pan back!

Cost is not always the best indicator of value. Look for sturdy pots and pans; despite the price tag, if something feels flimsy, it is. Your bakeware should feel sturdy and heavy. Remember, this stuff will be going in and out of a hot oven throughout its lifetime, so you want to choose equipment that can withstand the wear and tear of baking. And before using any new bakeware, be sure to wash it thoroughly in hot, soapy water. In the following sections, I'll give you the lowdown on what to look for in pans, pots, and the baker's essential appliances.

Baking Pans

You can't bake without pans. Don't worry, you won't need to make a huge investment, but you will need to acquire the basics. For items such as baking sheets, loaf pans, and cake pans, you will need a pair of them, so remember that when you're outfitting your kitchen. You don't want to skimp on getting set up, otherwise you may find yourself frustrated later.

Baking (Cookie) Sheets

To keep yourself sane, I recommend owning at least two cookie sheets. This way, you can always have a batch of cookies ready to go into the oven (you don't have to wait to remove the first batch from the sheet). If you become an avid baker, I recommend having four baking sheets. Choose heavy, shiny aluminum baking sheets. Avoid dark baking sheets; they tend to burn cookies faster. Cookie sheets will either have a small raised lip on one side of the sheet or have a lip running around all four sides. I prefer the baking sheets with the lip all the way around because they can serve so many purposes (place them under juicy pies as they bake and they'll catch the juice, preventing it from dripping into your oven).

Kitchen Utensil
If your cookies are burning on the bottom but raw on top, create your own insulated baking sheet. Stack two baking sheets together (one on top of the other) and continue baking as usual. This should prevent further burning.

Thin baking sheets will warp in the oven, so make sure the ones you choose are sturdy. If you have baking sheets with nonstick coating and find that they are browning your cookies too fast, reduce the oven temperature by 25°F. You can also buy insulated baking sheets, but they are expensive, and you may find you have to increase your baking time by a few minutes. They do help prevent the over-browning of cookie bottoms, however.

Baking sheet without lip.

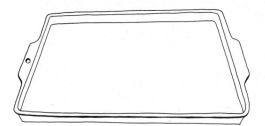

Baking sheet with lip.

Baking (Muffin) Tins

Baking tins contain six or 12 little cups pressed out of one sheet of metal. They are used for making muffins, cupcakes, and rolls, or for baking small cakes. Like other cake pans, these should be sturdy, made of heavy aluminum, and can have a nonstick coating. Specialty muffin tins are also available in mini-muffin size, and you can even get muffin-top pans (in which you get only the crunchy top of the muffin and not the cakey bottom). If you are using baking tins and don't have enough batter to fill all of the tins, place a few tablespoons of water in the empty tins to prevent them from burning while baking.

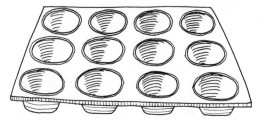

Baking tin.

Bundt and Tube Pans

Bundt and tube pans allow a hurried cook to make a beautiful, tall cake without the worry of layers. The secret is the funnel (the hollow tube in the center), which cooks the cake from the inside out. Bundt pans almost always have some sort of cut-crystal design molded into the pan and have tall sides with a hollow tube in the center. A tube pan has the funnel in the center, too, but the sides of this pan are smooth, which allows the batter to "climb" up the walls of the pan as it bakes. It's important for an angel food cake to cook this way so it doesn't collapse in the pan. Tube pans can also have "feet," little metal nubs that stick out above the rim of the pan, which allow the pan to be flipped over while it cools without smashing the cake inside.

> **Kitchen Informant**
> A *bundt pan* was originally the trademark name of a tube pan with the decorated, molded sides manufactured by the Nordicware Company. It has since developed into the generic name for that style of cake pan or for a cake that is baked in that style.

23

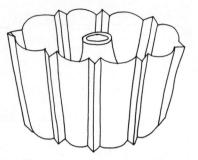

Bundt pan.

Tube pan.

Kitchen Utensil
If you don't know how many cups of batter your bundt or tube pan will hold, fill the pan to capacity with measured water to find out what its volume is. The same goes for any baking pan..

Cake Pans

Cake pans come in several sizes. The most common are 8-inch round and 9-inch round. Make sure the ones you choose are at least $1^1/_2$ inches deep. You will need two 8-inch or 9-inch-round baking pans to make a layer cake. I recommend heavy aluminum pans, with or without a nonstick coating, and with straight sides. Be sure your pans are sturdy; you don't want them to warp and produce an uneven cake. Remember, these pans will mold the batter you put into them, so you want the surfaces to be straight and flat.

Loaf Pans

Loaf pans come in two standard sizes: $9 \times 5 \times 3$ or $8^1/_2 \times 4^1/_2 \times 2^1/_2$. Either size is fine for the recipes in this book. You can find loaf pans made of glass, shiny metal, or nonstick aluminum. Glass pans and dark, nonstick pans have a tendency to brown your breads a bit faster than shiny metal, so you may have to lower the oven temperature by 25°F. You should always have two loaf pans for bread baking, because most recipes make two loaves of bread and you'll need both pans to put the bread in to rise; you can't really bake one loaf of yeast bread at a time. I also don't recommend baking quick breads one at a time. The leavening will become active when the wet ingredients are mixed together, and if the batter sits around for too long, the leavening may become inactive.

Pie Plates

The most common sizes for pie plates (also called pie pans) are 8 inches and 9 inches. Choosing the right plate for a recipe can be a bit tricky, because a 9-inch plate refers to the diameter of the bottom of the plate, not the depth, of the plate, so two "9-inch" pie plates can vary in the amount of filling that they will hold by almost three cups. I use glass pie plates because I like the finish it gives my bottom crust, but many people use aluminum or ceramic pie plates. If you use metal pie plates, be sure your pie plate has a dull finish. A shiny pie plate will reflect the heat and you will end up with a soggy bottom crust.

If you like fruit pies or quiches, look for a pie plate with a bottom that's at least an inch deep. Cream pies and meringues can be successfully made with a more shallow pie plate, about $1/2$-inch deep. You might want to have a selection of pie plates to use. If you're uncertain if the pie plate will hold the contents of the recipe you want to make, measure how many cups of water the plate will hold, then compare that to the volume your filling will make.

Springform Pans

Springform pans are the perfect pan for making cheese-cakes. They have a clasp on the side that allows you to remove the sides of the pan. This means that you don't have to invert your pan in order to free your cake for cutting and serving. The most common sizes for springform pans are 8-inch, 9-inch, and 10-inch pans. It's not uncommon to find sets of springform pans sold in these three sizes for about ten dollars. When shopping for a springform pan, make sure the bottom fits in tightly and the clasp is strong. It is not a pleasant experience to be carrying a cake to the oven and have your clasp give out on you—you're left wearing the cake. And believe me, it's even worse if it happens when the finished cake is going to the cooling rack!

Kitchen Utensil
To make sure your springform pan doesn't spring a leak, place it on a baking sheet when you place it in the oven. The baking sheet will help catch any drips. Besides, it allows you to transport your cake without any risk of the bottom falling from the cake pan.

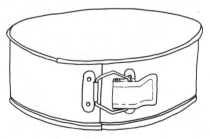

Springform pan.

Basic Pots

There aren't that many pots that you need when baking. However, you might have to melt chocolate for a cake, or cook up a filling for a pot pie or even a pudding for a pie, so I'll include a short list of essential pots to have in the kitchen. Again, I recommend heavy, stainless steel cookware (nonstick coating is your choice).

Double Boilers

The safest and easiest way to melt chocolate and make puddings is to use a double boiler. A double boiler consists of two stacked saucepans, or a saucepan with a fitted bowl that sits on top. The water in the lower pot is heated until it simmers (do not boil) and begins to steam, which warms the bottom of the upper pan or bowl. The bottom of the bowl should not touch the simmering water. This way, the chocolate melts and the pudding can cook with no risk of burning. This method of indirect heating is also used for making some creams and sauces. The top saucepan of a double boiler should not be used over direct heat, because the metal used to make the upper pan is not as sturdy as that of the bottom saucepan.

Double boiler.

Information Station

If you're in a pinch and need to make a double boiler, take two saucepans of different sizes or a saucepan and a heat-resistant bowl that you can insert on the top (the bowl should not float on the water). Fill the larger saucepan with about 2 inches of water and rest the smaller saucepan on top of the water (it's not so important that the second saucepan doesn't touch the water, because the bottom of a regular saucepan is sturdier than the bottom of a double boiler), or rest the bowl on the top of the saucepan. Use as you would a regular double boiler. A word of warning: Since the two pans will not be fitted, be careful none of the simmering water gets into the top saucepan. Also, if you're using a top bowl, be very careful when removing it—it will be HOT.

Dutch Ovens

The name of these large pots or kettles is said to have come from their Dutch ancestry. Usually made of cast iron, sometimes enameled, with molded handles, they can go from the stovetop to the oven, which is great if you're making pot pie or stew and dumplings.

Make sure your Dutch oven has a tight-fitting lid, which prevents steam from escaping, and is flameproof (oven-safe). Dutch ovens come in several sizes. Choose one that holds at least $4^1/_2$ quarts.

Saucepans

You should have at least a 1-quart and 2-quart saucepan on hand for stovetop procedures such as scalding milk or boiling water. Heavy-bottomed saucepans are better conductors of heat, and you are less likely to burn or scald the bottom than if you use thinner metals. I prefer stainless-steel saucepans because they are nonreactive and durable. They also don't pick up food odors or stain easily.

Information Station

The term *nonreactive* is used when talking about cooking equipment. Non-reactive equipment is made of a metal that will not react with acidic foods. Some examples of nonreactive equipment are stainless steel, ceramic, plastic, Teflon-coated, or glass. *Reactive* metals are aluminum and copper. When foods and metal equipment do react, generally the foods will turn an undesirable brown color. Tomato sauces, red-wine sauces, and lemon juice are a few examples of foods that will react with metals.

Electric Tools

While most baked goods do not require the use of electric gadgets, these convenience tools certainly speed along the process. Electric mixers help us speedily beat sugar and butter, whip egg whites, and mix batters. Food processors and blenders can chop and purée in no time.

Blenders

A blender is great for puréeing fruits, making cheesecake, crushing crackers or cookies for a crumb crust, and even grinding or chopping nuts. Also, there is no better tool than the blender when you need superfine (quick-dissolving) sugar and only have granulated sugar on hand. I dump the amount I need in the blender and whiz it for a minute or so, and voilà—superfine sugar. I once tried it in my food processor and the results were just not the same.

If you plan to buy a blender, look for one with at least a 4- to 5-cup capacity and a jar with a wide base that makes for easy scraping. Glass jars break, so you might want to shop around for a plastic container (they are also lighter). Blenders have come quite a long way in design, and you can find some with all sorts of bells and whistles, so pick one with the components you want and go from there. When you use your blender, remember: Never, ever, put anything but ingredients (no spoons of spatulas) into the blender jar while the motor is running.

Food Processors

The food processor is a wonderful tool in the kitchen because it is strong, simple to use, and quiet. The bad news is they are quite expensive. I absolutely love, love, love my food processor and use it all the time. It makes pastry dough, chops nuts or citrus zest, purées fruit, juices lemons and limes, and shreds carrots all in a fraction of the time it used to take me to do it by hand. If you are considering purchasing a food processor, don't skimp on quality. Make sure you purchase a reputable brand with a good, durable motor. The money you spend on it up front will save you money and time in the long run.

Food processor and blades: slicer (top), shredder (middle), and all-purpose (bottom).

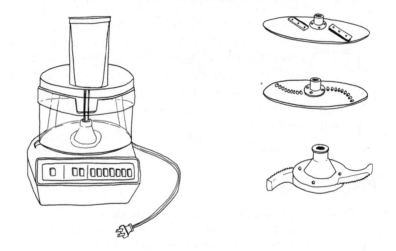

Hand-Held Mixers

Hand-held mixers are relatively inexpensive and great in the kitchen for whipping up cake batters and light cookie doughs. They are also perfect for whipping cream and egg whites. Their portability and easy cleanup (the beaters just pop off when you're finished) save you a great deal of time and frustration. While the motor in a hand-held mixer is not as strong as that of a stand mixer, there are sturdier, more expensive models that come with attachments for creaming thick cake batters and dough hooks for bread doughs. The advantage of a hand-held mixer is that it's portable, meaning it can be used wherever it's needed (as long as you can plug it in). Hand-held mixers have a choice of three speeds: slow, medium, and fast.

Stand (Table) Mixers

A good stand mixer is quite a workhorse in the kitchen. It can handle almost any work-load you can dish out because the motor is about six times stronger than that of any hand-held mixer. It also has a wider range of speeds than a hand-held mixer. The stand mixer should come with its own bowl attachment, which is always generous in size, and three attachments: a paddle, a wire whisk, and a dough hook. You can also purchase special attachments for some models of mixers, including a pasta maker, grinder, shred-der, slicer, and juicer. Stand mixers are not quite as convenient and do not disassemble as neatly as hand-held mixers, so they will more than likely be stored on the countertop or in an easy-to-access place.

There are many stand mixers available in a wide range of prices. My advice is to deter-mine how much baking you will be doing. If you bake about once a month, I recommend investing in a quality mixer, such as a KitchenAid. They are expensive, but well worth the money. My mother has had hers for well over 25 years and has never had any problems, and I plan on having mine for at least that long.

Stand mixer.

Other Essentials

So now you've got your pots, pans, and appliances covered. Before we get into the gadgets, there are a few other essential pieces of equipment you'll need to have on hand.

Cooling Racks

Cooling racks are wire racks that allow air to circulate around baked goods while they cool, preventing them from having a soggy or moist bottom. There are a wide variety of shapes and sizes available—just make sure your rack has feet on it so it will not lay flat on the countertop, which would defeat the purpose. Also, the wires on the racks should be close together. This will prevent delicate cakes from sinking too much and smaller cookies from slipping through the spaces.

Cooling rack.

Kitchen Scales

When recipes give ingredient amounts in weights (such as 5 pounds of apples), kitchen scales are great tools to have for weighing ingredients. There are two types of scales: balance scales and spring scales. The less common for the home baker is the balance scale, which has a platform for the weights on one side and a pan or bowl for the ingredients on the other. When the ingredient's weight levels out with the side with the desired weight, you have the right amount. Spring scales are more common and simple to use. Just place the item you need to weigh in the pan and read the face to tell you the weight.

Mixing Bowls

If you have a stand mixer, you probably already have a good mixing bowl (the one it came with). I have a wide variety of bowls at home. For mixing cake batters and cookies,

Bakers Beware!
When selecting a mixing bowl, consider what ingredients will be going into it. This is especially important when whipping egg whites or cream, because egg whites can grow up to six times their original volume and cream will at least double.

I like a wide, stainless-steel mixing bowl. These come in a variety of sizes, but look for bowls with flat bottoms and wide, sloping sides rather than straight sides. They make mixing easier and are less likely to tip over if you leave a whisk or spoon in them. Stainless steel is also durable, unbreakable, and nonreactive.

When I make bread, I like to use a heavy ceramic bowl to let the bread rise in. The ceramic bowl keeps my dough well insulated and at a more consistent temperature.

When choosing a mixing bowl, make sure you'll have enough room to fit all of the ingredients and still have space to mix them up. Of course, you don't have to go out and purchase new bowls; you can use any bowl you have on hand to make these recipes.

An assortment of mixing bowls.

Great Gadgets: The Right Tool for the Job

Following is a list of helpful tools for the kitchen. While it's not necessary to go out and purchase each and every one of these items, it's good to know they are out there to help make your life in the kitchen that much easier.

Apple Corers

An apple corer has a wooden handle attached to an elongated, curved piece of metal with a cylindrical bottom and a cutting edge. This tool is indispensable when you want to core an apple or pear without slicing into it, making it perfect for baked apples or pears. You just press down vertically into the apple with a slight twisting motion until you reach the bottom.

Another version of this tool cores the apple and slices it into segments. This tool has sets of metal spokes that meet in the circle in the center. Press directly over the apple and it slices and cores the apple easily.

Apple corer.

Bottle Openers

Bottle openers pry off the top of a bottle or jar. (I use mine when I open a jar of home-made preserves and don't want to damage the lid.) Most people have this utensil in their drawer already. If the opener does not bend the cap in half too much, the cap can be reused to re-seal the bottle. Bottle openers can also be found attached to a wine opener or even a hand-held can opener.

Box Graters

Graters are usually made of metal, although plastic ones are available, and usually have four sides that offer a choice from fine to coarse grating, as well as a slicing blade. I like to use it to grate cheese and carrots. If you don't already own a box grater, choose a sturdy one with four sides and comfortable handle. There are also flat graters, which usually only offer a choice of two holes, but I find them cumbersome to use and unsteady. In their favor, they take up less space and are easier to clean than box graters.

Kitchen Utensil
Clean your box grater from the inside out. Scrub the inside with a stiff brush, under running water, to push food through from the back instead of the front. Hang to air dry.

Box grater (left) and hand-held grater (right).

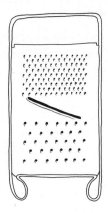

Cake Testers

Cake testers are thin plastic or metal needle-like instruments, sometimes with a round handle. They are inserted into the center of the cake to determine doneness. If dough clings to the tester, the cake is not yet finished. If the cake tester comes out clean, the cake is finished. Personally, I find that wooden toothpicks or even a thin, small knife work just as well, and they don't get lost as easily as a cake tester might.

Bakers Beware!
Can openers can be big-time bacteria harbingers. Make sure you wash your can opener with hot, soapy water and allow it to air-dry after every use to prevent bacteria from building up.

Can Openers

Can openers can be hand-held or electric. I prefer the compact hand-held can opener to electric, but not just any hand-held can opener will do. After years of struggling with can openers that dull easily, I've found a heavy-duty, gear-driven can opener with a sturdy handle and comfortable crank. Without hesitation, I recommend throwing out any dull can openers with wimpy cranks you may be keeping around, wishing they would miraculously sharpen, and search out this can opener. I have seen this variety available in discount stores and kitchen-supply stores, so I don't think you'll have to look far to find it. It usually costs more than the flimsy metal variety, but less than an electric opener. I have had mine well over five years. It's opened hundreds of cans, and it still keeps going strong.

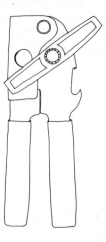

Can opener.

Citrus Juicers (Reamers)

A citrus juicer is a tool that allows you to juice citrus fruits without getting seeds or too much pulp in your juice. There are some that you place over a bowl, some that are hand-held and strain out the seeds and pulp so only the juice falls into the bowl, and others that collect the juice in a base. Citrus juicers come in many different shapes and sizes, so choose one that works well for you. Because my food processor has a citrus juicing attachment, I rely on its speedy work.

If you don't have a citrus juicer and you need to get more juice out of a lemon or other citrus fruit than squeezing will allow, use a teaspoon to help. Squeeze the lemon, then insert the teaspoon and gently squeeze again, while twisting the spoon around the inside of the lemon; or you can just press the lemon against the spoon inside the lemon. This will help release additional juice. You can also roll a lemon or lime on the table several times (pushing down with your palm) to release the juices before you cut it in half.

Citrus juicers.

33

Colanders

There are not many tools in the kitchen quite as useful as a good, sturdy colander. A colander is a bowl with holes in it, which allows you to wash small things such as blueberries, and not run the risk of them dropping down the drain. Colanders are also useful for thawing foods that produce a lot of liquid, such as frozen fruits. Allow the fruits to thaw in a colander, set over a bowl to catch the liquid, and you will not have waterlogged berries. And, of course, colanders are indispensable for draining pasta or cooked vegetables.

Colander.

Cutting Boards

Cutting boards offer smooth, even surfaces for many tasks such as chopping, cutting, peeling, and rolling out doughs. A wooden cutting board is your best choice for preserving the sharp edges of knives since they don't blunt as quickly as on plastic, metal, or marble. Don't place your wooden cutting board in the dishwasher, or let it soak in water for any length of time. The heat from the dishwasher will warp your board, and the water will soften the bonded sections of the board. Keep one side of your cutting board nick-free and smooth, so it will be suitable for rolling out cookie or pastry dough.

Bakers Beware!
Some cutting boards (mostly wooden ones) can trap strong food odors, such as onions and garlic. Make sure you don't use the same board to chop your onions as you do to roll out your delicate doughs!

Another good choice for a cutting board is a plastic polyurethane board. These will not warp when exposed to water and are soft enough for knives to be used without dulling. They can also be sterilized in the dishwasher.

Flour Sifters

A flour sifter will remove any lumps or debris in your dry ingredients by sifting it through a fine mesh. Although most of the flour you find today is pre-sifted, it has a tendency to settle during storage, so it's a good idea to sift it, especially cake flour. Sifting is also a good way to evenly blend all dry ingredients and aerate your dry ingredients.

Some flour sifters work by turning a crank, which aerates the ingredients and pushes them through the fine mesh. Others have a handle you squeeze, which shifts a plate and sifts the ingredients through the fine mesh. If you have arthritic hands, you might find the crank more comfortable. Try several different models to find the one you are most comfortable with.

Flour sifter.

Funnels

There are many uses for funnels in the kitchen. They are ideal for hanging an angel-food-cake pan over for cooling, for filling salt shakers, or for pouring liquids into narrow-necked containers. They come in metal or plastic. While they're not the most essential gadget to have in the kitchen, when you need one, no other tool will do.

Kitchen Scissors

It's always a good idea to keep a set of scissors in the kitchen for food-related jobs. Kitchen scissors are perfect for trimming pastry dough, cutting paper to line a pan, opening plastic bags, cutting fresh herbs, and snipping strings. The heavier and stronger the scissors you have, the better they will help you in the kitchen.

Kitchen scissors.

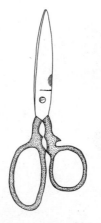

35

While the sharp edge of a knife can be dangerous, dull knives are even more so. The dull knife will need more pressure applied to it, increasing the chances of slippage and injuring the user. Always tuck your fingertips under when cutting with a knife so that if your knife does slip, it will cut your knuckle, not your fingertips.

Knives

A good sharp knife can be your best friend in the kitchen. Top-quality, professional knives are quite expensive, and not really necessary for the home baker. Basically, you should have four knives in your kitchen: a large chef's knife, a serrated knife, a medium-size (6- or 8-inch blade) knife, and a paring knife. The large chef's knife is perfect for chopping and you can use its broad side to crush cloves of garlic. The serrated knife is great for slicing breads and delicate cakes. The medium-size knife is the perfect size for slicing cakes, cutting pastry, and for less heavy work than the chef's knife. The paring knife is ideal for cutting small things, peeling fruits, hulling strawberries, and performing many other detail-oriented tasks.

From left: medium-sized knife, chef's knife, paring knife.

How to hold a knife when cutting.

Ladles

A ladle has a long handle and a large bowl for reaching into pots or pans and scooping up liquid. They are available in either metal or plastic. A ladle is great for pouring or serving sauces or other hot liquids.

Measuring Cups

Measuring cups are essential for every kitchen. There aren't many recipes that do not require measurements of some kind. There are two types of measuring cups available: graduated and glass. Graduated cups range in size from $^1/_4$ cup to 1 cup, and can range from four to six cups in a set. Use graduated cups to measure dry ingredients and solid fats such as shortening. Glass cups are available in a wide range of sizes, the most common being 1, 2, and 4 cups. Use these cups for measuring liquids. Make sure you read your measurement at eye level, and that the cup is on a flat surface. I'll talk more about this in Chapter 8.

Measuring Spoons

Graduated measuring spoons usually come in sets of four or six, ranging from $^1/_4$ teaspoon to 1 tablespoon. Sometimes sets will have $^1/_8$ teaspoon and $1^1/_2$ tablespoon, too. Use the measuring spoons for both dry and liquid measure.

Nutmeg Graters

This is a fun but not necessarily essential item for the kitchen. Fresh spices are so much more flavorful when freshly ground, and fresh ground nutmeg is no exception. A nutmeg grater is a small tool used to turn the whole egg-shaped nutmeg seed into a ground spice. The surface of the slightly curved surface has a fine rasp, and you rub the seed across the surface to grate it. There is a little door that slides open in the back of the grater that stores the nutmeg seeds for you.

Nutmeg grater.

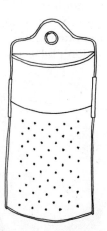

Oven Thermometers

If you were to run out right now and purchase just one item for the kitchen, it should be an oven thermometer. A good oven thermometer is inexpensive and can save you from ruining your baked goods. Because we rely on our ovens for baking, it's essential that the heat is accurate. Many home oven thermostats are not always true, so the best way to monitor your oven's temperature is with a thermometer. Look for one with a hook for hanging. I hang my thermometer on the center rack in the oven so I can easily double-check the temperature. Installing an oven thermometer is the best thing you can do for your oven and the success of your baking. (See Chapter 6 for more on ovens.)

Oven thermometer.

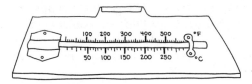

Pastry Bags and Tips

If you like to decorate cakes, you'll need a pastry bag and a small assortment of tips. I like a sturdy cloth (nylon) pastry bag for decorating cakes. If you are going to purchase one, I suggest getting one slightly larger than you think you'll need. Pastry tips are hard little metal cones that are either dropped into the pastry bag (coming out the small end) or screwed on the coupler on the outside of the bag (making switching tips easy). The pattern you pipe onto the cake is determined by the tip you choose to use. (See "Tips on Tips" in Chapter 11 for more about pastry bags and tips.)

Pastry Blenders

A pastry blender is a hand-held tool with a set of steel cutters on the bottom. It's used to cut fats into flour quickly and without the addition of heat, so your dough remains tender. To use a pastry blender, press it into the fats using a rocking, up-and-down bouncing motion. The blender will incorporate the butter into the flour and the end mixture will resemble coarse meal. If you don't have a pastry blender, you can use two knifes, or two forks, to cut in the fat.

Pastry blender.

Pastry Brushes

Pastry brushes are great for spreading melted butter, glazing pastry, or brushing breads with egg wash. They are a small tool that makes life a lot easier in the kitchen. If you enjoy working with phyllo dough or pastry, you'll definitely want to purchase a pastry brush. Look for one with very soft bristles. Rough or stiff brushes will tear your pastry. Wash your brush with hot, soapy water after each use and hang to dry. Do not store with the weight on the bristles, or they will curve and not brush effectively anymore.

Pie Weights

When you pre-bake an empty pie shell (also called blind baking), you'll need to weigh down the crust with pie weights to prevent it from bubbling up. (You can prick the bottom with a fork instead of using weights, but you may not want to use that method if you're making a fruit-filled pie.) Pie weights are available at any kitchen-supply store and are usually ceramic or metal round pellets. To use them, pour them onto an unbaked, foil-lined pie crust and place the crust in the oven. About five to ten minutes before the pie has finished baking, remove the weights by lifting out the foil and return the crust to the oven to finish browning.

> **Kitchen Utensil**
> If you don't have pie weights, you can use dried beans instead. Just follow the same directions as the pie weights. Keep the beans in a special jar since they can be reused many times. Unfortunately, once used in place of pie weights, the dried beans can no longer be cooked because they will have dried out too much.

Pie weights on pie crust.

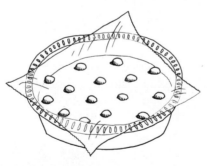

Potholders (Oven Mitts)

Potholders enable you to hold hot baking sheets and pans without burning yourself. I like to have both the mitt and square pad potholders on hand for different tasks. I use the mitt holder if I'm reaching into the oven and run the risk of burning my whole hand. I choose the square pads when I need to hold the sides of dishes, such as a soufflé.

Bakers Beware!
You should always have two sets of potholders. No matter what kind of potholder you have, if it gets wet, don't use it. It can no longer protect your hands.

Potholders play a very important role in baking, since they save your hands from becoming seriously burned. Therefore, I highly recommend you forgo the decorative potholders that are so commonly found in houseware departments of stores, or if you have them, use them for display. Make a special trip to your kitchen-supply store and purchase insulated potholders. They are slightly more expensive than regular potholders, but I trust them in every situation; whereas the decorative holders wear in strange spots and you can end up burning your hands.

Rolling Pins

A rolling pin is used to roll out pastry dough. There are many types available; I recommend a relatively heavy pin with handles. The weight of the pin helps to distribute the dough evenly, so you should not push down on the pin when using it. There are such things as "cool" pins, made of plastic or marble; some you can even fill with water and freeze. All of these ensure that your dough stays cool while you are working with it. I don't recommend buying a "cool" pin unless you have worked with one and found that you really like it. Stick with a sure thing. Always lightly dust your rolling pin with flour before using it and wipe it clean when you are finished. Never put your rolling pin in the dishwasher.

Rolling pin.

Sieves (Strainers)

Sieves are great for sifting flour, dusting cakes with confectioners' sugar, or straining liquids from solids. Sieves generally have a bowl-shaped bottom made of fine mesh and a long handle. You can also mash soft fruits through the mesh to make a purée; this is especially good for removing all the seeds from a raspberry purée.

Sieve.

Spatulas

There are two kinds of spatulas that are important in baking: rubber and metal. The rubber spatula is great for scraping down the sides of bowls during mixing, getting all the batter into pans, and folding together ingredients. Choose a spatula with a flexible but stiff blade. The stiffness in the blade gives you more scraping control. Don't expose your rubber spatula to heat, because it will melt or crack. (Although you can put a rubber spatula in the dishwasher, it will shorten its life.)

A metal spatula has blunt edges and a rounded tip and is the perfect tool for spreading frostings and fillings. Metal spatulas are available in a wide range of sizes, but for finished cakes, you might want to have a 10-inch blade so you can sweep across the entire top of the cake for a smooth finish. Make sure the blade fits snugly in the handle and that the handle is comfortable to hold.

Spoons

You should have two types of spoons in your kitchen: metal and wooden. You should have at least two metal spoons, one solid and one slotted. They are essential for stirring, and a slotted spoon makes it easy to lift foods from hot liquid. Wooden spoons are great for stirring custards and sauces made in nonstick pans, as well as for stirring batters and doughs. Nothing beats a sturdy wooden spoon. They are not expensive, so you might want to get two or three.

Timers

A timer is an inexpensive item that can actually save you money in the long run by always reminding you when to take your cakes and cookies out of the oven, therefore preventing any wasted batches. Always set your timer for the minimum amount of time given in a recipe, and check for doneness.

Tongs

Think of your tongs as an extension of your hands. Tongs are great for retrieving foods from hot water, flipping foods during cooking, and lifting hot lids.

Trivets

A trivet can be made of wood, cork, or ceramic, and is usually round or square. Trivets are placed underneath the bottom of hot pots and pans to prevent them from burning the surface they are placed on. They also protect glass and ceramic baking dishes from the sudden shock of cold surfaces, which can cause the dishes to break.

Vegetable Peelers

There's nothing like a comfortable vegetable peeler. When I worked in a bakery as a pastry chef, every Sunday I would have to peel a case of apples to make apple filling for that week's supply of croissants. We had cheap, flimsy metal peelers and when I finally finished, my hand would be completely cramped up. One day someone brought in a

Good Grips brand vegetable peeler with a big, fat, soft, black handle and super-durable blade. After using that, my hand stopped hurting and I could peel without any discomfort or pain. That Christmas, everyone in my family received Good Grips peelers as presents. When shopping for a vegetable peeler look for a stainless steel blade so it will not react with acids. Not only is a vegetable peeler good for removing the skins of fruits and vegetables, it also makes great chocolate curls.

The Least You Need to Know

➤ Don't go hog wild and purchase every piece of baking equipment your kitchen store has to offer. Begin with easy baking projects and build up your equipment from there.

➤ Department-store sales and outlet shopping centers are great places to pick up quality baking supplies.

➤ The right tool for the right job does add ease to baking, so make sure you have them before embarking on baking projects.

Part 2
The Lingo

Part of what's intimidating about baking is the foreign language recipe writers seem to speak. Sure, you are familiar with terms like "beat," "blend," "mix," and "whip," but when the recipe calls for the dough to "come together" or asks you to "blanch" your almonds, "hull" your strawberries, or "zest" lemons, you may start feeling faint and begin searching for the number of the nearest bakery. Well, put down the phone and get ready to learn! When you get through the chapters in this part, you'll be able to talk shop with the best of them. You'll also learn about the role of basic ingredients. The more familiar you become with what they do, the less intimidating baking as a whole will become.

Bakerspeak: What They Mean When They Say...

In This Chapter

➤ A comprehensive glossary that defines food terms

For the most part, baking recipes are pretty straightforward. You're probably familiar with terms such as *beat*, *whip*, and *bake*. But from time to time you come across words like *scald*, *flute*, or *macerate*, which set your head spinning and make you want to put down this book and go to the local bakery. Here is a list of more than 75 of the most commonly used cooking and baking terms to clear up any confusion in the kitchen.

Bain-marie   See "Water bath."

Bake   To cook in a hot, dry environment in a closed area (your oven!). Foods are baked uncovered for dry, crisp surfaces and covered for moistness and to prevent excess browning.

Batter   An uncooked semi-liquid mixture containing flour and other ingredients used to make a cake or bread. Generally a batter contains more liquid and sometimes more fat and/or sugar than a dough.

Beat   A mixing method in which ingredients are vigorously agitated to incorporate air and develop gluten (a protein found in wheat flour, among other varieties, that, when beaten, becomes more elastic and gives a cohesiveness to the dough). A spoon, beater, or mixer with a paddle attachment is generally used.

Bind   To add an ingredient that holds other ingredients together; most commonly, when an ingredient (flour, eggs, cream, cheese) is added to a hot liquid and causes it to thicken.

Blanch   A technique in which food is plunged into boiling water for a short time (about 30 seconds), then sometimes plunged into ice water to stop the cooking. This preserves the color, taste, and texture of the food. This technique is also used to remove the skins of harder-to-peel fruits, vegetables, and nuts.

Blend   A mixing method in which two or more ingredients are combined just until they are evenly distributed; a spoon, rubber spatula, whisk, beater, or mixer with a paddle attachment is generally used.

Boil   To heat a liquid until bubbles rise to the surface and break and steam is given off. At sea level, water boils at 212°F. A *rolling boil* means the bubbles are forming rapidly and cannot be stopped when stirred.

Broil   To cook foods directly under a very hot heat source. Generally, this technique is used for quickly browning tops of dishes or cooking meats and fish with little or no added fat.

Caramelize   To cook sugar over medium heat until it liquefies and turns a rich caramel brown.

Chill   To place hot or room-temperature foods in the refrigerator or freezer. Gelatin and puddings will change from liquids to solids when chilled. Creams will also thicken upon chilling.

Chop   To cut foods into coarse or fine pieces using a large chef's knife, food processor, or blender.

Coat   To cover food evenly with flour, sugar, a crumb mixture, or sauce.

Come together   A term used in pastry making. When small amounts of water are added to the crumbled mixture, it "comes together" and forms a rough dough.

Cool   To allow hot foods to come to room temperature. Putting food on a wire rack allows air to circulate around it; stirring hot liquids cools them faster because it allows the steam to escape. You can also cool liquids in the refrigerator.

Core   To remove the center of fruits, usually apples, pears, or pineapples.

Coring an apple.

Cream   A mixing method in which a softened fat and sugar are vigorously combined to incorporate air; used for quick breads, cookies, and some cakes. Creaming can be done with a wooden spoon or electric mixer.

Crush   To press into very fine bits.

Curdle   The separation of milk or egg mixtures into solid or liquid components; caused by overcooking, high heat, or acidic ingredients (such as lemon juice or vinegar). If you add lemon juice to milk, the milk will thicken and curdle. This is fine if you are making sour milk or buttermilk.

Cut-in   A mixing method in which solid fat is incorporated into dry ingredients, using either a pastry blender, two knives, or a fork, resulting in a coarse texture, as when making pie crust, biscuits, crumb toppings, etc.

Dash   Less than ⅛ teaspoon of an ingredient. (See also "Pinch.")

Dice   To cut food into squares smaller than ½ inch.

Dilute   To make a liquid or food weaker with the addition of water or another liquid.

Double boiler   A double boiler consists of two stacked saucepans, or a saucepan with a fitted bowl that sits on top. The water in the lower pot is heated until it simmers (do not boil) and begins to steam, which warms the bottom of the upper pan or bowl. A double boiler cooks or melts delicate foods that burn easily, such as chocolate, puddings, and custards.

Dough   A mixture of flour and other ingredients used in baking; it has a low moisture content and is often stiff enough to hold a shape.

Drain   To remove excess liquid by placing the food in a colander or strainer that has been set over the sink, or over a bowl if you want to reserve the liquids you are draining.

Drizzle   To pour a liquid (such as a sauce, frosting, or topping) in a thin stream over food. Usually, this is done quickly and not a lot of liquid is used.

Dust   To sprinkle lightly with flour, confectioners' sugar, cocoa, and the like.

Dusting a cake with confectioners' sugar.

Egg wash   A beaten egg (sometimes mixed with a little water or milk) brushed on top of either pastry or dough. It is used to give a sheen to bread, pie crusts, pastries, etc. when baked.

Finely chop (mince)   To cut into very small pieces. Done with a knife or in a food processor or blender.

Bakers Beware!
Sleeves should always be rolled up and hair tied back when flambéing foods. Be sure to have a large, heavy lid on hand to extinguish flames.

Flambé   Food served flaming, generally produced by lighting alcohol such as brandy or rum.

Flute   To pinch pastry edges with your fingers to make a decorative edge, and also to extend the height of the crust edge to better hold in juicy pie fillings.

Fold   A mixing method used to gently incorporate light, airy products into heavier ingredients (for example, mixing beaten egg whites into a cake batter). Usually a rubber spatula is used. First you cut down vertically through the mixture, then you slide the spatula across the bottom of the bowl and up the other side, turning the mixture over. You continue this down-across-up-over motion while rotating the bowl a quarter-turn each time. This should be done just until the ingredients are incorporated. Do not use a stirring motion.

Folding ingredients together.

Garnish   Any food used as an attractive decoration. Popular garnishes for baked goods include chocolate curls, whole strawberries, edible or sugar flowers, chopped nuts, and orange halves.

Glaze   A shiny coating applied to food or a thin, sometimes flavored, coating poured or dripped onto cake or pastry.

Grate   To shred food (such as cheese) by rubbing it against a serrated metal plate known as a grater.

Grease   To rub the inside of a baking pan with a thin, even coating of butter, margarine, or shortening, or to spray with a nonstick cooking spray, to prevent foods from sticking to the pan while baking. Generally used for cakes. Use shortening, not butter, if baking sheets need to be greased for cookies.

Grind   To pulverize or reduce food to very small particles using a mechanical grinder, mortar and pestle, or food processor.

Hull   To remove the caps from strawberries. This can be done with a small knife, an inexpensive tool called a strawberry huller (short, fat tweezers), or a straw. With the knife or huller, just pinch off the green cap. To use the straw, insert it in the narrow end of the strawberry and push it through to the top of the strawberry. The green cap should pop right off.

Knead   To work dough to develop the gluten present in the flours. During kneading, the gluten strands stretch and expand throughout the dough, which enables the dough to hold in the gas bubbles released by the leavener (usually yeast). You can knead by hand by following these steps: Press into the dough with the heel of your hand, fold the dough in half, and then give it a turn and repeat. You can also use a large mixer with a dough hook or a food processor equipped with a plastic blade. Well-kneaded dough is smooth and elastic.

Macerate   To soak foods in a liquid (often juice or liqueur) to soften them, absorb the flavor of the soaking liquid, and release their flavor. Both liquids and solids are used for the dish, as in a dessert fruit topping.

Melt   A process in which certain foods, especially those high in fat, gradually soften and then liquefy when heated.

Meringue   A stiff, glossy foam made of beaten egg whites and sugar.

Mince   See "Finely chop."

Mix   To combine ingredients by hand or with an electric appliance so they are evenly dispersed.

Nonreactive   Used when talking about cooking equipment. Nonreactive equipment is made of a metal that will not react with acidic foods. Some examples of nonreactive equipment are stainless steel, Teflon-coated, plastic, ceramic, or glass. Reactive metals are aluminum and copper. When foods and metal equipment do react, generally the foods will turn an undesirable brown color. Tomato sauces, red-wine sauces, and lemon juice are a few examples of foods that will react with metals.

Pare   See "Peel." A paring knife is a small, short knife.

Kitchen Utensil

Here's a fool-proof method for peeling a peach. Cut a shallow X in the peach's skin. Drop the peach into boiling water (enough to cover it) for 30 seconds (you'll see the skin start to detach where it is cut). Remove the peach from the water with a slotted spoon and plunge it into a bowl of ice water for 30 seconds. The skin should slip off easily. If not, repeat the procedure.

Patch To repair pastry dough by placing a small scrap over the ripped dough and gently pressing the pieces together.

Peel To remove the outer covering of fruits and vegetables, using a knife, vegetable peeler, or your fingers.

Pinch Used in measuring dry ingredients, usually spices or salt. Less than ¹/₈ teaspoon (the amount you can grab between your finger and thumb is an accurate amount).

Pipe To force a softened mixture (frosting or whipped cream) through a pastry bag in order to decorate a cake.

Piping frosting onto a cake.

Pit To remove the hard seeds from the center of fruits.

Preheat To allow the oven to reach its proper baking temperature before food is placed in it. An oven will take between 10 and 20 minutes to properly preheat.

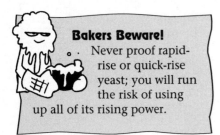

Bakers Beware! Never proof rapid-rise or quick-rise yeast; you will run the risk of using up all of its rising power.

Proof A test given to yeast to determine whether it is alive. The yeast is dissolved in warm (wrist temperature, not above 115°F) water with a pinch of sugar, then set aside for about five minutes. If the mixture becomes foamy, it is alive.

Pulse Short on-and-off bursts of a food processor. Pulsing is generally used to chop or mince foods.

Punch down To firmly push your fist into risen dough to deflate it so it will become more tender and even-grained.

Purée To process food into a smooth pulp. Usually done with a food processor, blender, or by pushing softened foods through a fine mesh strainer or food mill.

Reduce To cook a liquid until its quantity decreases due to evaporation. Typically this is done to intensify flavors and thicken the liquid.

Rest   To allow dough to stand for a certain period of time before forming it into a shape such as a roll or braid. The dough will relax and be easier to work with after a rest.

Scald   To heat liquid (usually milk) uncovered, to just below the boiling point.

Score   To cut very shallow slits across food before cooking. Scoring can be decorative, as when making French bread, or it can be used to help loosen skin if you will be peeling peaches or tomatoes.

Seed   To remove the seeds from a fruit or vegetable.

Set   To chill a custard or gelatin, transforming it from a liquid to a solid.

Shave   To cut in very thin layers with a vegetable peeler (usually done with chocolate).

Shell   To remove the hard outer casing of nuts.

Shred   To cut into thin but irregular pieces. Often done with a grater or food processor with a shredding disk.

Sift   To shake a dry ingredient (such as flour or sugar) through a sieve or sifter to remove lumps and incorporate air. Sifting is also used to combine dry ingredients.

Sifting dry ingredients.

Simmer   To maintain the temperature of a liquid just below the boiling point. Small bubbles continually but gently break the surface of the cooking mixture.

Slice   To cut an item into relatively broad, thin pieces.

Soften   To allow food, usually butter, cream cheese, or margarine, to stand at room temperature until it is no longer hard. Perishable foods should not sit at room temperature any longer than 30 minutes.

Sprinkle   To scatter something, usually a garnish, lightly over the surface of food.

Steep   To soak foods in a hot liquid in order to extract flavor or to soften texture, such as when you make tea.

Stir   A mixing method in which ingredients are gently combined until blended.

Strain   To pour foods through a sieve, mesh strainer, or cheesecloth to separate or remove the liquid or smaller particles from larger particles.

Temper   A technique used with chocolate to prevent it from separating. It is a precise technique of heating, cooling, and reheating chocolate to create a smooth, shiny coating for decorating, dipping, etc.

Toast   To brown food in an oven or broiler. Nuts and spices are toasted by cooking them in a dry skillet over very low heat for several minutes, stirring often, until they brown slightly and become aromatic.

Unmold   To remove food—usually a cake, custard, or gelatin—from its container and place it on a serving plate.

Water bath   Also called a *bain-marie*, a large baking dish filled with hot water in which food in individual cups is gently baked. Usually used for custards and baked puddings.

A water bath. Note that the water comes halfway up the sides of the custard cups.

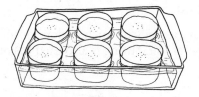

Whip   A mixing method in which foods are vigorously beaten in order to incorporate air. A hand-held whisk or an electric mixer with a whisk attachment is used.

Whisk   A wire whip used to beat foods to incorporate air into them.

Work in   A mixing method in which an ingredient is incorporated into other ingredients, resulting in a uniform mixture. Butter is worked into flour to create a delicate pastry.

Yield   The total amount of a product made from a specific recipe or the number of servings a recipe will produce.

Zest   The outer skin of citrus fruits that contains the fragrant oils. You want to avoid the white underneath (the pith), which tastes bitter.

Chapter 5

The Basics of Basic Ingredients

In This Chapter

➤ Understanding the role ingredients play in making your final product

➤ Learning to choose the best ingredients

➤ Handy substitutions in case you run out of something you need

➤ Tips on selecting and storing fresh fruits

A pinch of this, a cup of that, a few incantations whispered over the bowl, and voilà—a cake is ready. If only it were that easy. When you mix, blend, beat, and stir, stuff is going on with the gods of baking that mere mortals can't begin to understand. What you do need to understand, though, is the role each ingredient plays in the final product. Baking is a science, the kitchen is your laboratory, the ingredients are your elements, and it is your job to mix them together properly so you don't have a huge explosion—or even a small fizzle.

In this chapter I'll tell you what you need to know about the basic baking ingredients. You'll learn how to choose the best ones for your recipes, what to substitute when you're out of something and the store is closed, and how to store your ingredients so they stay as fresh as possible.

Flour Power

Flour is the primary ingredient for most cakes, cookies, pastries, and breads. While it is one of the most basic baking ingredients, it can also be the most confusing because of the wide variety available on your grocery store shelf. Some flours possess qualities perfect for bread baking but disastrous for pie crusts or tender pastries. What makes a flour good for

Kitchen Informant
Gluten is the protein that forms web-like structures present in wheat and other flours. When the flour is moistened and the bread is kneaded or doughs and batters are mixed together, gluten forms and adds an elastic and cohesive nature to the food. This elasticity allows the dough to expand and trap the carbon dioxide, produced by the leavening, which makes the dough rise and stretch for bread, but too much gluten in your delicate pie crusts or biscuits will make them tough.

one recipe and bad for another? It's the amount of protein it contains. The more protein, the more *gluten* a flour will produce when it is kneaded. The more gluten you have, the less tender your baked good will be.

There are three basic types of flour that you'll need to become acquainted with: all-purpose flour, cake flour, and bread flour.

➤ *All-purpose flour.* This is a blend of hard and soft wheat flours. It ranges between 11 and 13 percent protein, which is average. The presence of more and tougher gluten in the hard wheat results in a rather elastic product. This produces the texture you want for cakes and cookies. Bleached and unbleached all-purpose flours can be used interchangeably, but unbleached flour has a higher nutritional value. Southern flours, such as White Lily, are made with a softer wheat, which means they have cake flour-like qualities. Southern flour is great for tender biscuits and pie crusts.

➤ *Cake flour.* This flour is made with soft wheat, producing less gluten when mixed, so your cake will be more delicate with a slightly crumbly texture. The protein percentage of cake flour is 9 percent. When purchasing cake flour, be sure you don't purchase self-rising cake flour unless the recipe calls for it. If you do buy it by mistake, omit the baking powder or baking soda and salt from the recipe.

An assortment of flour.

➤ *Bread flour.* The type of flour has a higher gluten-forming protein content, around 14 percent, making the dough nice and elastic. This makes it ideal for bread making.

Store all of your flours in airtight containers in a cool, dry place. They can last up to a year. If you use flour slowly, you can store your flour in the freezer. Double-bag the flour in sealable freezer bags and be sure to label it. Flour stored in the freezer can last several years.

Kitchen Utensil

If your recipe calls for cake flour and you only have all-purpose flour on hand, you can substitute 1 cup *minus* 2 tablespoons all-purpose flour for 1 cup of cake flour. If you need all-purpose flour and only have cake flour on hand, substitute 1 cup *plus* 2 tablespoons cake flour for 1 cup of all-purpose flour.

Gimme Some Sugar

Sugar, another basic in baking, gives tenderness and sweetness to doughs and batters. Sugar also causes browning, as it *caramelizes* (turns brown) when heated. Sugar is also a food source for yeast, making it rise. When baking, there are three different types of sugar you will need.

An assortment of sugar.

➤ *Granulated sugar.* This is standard white sugar, either from sugar cane or sugar beets, and is the most popular and readily available sweetener in baking. Superfine sugar is a form of granulated sugar that dissolves easily in liquid. You can make your own superfine sugar: Place 1 cup of granulated sugar in the blender, cover and process for one minute. Let it sit for about one minute longer to let the "dust" settle.

➤ *Brown sugar.* Brown sugar, both light and dark, is a mixture of granulated sugar and molasses. The color of the sugar depends on the amount of molasses mixed in; dark brown sugar has the most. Brown sugar has a deeper flavor than granulated sugar. When measuring brown sugar for recipes, be sure to pack it firmly into the measuring cup for accurate measuring.

When exposed to air for an extended amount of time, brown sugar has a tendency to harden. If this has happened, there's a quick fix. Place the hardened brown sugar in a heat-proof bowl and place the bowl in a baking pan containing about an inch of water. Tightly cover the entire baking pan with aluminum foil and place it in a 200°F oven for 20 minutes or until softened. You can also soften it in the microwave: Place hardened brown sugar in a microwave-safe dish. Add an apple wedge. Cover the dish tightly with plastic wrap and heat at HIGH for 35 seconds. Use the softened brown sugar immediately as it will re-harden when it cools.

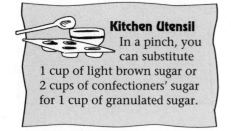

Kitchen Utensil
In a pinch, you can substitute 1 cup of light brown sugar or 2 cups of confectioners' sugar for 1 cup of granulated sugar.

Kitchen Utensil
To make your own brown sugar, use 1 cup granulated sugar plus 2 tablespoons of molasses or dark corn syrup for 1 cup of brown sugar.

➤ *Confectioners' (powdered) sugar.* Confectioners' sugar is granulated sugar that has been refined to a powder and contains a small amount of cornstarch to prevent lumping. Confectioners' sugar dissolves instantly in liquid and has a smoothness that makes it a popular choice for frostings, icings, and whipped toppings. It's also perfect for dusting cake tops and brownies. If your confectioners' sugar becomes lumpy, you can sift it. Store confectioners' sugar in an airtight container.

Extraordinary Eggs

Eggs thicken custards and sauces, help cakes to rise and be tender, and enrich and add sheen to baked doughs. Eggs come in two different colors, white and brown, but there is no difference nutritionally between them. Feel free to use free-range or organic eggs in any of these recipes, as long as they are the right size.

Always buy the freshest eggs available.

Information Station

Care must be taken when handling eggs because they can carry salmonella, a dangerous bacteria that can cause food poisoning. While salmonella is rare, prevention is the best cure. Here are some tips that can help:

➤ Always buy the freshest eggs possible. Buy only the number of eggs you will use within two weeks' time to ensure the freshness of your supply. If you don't use eggs that often, buy them by the half-dozen.

➤ Be sure to wash your hands with hot, soapy water before and after handling raw eggs. If you use a bowl to hold raw eggs, wash and dry the bowl before reusing it for another purpose.

➤ Salmonella does not grow in temperatures of less than 40°F. It is killed at temperatures above 160°F. Don't store eggs in the egg holder on the door of the refrigerator. It might be convenient, but it's also the warmest part of the refrigerator.

➤ Never use an egg with a cracked shell. If there is an off-odor after you have cracked an egg, discard it immediately.

➤ If a recipe calls for eggs at room temperature, don't allow the eggs to sit at room temperature for more than 20 minutes. Never use eggs left at room temperature for more than two hours.

You can freeze egg whites, egg yolks mixed with a pinch of salt or sugar per egg, or whole eggs, lightly beaten, with a pinch of salt or sugar added per egg. Ice-cube trays make convenient holders for freezing eggs. Never freeze eggs in their shells. Thaw frozen eggs in the refrigerator overnight, and never refreeze eggs once thawed. Be sure to label your containers so you know exactly how many eggs you have stored. Three tablespoons of beaten whole egg equals one large egg (or make up a whole egg by combining 1 tablespoon yolk with 2 tablespoons of white).

All the recipes in this book have been tested with Grade A large eggs. Egg sizes are determined by their weight and volume, so substituting one egg size for another can affect the outcome. For example, two large eggs equal approximately $1/2$ cup. It takes three medium eggs to equal the same $1/2$ cup.

Eggshell color (brown or white) and color of the yolk (light yellow to deep orange) are the result of the breed and diet of the chicken and don't say anything about the nutritional value or quality of the eggs.

Fats, the Good Guys With a Bad Rap

Fat is just the generic way of referring to butter, margarine, lard, oil, and shortening. How rich a cake, pastry, cookie, or other baked item tastes depends largely on the type of fat used in it and how it was incorporated. Although fat has gotten a bad reputation lately, it really does play an important role in baking, adding tenderness and flavor to baked goods. It also retains moisture and helps the leaveners in batters.

*The different types
of fat.*

There are several different types of fats used in cooking. While butter, stick margarines, and shortenings are fairly interchangable, it's always best to use the ingredient the recipe calls for.

➤ *Butter.* Of all the fats, butter has the best flavor for baking. Most professional bakers would not think of baking with anything else. It is made from the richness of cream and gives a wonderful melt-in-your-mouth taste to baked goods.

Butter varies in taste from brand to brand, so it's important to find the brand you like. Because butter can be expensive compared to your other choices (margarine, oil, shortening, etc.), your best choice is usually the brand that is on sale. At the market, butter comes in sticks or whipped in tubs. For baking, choose the stick form—whipped butter will give a much different texture to your baked goods because it has air whipped into it. You'll also have to choose between salted and unsalted. For the recipes in this book, it doesn't really matter which one you use, although you might want to chose unsalted butter for less salt content in your baked goods.

Keep butter wrapped in the refrigerator, away from any strong odors (the butter compartment of your refrigerator is always a good choice). You can also freeze butter (which offers great inspiration to load up when there's a sale). Just remember that butter is a sponge for odors (which can dramatically change its flavor), so wrap your butter in aluminum foil or seal well in plastic wrap or plastic bags before freezing and rotate your stock (first in, first out). Butter will keep frozen for up to one year, and in the refrigerator for several weeks. If you're in doubt about the freshness, just give it a taste. It should taste like nothing but butter.

➤ *Margarine, butter blends, and vegetable spreads.* A wide variety of oils and solid fats is used in making margarine, which gives the consumer an unsaturated butter substitute with no less than 80 percent fat. Butter is 100% saturated fat, which is a drawback for many. For the most part, stick margarine can be used in place of butter. Because of the oils that are added, margarine has a higher melting point than butter (110°F compared to 96°F). This also means it remains softer even when refrigerated. Textures and flavors vary, so you might have to try several brands before you find one you prefer. Butter blends are a combination of about 60 percent margarine and 40 percent butter and can be used interchangeably with butter or margarine.

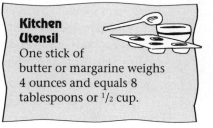

Kitchen Utensil
One stick of butter or margarine weighs 4 ounces and equals 8 tablespoons or $1/2$ cup.

Margarine and butter blends come in sticks and in tubs. Use the sticks for baking, since the margarine in the tub is too soft. Do not use reduced-calorie or low-fat butter or margarine for baking. There are margarine products called vegetable oil spreads that are lower in fat and cholesterol than butter or margarine. They are available in sticks, tubs, or as liquid spreads. Because there is less fat and more water in these products, I don't recommend them for baking—you won't like the results! If you must use them for health reasons, don't use any product with less then 65 percent fat for baking, and choose only the sticks. These products will affect the texture and quality of any baked item. Never should a liquid spread be used for the recipes in this book.

Information Station

Margarine was invented by a French chemist during the late 19th century, when Napoleon III needed a long-lasting and inexpensive fat for his army. It was patented in America in 1873 and has been on our store shelves ever since.

➤ *Shortening.* Shortening is 100 percent fat and is great for creaming and whipping because it doesn't break down or melt (like butter or margarine can) from the friction created by creaming fats. Many bakers swear by vegetable shortening for the flakiest pie crusts. Solid vegetable shortening is great for incorporating air into the batter, which gives added volume to cookies and cakes and makes them softer and spongier. Unfortunately, shortening does not impart much flavor to baked goods. Although there are butter-flavored shortenings, they still fall short of the real thing. Shortening is a good choice when the flavor of the fat is not that important. For example, you might want to use shortening for a spice or chocolate cake, and it makes a great choice for crunchy chocolate chip cookies. It's a bad choice for sugar cookies, however, since butter is an important flavoring ingredient in that recipe. Substitute shortening for butter, measure for measure.

➤ *Lard.* Lard is rendered pork fat, which is 100 percent animal fat and means that, like butter, it contains cholesterol. Lard makes a great flaky pie crust, and the pork fat gives good flavor and is inexpensive. Pie crusts aside, lard is not recommended for cakes, cookies, or other baked goods because of the strong flavor of the pork fat. When serving, you might want to inform your guests that there is lard in the crust, in case there are any vegetarians in the crowd. To substitute lard for butter, use 15–20 percent less.

➤ *Oil.* Oils are generally used for cakes, muffins, and quick breads. They impart a tenderness and moistness to the baked item. When an oil is called for in a recipe, be sure to choose one with a very mild flavor, such as safflower, canola, vegetable, peanut, or corn. I learned this the hard way. When I was a beginning baker, I once decided to make fresh blueberry muffins for guests visiting from Russia. The only oil I could find in the kitchen was olive oil, so I used it. While the muffins looked fine, the assertive flavor the olive oil gave to the muffins made them pretty unpleasant-tasting (although the jolt was better than coffee!). Our guests were extremely gracious, and even sampled one or two, but in the end we used the muffins to feed the birds.

Vegetable oils are a good choice in baking because they are low in saturated fat and contain no cholesterol. Oils can be stored at room temperature for several months. You can also refrigerate oils for even longer storage. When baking, use oil only when a recipe calls for it. Because oil mixes up differently than solid fats, the outcome of using it when it wasn't called for might be undesirable.

Cocoa and Chocolate, a Chocoholic's Dream

Chocolate comes from cocoa beans that have been fermented, roasted, and crushed into nibs. These nibs are then reheated and ground into a paste called chocolate liquor, which contains approximately 53 percent cocoa butter. All chocolate and cocoa starts out this way, but develops into many other products.

The different chocolates: a slab of chocolate, cocoa, chocolate chips, and a 1-ounce square.

Cocoa

Unsweetened cocoa comes from pure chocolate liquor that has been separated into cocoa butter and solid cocoa cakes. These cakes are ground into cocoa powder. Unsweetened cocoa is much different than cocoa for hot chocolate drinks, which has milk powder and sugar added. They cannot be substituted for one another.

Chocolate

Solid chocolate used for baking and eating comes in many varieties. Their differences lie not only in their varying proportions of chocolate liquor, sugar, and cocoa butter, but also in the addition of vanilla and sugar.

➤ *Unsweetened chocolate* is pure chocolate liquor, containing at least 50 percent cocoa butter and no added sugar.

➤ *Bittersweet, semisweet,* and *sweet chocolate* vary from one another by the amount of sugar, cocoa butter, and vanilla added to the chocolate liquor.

➤ *Milk chocolate* has dried milk powder, cocoa butter, and sugar added.

➤ *White chocolate* is not really even chocolate, since it does not contain any chocolate liquor, but most brands have cocoa butter. White chocolate is also called "vanilla chips" or "vanilla baking bar."

Stored properly, chocolate has an extremely long shelf life—up to one year. It should remain at a constant

Bakers Beware!
When a recipe calls for a specific type of chocolate, don't substitute any other type. You run the risk of a bad baking outcome. Different brands of chocolate have a wide range of tastes and textures. Experiment with various brands until you find a type you like.

Kitchen Utensil
One ounce solid unsweetened chocolate equals 3 tablespoons unsweetened cocoa plus 1 tablespoon vegetable oil or shortening.

temperature, between 65° and 78°F, and stored well wrapped in aluminum foil or plastic wrap. If stored at a high temperature, the chocolate will *bloom*, which means the cocoa butter will separate from the solids and your chocolate will have a grayish exterior color. Not to worry, though—the quality of the chocolate is not affected. When melting chocolate, never do so over direct heat. It is very delicate and burns easily. See "Melting and Tempering Chocolate" in Chapter 9 for the correct procedure.

Leaveners, a Baker's Best Pick-Me-Up

Leaveners cause a dough or batter to rise by producing carbon dioxide (a gas), which rises throughout the batter and gives it a light, porous texture. There are two types of leaveners, chemical and yeast. Chemical leaveners include baking soda, baking powder, and cream of tartar. Yeast is just that, yeast—which, if you wanted to get technical, is a fungal leavener.

A variety of leaveners.

Now for a quick bit of Chemistry 101: When an acid and an alkaline are combined in the presence of a liquid, carbon dioxide is formed. All three elements are needed to produce the rise. Once combined, the reaction is immediate, and, thanks to the heat of the oven, the gases in the batter expand, acting as another rising agent. There you go. Too much rise is not desirable, because then the cake or bread or whatever you are baking will collapse into itself.

There are a variety of leaveners commonly used in baking. Be sure to use the one called for in the recipe.

➤ *Baking soda.* Otherwise known as sodium bicarbonate, baking soda is an alkali that must be mixed with something acidic (such as lemon juice, buttermilk, chocolate, or molasses) in order to react. Because baking soda reacts immediately, you should place the batter in the oven as soon as you have finished putting it together. Baking soda and baking powder should not be substituted for one another. If you taste baking soda, you will feel it tingle on your tongue. If your baking soda is particularly lumpy, you can sift it.

Sometimes I store my baking soda in clear, airtight glass jars instead of the box it comes in to increase its shelf life. I often neglect to label the jar, and have to depend on my memory and the tingle taste-test when it comes time to bake. I think I picked up this habit from my mother, who keeps glass jars a-plenty in her kitchen. On one visit, I decided to bake up some banana bread. I found a jar of white powder and tasted it. It tingled, so I proceeded to make the bread. A few hours later, I heard a great clamoring in the kitchen and went to see what the problem was. On the counter was a *huge* raccoon that had climbed through the open window, feasting on my banana bread! When my mom came home and I related the story, she was surprised to learn that I had even been able to bake because she thought she was out of baking soda. I retrieved the jar and showed it to her. She then informed me that in fact it was not baking soda that I had used, but laundry detergent *with* baking soda!! I still wonder how that poor raccoon's stomach felt. The moral of the story is: Label your jars!

➤ *Baking powder.* Baking powder contains both an acid and an alkali (which is almost always baking soda), so just the addition of liquid is necessary to create a rise. Double-acting baking powder is true to its name—it reacts twice—once when the liquid is mixed in, and then again when the batter is placed in the oven. Today, almost all baking powder sold is double-acting. Although baking powder contains baking soda, don't substitute one for the other. Too much baking powder will make your baked goods taste acidic and may cause the finished product to collapse.

➤ *Cream of tartar.* After the manufacturing of wine, the acid left in the wine barrels is made into cream of tartar. Not widely used in baking, cream of tartar is generally added to egg whites when whipping to help stabilize them. It is also often used in candy making.

➤ *Yeast.* Mostly used in bread making, yeast gets its rising powder from the combination of the right amount of warmth, food for it to eat (sugar), and liquid, which causes the yeast to release carbon dioxide. In general, there are two types of yeast:

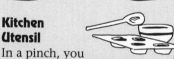

Kitchen Utensil
In a pinch, you can make your own baking powder. Combine $1/4$ teaspoon baking soda and $1/2$ teaspoon cream of tartar to equal 1 teaspoon baking powder. Or you can use 1 teaspoon baking soda plus 2 teaspoons cream of tartar for each cup of flour called for in the recipe. If you do make your own baking powder, make just what you need for the recipe; it can't be stored.

active dry yeast and fresh compressed yeast. Active dry yeast, which I use for all the recipes in this book, is available in most supermarkets in premeasured packets, containing $1/4$ ounce (or about 1 tablespoon). You can also buy active dry yeast in jars that contain larger amounts. Active dry yeast should be dissolved in lukewarm water, no hotter than 110°F, which is actually just slightly warmer than lukewarm. Test the water on the inside of your wrist or run the tap over a candy thermometer until you reach this temperature. If you're unsure, it's better to err on the side of cooler water than hotter because all yeast will die if exposed to temperatures over 120°F.

Kitchen Utensil

Before starting any recipe, be sure to check the expiration date on your package of yeast. Don't bother trying to use yeast that has passed that date.

Fresh compressed yeast is moist yeast, available in 0.6-ounce squares. A square of fresh yeast can be substituted for one package of active dry yeast.

There is also bread machine yeast, which I don't recommended for any of the recipes in this book. It's a special strain of fine-granulated, dehydrated yeast, specially designed to dissolve during the kneading and mixing processes of bread machines.

A final type is rapid-rise or quick-acting yeast, which is another strain of dehydrated yeast. While this type of yeast can be substituted for active dry yeast, measure for measure, I don't often use it. I haven't found it to significantly reduce rising time for my breads and am somewhat wary of its sustained rising power. If you do choose to use this variety of yeast, DO NOT proof it. It may expire before your dough finishes rising.

Liquid Assets

Liquids are added to a batter to help dissolve the salt and sugar and to create steam, which helps a cake rise and adds to its texture. Liquids also moisten the leaveners, which helps to activate it. While liquids include everything from water to fruit juice, the liquids I will define here are dairy liquids, since these are the ones you'll come in contact with most often.

➤ *Fresh milk.* When milk is called for in a recipe, it refers to cow's milk. There are several varieties of fresh milk available in the market: whole, low-fat, and skim. While all the recipes in this book were tested with whole milk, unless otherwise specified, you can substitute the milk of your choice.

➤ *Buttermilk.* This milk contains no butter, but was once a by-product of butter-making. Most commercial buttermilk is fermented from milk mixed with lactic acid (like yogurt and sour cream). Buttermilk adds a tangy flavor to doughs and batters and it is lower in fat than whole milk.

➤ *Evaporated milk.* Available in small cans, evaporated milk is whole milk with half of the water removed. The mixture is slightly thicker than whole milk. Skimmed evaporated milk is widely available and can be used interchangeably.

➤ *Sweetened condensed milk.* Also available in small cans, this is similar to evaporated milk with sweetener added. It is often used for cream pies and candy making.

➤ *Cream.* Cream is produced when the butterfat of milk is separated out of the liquid. The different types vary depending on the amount of butterfat in them. *Heavy (whipping) cream* is the richest of all the creams, containing between 36 and 40 percent butterfat. It is used for making whipped cream, but if you beat it too long it will turn into butter. *Light cream* is only about 20 percent butterfat and can't be whipped up like heavy cream. Light cream is good for making sauces or baking when you don't want all the richness of heavy cream. *Half-and-half* is a mixture of light cream and milk and contains between 10 and 12 percent butterfat. If you ever run out of milk, half-and-half makes a great substitute for baking.

Kitchen Utensil
If a recipe calls for buttermilk and you don't have any on hand, you can substitute 1 cup of regular milk plus 1 tablespoon vinegar or lemon juice for 1 cup of buttermilk. Let it sit for a few minutes before using. You can also substitute plain yogurt, measure for measure.

Kitchen Utensil
It's always a good idea to keep a can of evaporated milk on hand. If you ever run out of fresh milk while baking, just mix equal parts evaporated milk and water to make up the amount of milk you need.

A variety of liquid ingredients.

Air: It's Not Just in Your Head

One of the most important ingredients in baking is the one you can't see—air! Air is what leavens your batter, lightens your cakes, and can send your batter pouring over the sides of the pan. Unfortunately, you have the least amount of control over this element since it can't be measured and you have to rely on technique or other ingredients to incorporate it. Air bubbles beaten into fat or eggs are one leavening agent. These are created when you beat sugar into butter. In the heat of the oven, the air in these bubbles expands, making the cake rise. The steam given off from the liquids makes the air expand and it rises even more. Although you may not be able to see air, you can certainly see its effects.

The Baking Spices (and Extracts) of Life

Spices and extracts add flavoring to baked goods. The most common spices used in baking are cinnamon, allspice, ginger, mixed spice (also called apple pie spice), cardamom, cloves, and nutmeg. Spices come from the seeds, bark, roots, and nuts of different plants. Recipes usually call for ground spices. When spices are ground, the oil that gives them their fresh flavor evaporates over time. For best results, buy small quantities of ground spices and store them in tightly closed containers (glass is best) in a cool, dry place (not near the stove). This will minimize the loss of the oil, but you should still consider replacing spices you've had for more than one year.

Examples of extracts and spices.

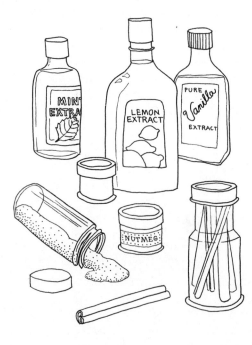

Extracts are a mixture of ethyl alcohol and flavoring oil, such as orange, lemon, or almond. The most common extract used in baking is vanilla. At the market you will have a choice of pure or imitation extracts. For the best flavor, you should always choose pure extract. Although it can cost almost twice as much as imitation, it's a smart investment because the flavor it gives your baked goods is so much better than that of imitation. Some extracts, such as root beer and maple syrup, don't come in a pure form, so you don't have a choice. Because alcohol evaporates, be sure you keep the lid on tight and store your extracts in a cool, dry place.

Kitchen Utensil

It's much less expensive to buy spices in bulk than at grocery stores or supermarkets. Check out your local natural-food store or baking supply shop to see if they carry loose spices. Just don't forget to label the jars you store them in.

Information Station

Believe it or not, you can actually make your own vanilla extract. It's easy. Get four whole vanilla beans, available at gourmet stores and baking supply stores (make sure they are soft and pliable, not hard and stiff). Slit each bean in half lengthwise. Soak the beans in 2 cups of vodka in a covered glass jar for at least two weeks. You can strain the liquid or just leave the beans in, it doesn't matter. Use it measure for measure when vanilla extract is called for. This also makes a great gift for a baker.

The Nuts and Bolts of Nuts

Ever notice how many oils come from nuts? Peanut oil, walnut oil, almond oil—the list goes on. That's because nuts get most of their flavor from the oils they contain. But be careful, because these same oils make the nuts go rancid if not properly stored. Nuts add a wonderful flavor to baked goods, and they can also double as decorations. Be sure to get the freshest nuts possible. Store all your nuts in airtight containers in a cool, dry place if you will use them in less than a month. Otherwise, pop them into your freezer, away from strong odors, where they can keep for up to one year. I usually buy my nuts in bulk, since there is great savings in doing so, and they are readily available in the bulk section of many grocery stores. Don't grind or chop your nuts until you are ready to use them. Here's a list of the nuts most commonly used in baking:

Kitchen Utensil

It's easy to blanch your own almonds. Just place the almonds in boiling water for 30 seconds to 1 minute. Drain and run under cool water, if desired, then rub them in a clean kitchen towel to loosen the skins. You can also pop them straight out of their skins by just squeezing them a little.

➤ *Almonds*. Almonds are oval-shaped with a light brown exterior. Almonds are available in or out of the shell, blanched (skinned) or unblanched ("raw"), halved, sliced, slivered, toasted, smoked, buttered, or salted. Whew!

Almonds.

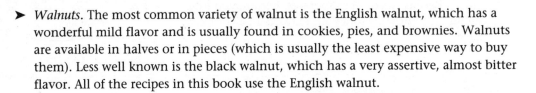

➤ *Walnuts*. The most common variety of walnut is the English walnut, which has a wonderful mild flavor and is usually found in cookies, pies, and brownies. Walnuts are available in halves or in pieces (which is usually the least expensive way to buy them). Less well known is the black walnut, which has a very assertive, almost bitter flavor. All of the recipes in this book use the English walnut.

Walnuts.

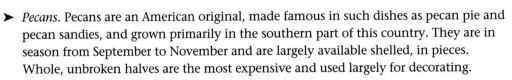

➤ *Pecans*. Pecans are an American original, made famous in such dishes as pecan pie and pecan sandies, and grown primarily in the southern part of this country. They are in season from September to November and are largely available shelled, in pieces. Whole, unbroken halves are the most expensive and used largely for decorating.

Pecans.

➤ *Hazelnuts*. Also called filberts, hazelnuts seem to be the nut of the decade. You can find just about anything flavored with this nut, from coffees to gourmet desserts. Their round shape makes them perfect for garnishing, too. Hazelnuts have a light brown skin and can be used whole, ground, chopped, or as a paste to flavor fillings for desserts.

Hazelnuts.

➤ *Pine nuts.* Also called piñon, these buttery-tasting nuts have grown in popularity in recent years because of their starring role in pesto. These little nuts, shaped like a tiny ivory teardrop, have a high oil content, so they should be stored in the freezer and used within six months of purchase. While the pine nut is grown worldwide and there are many varieties available, don't purchase the Chinese pine nut, which has a strong, piney flavor.

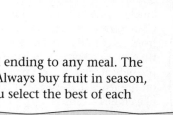

Kitchen Utensil
To skin hazelnuts, spread them out on a baking sheet and bake at 350°F for 10 minutes or until the skins begin to crack. Rub the nuts in a clean kitchen towel to remove the skins.

Toasting nuts helps bring out their wonderful flavor and removes some of their "raw" taste. To toast nuts, place the nuts in a shallow baking dish and bake in a 350° oven, stirring often, until they are golden brown, 5 to 10 minutes, depending on the nut. Don't overbake them or their flavor becomes bitter.

Fresh Fruits and How to Pick 'Em

Cakes, pies, and tarts made with fresh fruit make a wonderful ending to any meal. The better the fruit you choose, the better the end result will be. Always buy fruit in season, at the peak of ripeness. The following guidelines will help you select the best of each season's crop:

➤ *Apples.* Choose apples that have a fresh, bright look and smooth, tight, unbruised skin. They should be firm and crisp. The best apples for baking are the more tart or sturdy varieties, such as Granny Smith, Winesap, McIntosh, and Golden Delicious. I try to buy my apples at the local farmers' market to ensure I am getting the best quality. I usually find a better variety of apples there than at my local supermarket. Keep in mind, red delicious apples may look pretty and are great for snacking, but they are not a good choice for baking.

Kitchen Utensil
Always store apples in the refrigerator. At room temperature they will ripen up to ten times faster and turn mealy. Yuck!

➤ *Bananas.* Bananas should be lightly firm and golden yellow with speckles of black spots; you don't want green stems or tips. If your bananas have green tips, just let them ripen at room temperature for a few days.

➤ *Berries.* All berries, especially raspberries, are highly perishable and should be refrigerated and used within a day or two of purchase. Don't wash berries until you are ready to use them. Inspect packages of berries carefully; there should be no sign of mold. Fresh berries should give off a pleasant, fresh, aromatic smell. If there is not much smell, there will not be a lot of flavor. Store delicate berries in a single layer to extend their storage life.

➤ *Cantaloupe.* Choose a cantaloupe with a beige, not green, color. The blossom end (the end with the dimple) should give just a little when it is pressed. If the cantaloupe is ripe, it will have a sweet, ripe aroma.

➤ *Citrus fruits.* This category includes lemons, limes, grapefruits, and oranges. Choose fruits that are firm and feel heavy for their size. The heaviness comes from the fruit being juicy. Avoid lemons and oranges that have tinges of green skin. Always wash the fruit if you plan on using it for zest.

Kitchen Informant
North America has very few indigenous fruits, and the cranberry happens to be one of them (along with the blueberry and Concord grape). Cranberries got their name from early settlers, who called them "crane berries" because the delicate red berries grew on branches that were shaped like cranes' heads.

➤ *Cherries.* Unfortunately, cherries have an extremely short season—July and August—so grab them while you can. Look for firm, plump, glossy cherries with a dark maroon color. Avoid soft or brown cherries; that means they are overripe. Wash them only when you are ready to use them (within a few days of purchase).

➤ *Cranberries.* You can usually only find cranberries in the autumn, and they are often sold in plastic packaging. Look for bright, plump, glossy cranberries. Shriveled or soft berries are a sign of age, and certainly steer clear of any brown or moldy packages. Rinse fresh cranberries before using. Cranberries freeze very well, so consider stocking up on them for a year-round supply. Just don't defrost them before baking.

➤ *Dried fruits.* Dried fruits such as apricots, dates, raisins, cherries, blueberries, and cranberries are great for baking because they have a long shelf life and can be added to many recipes. When choosing dried fruits, make sure they are soft and pliable and have a nice aroma. Soak dried fruits in hot water or flavored water (water with a teaspoon of vanilla, rum, brandy, etc.) for up to 30 minutes to add some moisture and additional flavor to any dried fruit. Store all dried fruits in an airtight container for up to six months. You can also freeze them to prolong their shelf life—just thaw them before using.

➤ *Honeydew.* Choose melons with creamy white skin or pale yellow skin. Both ends should give a little when pressed, and the smell of the fruit should be sweet. Feel the skin of the honeydew. If it is a bit sticky or tacky, it means the fruit is sweet, since the sugar of the fruit rises to the surface.

An assortment of fresh fruits.

➤ *Mangoes.* Mangoes are becoming more and more popular and finding them is no longer such a chore. Purchase your mango while it is still slightly firm but gives a bit when pressed. Look for a smooth skin with red and yellow coloring. A little touch of green is okay, but avoid mangoes that are all green.

➤ *Nectarines and peaches.* Choose fruits with an orange yellow or creamy yellow skin with a nice red blush and a fragrant smell. The red blush of a peach, however, is not an indication of ripeness. It is caused by the exposure to the sun. Judge the ripeness of a peach by the yellow or creamy color. Any green tint to the skin means the fruit was picked unripe and will never sweeten or ripen. If the fruits have nice color (no green tint), but are slightly hard, set them out at room temperature for a few days to ripen. Refrigerate the peaches once they have ripened.

➤ *Pears.* Since pears bruise so easily, choose your fruits slightly firm. They will ripen at room temperature in a few days. Avoid very green or bruised fruit. A good pear will have a nice pear-like fragrance.

➤ *Pineapple.* Choosing a good pineapple can be tricky, since the fruits will not continue to ripen, or sweeten, once picked. Some pineapples are labeled "field ripened" and they should be your first choice. Otherwise, look for fresh-smelling, deep-green leaves. Pineapples should be firm but give slightly when squeezed. Pulling a leaf from the center of the pineapple is not a good indicator about the freshness or sweetness of the fruit, which is a popular misconception. Avoid any pineapples that are soft or smell like they are beginning to ferment.

The Least You Need to Know

➤ Each ingredient plays an important role in your finished product. Make sure you choose the right ones.

➤ Don't panic if you run out of something; there are substitutions for many ingredients.

➤ Freshness counts, so take care when choosing the ingredients for your recipes.

➤ Proper storage prolongs shelf life.

Part 3
Getting Down to the Nitty-Gritty

You know you have an oven, but do you know how it works? This section preps you for the process of baking. There is information here for getting your oven in top working order and for working with an oven that's troublesome. You'll also find advice on how to read recipes, and how to avoid getting yourself in over your head if you are a beginning baker. There are tips on how to measure all kinds of things from flour to fats. You'll also find information on the basic techniques you'll need to perform when you want to try out some of the intermediate to challenging recipes—everything from whipping egg whites to melting chocolate. This sections unlocks many of the mysteries of the kitchen and gets you ready to go.

Chapter 6

Ode to the Oven

In This Chapter

➤ Understanding how your oven works

➤ The different types of ovens

➤ How to avoid hot spots in your oven

➤ Tips on how to make sure your oven is the right temperature

➤ Knowing how to position your racks

Ah, the oven. Without it, baking would be impossible. Many bakers take the oven for granted, however, thinking it will always be relatively trouble-free. You turn the dial, the oven heats up, you put your item in to bake, and that is just about all the thought you give to it. But, really, the oven is almost magical. In this chapter, I'll explain what goes on when you close the oven door, and I'll pass along some hints on what to do if your oven begins acting up.

What's Going On in There?

The oven is an appliance everyone's familiar with, but have you ever given much thought to how your oven works? Food cooks in an oven because it is surrounded by hot, dry air. How quickly or evenly the food cooks depends on the temperature of the oven. Food is baked in the oven due to *conduction* (or transfer) of energy (heat) from the air to the batter or dough.

The foods we bake are made up of many elements: proteins, starches, sugars, water, and fats. Heat has an effect on all of these elements, producing specific and necessary reactions in each.

Conduction is actually pretty straightforward: The food is surrounded by the heat of the oven. Slowly, the heat from the air is transferred to the food and penetrates it from the outside inwards (that's why the outside of a cake may look cooked, but it may still be wet and gooey inside). The metal pan also retains the heat from the oven and acts as an insulator for the heat.

Heat affects the batter in several ways:

➤ The proteins (eggs and gluten) begin to lose moisture, shrink, and coagulate.

➤ The liquid that has been mixed into the starches becomes gelatinous and firms up (in other words, the flour begins to absorb the liquids and becomes firm and dry).

➤ The sugars begin to caramelize, which is why baked goods turn golden brown. The type of sugar used determines how brown the food becomes.

➤ Water evaporates, which can happen rapidly as the internal temperature of the food increases.

➤ Fats begin to melt and give the baked good tenderness.

➤ The air that has been incorporated into the batter (either by beating or by the gases produced by the chemical leaveners or yeast) begins to expand, which allows cakes and cookies to rise.

So, basically, the food is put into the oven, the surface begins to lose the moisture and firms up, and the food browns, which completes the cooking process. Pretty neat, huh?

Taking all of this into consideration, you can imagine how important a properly working oven is.

All About Ovens

There are three different types of ovens on the market: gas, electric, and convection. Gas and electric ovens are the varieties most commonly found in homes. Convection ovens are generally found in professional or very top-of-the-line kitchens, because they are so expensive and because most people who bake don't really need a high-performance convection oven.

Information Station

Before conventional ovens were in homes (the first gas stove was introduced into American homes in the 1850s), the majority of cooking was done over open fires and the baking was done in beehive-like ovens usually above or behind an open fire. Temperature was regulated by touch—how long your hand could remain in the oven—instead of by a thermometer. Judging when an oven was hot enough was one of the baker's most difficult challenges.

I have always used a gas oven, unless I was baking professionally and was therefore privileged enough to have a convection oven for my use. Gas ovens generally have a constantly running pilot light and the heat comes from a perforated bar that runs down the center or in a "T" shape in the bottom of the oven. This bar is usually covered by a false bottom of the oven.

Electric ovens have large, exposed coils on the top and bottom of the oven, called a dual-element, so that they heat from both areas (unless you broil, when only the top element does the heating). Because electric ovens heat from the top and bottom and gas ovens heat only from the bottom, many people claim that electric ovens supply more even heat, which results in more even cooking. However, the heat of a gas oven will surge on and off to maintain the temperature, something electric ovens don't do.

Kitchen Utensil

If your oven seems to cook food unevenly, give the food a half-turn halfway through the baking time, so that what was in the back is now in the front and what was on the left is now positioned on the right.

Convection ovens use an internal fan to circulate the hot air, so every part of the oven is the same temperature. In professional kitchens, they are almost always free-standing and have many racks. An in-home convection oven looks more like a standard oven. Some ovens can function as either a convection oven or an electric oven at the flick of a switch, which I think is pretty cool. Because every part of the oven is the same temperature, convection ovens can cook a lot of food at one time. That's why they're popular in professional baking. In general, convection ovens cook food more quickly than conventional ovens, so if you're using one, you may have to reduce the heat called for in a standard recipe by 25 to 50°F, or reduce the baking time by 25 percent.

If you're in the market for a new oven, figure out what features you like. Newer ovens come with all kinds of bells and whistles that can add a fun new dimension to your baking. (My aunt just purchased a new oven that beeps when it has reached the required temperature!) Think seriously about the amount of space you want your oven to have, and whether you want to pay extra for the convection feature. And always measure the oven to make sure it will fit in your kitchen. A good oven will soon become your best friend.

The Heat Is On

If you've been experimenting a bit with baking and have been having bad results, it may not be the recipes, but the temperature of your oven. DO NOT trust the oven dial with which you set the temperature. Ovens which have been tried and true for many years may suddenly become uncalibrated and without warning increase their temperature by 25 to 50 degrees!

There is no way an unsuspecting cook would know without having an additional auxiliary thermometer placed in the oven. You can find oven thermometers in any kitchen supply store or hardware store and they should only cost a few dollars. The time and frustration they will save and the peace of mind they give even a casual baker is certainly worth every dime. Place your oven thermometer in a central location in your oven. You can hang it off the center of your oven if you like (don't place it on the floor of the oven; it will give you an inaccurate reading). If you are convinced you have a tricky oven, you might want to invest in two thermometers, one for the front of the oven and one for the back of the oven, to make sure the temperature is even throughout your oven.

What Happens if Your Oven Is Too Cool or Too Hot

Let's say you're baking a cake. If the temperature of your oven is too cool, the surface of the cake will dry out too quickly, leaving the middle still uncooked. Or, when it does cook through, the cake will be too dry because too much of the moisture has evaporated.

If the temperature of your oven is too hot, all the chemical reactions happen too quickly. The cake can rise unevenly or too quickly and the outside of the cake will be cooked and browned while the inside is still raw batter.

Why Preheat?

You will notice that all recipes say to preheat the oven. You may think this is just a frivolous step, but it's actually very important.

Kitchen Utensil
Turn on your oven when you begin your recipe, and it will have reached the proper temperature by the time you're ready to put in your goodies.

It takes about 15 to 20 minutes to properly preheat an oven. A preheated oven allows the ingredients to react properly, ensuring a good finished product. If you place anything to bake in a cold oven, the ingredients will react much differently with each other and the results will be most undesirable. You need a heated oven to give breads their final growth spurt, soufflés a good push up, cakes a good rise, and to make cookies that won't spread all over the pan.

Rack Chat

All of the recipes in Part 6 of this book have been tested with the rack of the oven being placed in the center of the oven.

While it may sound odd to you, there really is a temperature difference between the racks of your oven. The center of the oven is where the temperature is most moderate, giving your baked goods the best chance for even cooking. The type of oven you're using—gas or electric—determines where the hot spots are in the oven. In general, the lower third of a gas oven is hotter than the middle (since that's where the heat comes from), and the top third is also hotter than the middle but not as hot as the floor of the oven. An electric oven heats from the top and bottom, which tends to make it equally hot at the top and bottom and moderate in the middle.

Hot spots in the oven result in uneven cooking. There really isn't much you can do about that. However, if you notice you need some extra protection, try placing all of your pans on baking sheets before you put them in the oven. The baking sheet will insulate the pans and help bake food more evenly.

I recommend using only one rack—the center rack—when you bake, unless of course you have a convection oven, in which case you can use all of them. However, if you want to use two racks, position the racks as close to the center of the oven as possible (usually that means one rack will be in the center, and one rack will be positioned directly below). Don't place the pans one on top of the other, but position them off-center so air can circulate around both pans. Halfway through baking, rotate the top and bottom pans and turn them back to front so they will bake most evenly. You may notice that with two pans in the oven at once, you will need an increased baking time.

Check the table on the following page for some common baking problems and their possible solutions:

Bakers Beware!
If you need to adjust the racks in your oven, do so while the oven is cool. Racks usually don't slide in and out easily, because most are designed to pull out and still support the weight of the food without tipping forward. There is usually some sort of up-and-over motion you have to finesse when removing the racks from each level. Don't try to manipulate tricky racks when they're hot.

Bakers Beware!
Each time you open the oven door, you are changing the oven's temperature. If you open the oven door too many times during baking, your item will take longer to bake and it may not turn out as you want it because of the many temperature changes. If your oven is equipped with a light, use that to monitor the baking process. You should only peek in on your item when you think it's ready to come out of the oven.

For even baking, position pans off-center from one another so heat can circulate around them.

Problem	Possible Solution
Item is burnt on the bottom, but top is not cooked	Adjust your rack so it is not so close to the bottom of the oven. Check oven temperature with an auxiliary oven thermometer to make sure it is accurate.
Item is burnt on the top, but bottom is not cooked	Adjust your rack so it is not so close to the top of the oven. Check oven temperature with an auxiliary oven thermometer to make sure it is accurate.
Item seems to burn before the recommended baking time is finished	Check oven temperature with an auxiliary oven thermometer to make sure it is accurate.
Item cooks unevenly	Rotate the baking tray a halfturn halfway through baking to ensure even cooking.

The Least You Need to Know

➤ The proper oven temperature can be the difference between success and failure in the kitchen.

➤ Make sure your oven is preheated to the correct temperature before you bake.

➤ It's a good idea to place an additional oven thermometer in your oven.

➤ Position your rack in the center of the oven for the most even baking.

Getting Ready to Get Started

Okay, now that you've read this far, you should have a good idea about the wide variety of things you can bake. It's time to start baking! The best way to become proficient and comfortable with baking is to practice and practice some more. Don't select a recipe that's too challenging. At first, choose one that includes just a few ingredients and techniques that you're familiar with. Once you master that recipe, move on to more challenging recipes, maybe trying a recipe where you have to pick up an unfamiliar ingredient or try a new technique. If you continue progressing in a slow and steady manner, in time you will become an expert baker, and maybe even launch a new part-time career (or at the very least you'll wonder why you ever bought a cake from the grocery store).

Recipe Rundown

If you know how to read, you can read a recipe. However, there are a couple of things to keep in mind as you're reading through a recipe to make sure there won't be any surprises along the way.

It's helpful to understand how a recipe is written. What's crystal clear to recipe writers may not always be so easy for the reader to understand, especially for less-experienced bakers.

If you run across any words that you are unfamiliar with in a recipe, be sure to look them up in Chapter 4 of this book or in a dictionary.

Sometimes, it's the wording of a recipe that can confound a beginning baker. Let's say your recipe calls for "1 cup walnuts, chopped." You may wonder: Does this mean to chop the walnuts and then measure them, or measure out 1 cup of walnuts and then chop them? The answer is simple. When you are supposed to do something to an ingredient *after* it is measured, it will be listed *after* the ingredient; if you are supposed to do something to the ingredient *before* it is measured, it will be listed *before*. Therefore, "1 cup walnuts, chopped" means you should measure the whole walnuts and then chop them. If you were supposed to measure first, the recipe would call for "1 cup chopped walnuts."

After you have selected your recipe, you should always read through it once before starting. You need to make sure you're familiar with all of the terminology used in the instructions. If there are some ingredients or methods you need to look up, you should take the time at the beginning to familiarize yourself with what you are about to do. It will be harder to leaf through the book when you are up to your elbows in batter!

Once you have read through a recipe, it's time to assemble all of your ingredients. Woe is the baker halfway through a recipe when he realizes he's out of an ingredient. If you're lucky (like me), you live near a market. When I run out of something, I have to prevail upon whomever is in the apartment to run out and pick up what I'm missing. Believe it or not, sometimes they even have to make two trips! This could all be avoided if I would heed my own advice (as you should) and do an inventory check before beginning to bake.

After you have read through the recipe once, make up your shopping list. Go over the ingredients again and double-check to make sure you have the correct amount in the pantry and refrigerator. If you bake infrequently, your flour supply might be lower than you remember. Often I think that I have more eggs and butter in the refrigerator than I really do. It takes a second to check, and it will save you a lot of time in the long run. Start composing a shopping list, if you need one.

Information Station

Be a smart shopper by composing a shopping list before you head for the store. When I rely on my memory, I tend to leave off at least one item, which means another trip to the store. There are also a lot of "impulse buys" one should be wary of. Grocery stores are filled with all kinds of distractions, so go with your list in hand, eat a snack before you go if you are feeling hungry, and stick to your written word. You will come out of the store faster and with more cash in your pocket.

After you have reviewed the ingredients, your next step is to get out the equipment you will need. If you're using a food processor, assemble all the parts. Check to make sure your mixing bowl is not being used for something else. Find the parts to the hand mixer, clear off the counter, and get ready. Assemble the baking tools you will need. Make sure everything is clean and ready to go. This is also a good time to grease baking pans or sheets. That way, the pans will be ready as soon as you've finished mixing the batter.

Sometimes, during this stage, you might discover you are out of materials. You may be low in shortening to grease the sheets, or perhaps you need more nonstick spray. These things might not be listed in the recipe's list of ingredients, but they are just as essential to having it turn out right as any of the ingredients you are adding. Assembling the tools and going over ingredients are two sure-fire ways to make sure you will have a successful baking experience.

Once you've taken inventory of what you will need, it's time to shop. (Perhaps you can send someone out on an errand to the store. I find that people are more willing to run a quick errand if they know their reward will be a warm, gooey cookie, a slab of cake, or a fresh slice of bread.) When all the ingredients are assembled, it's time to start baking.

Kitchen Utensil
Don't be discouraged if something doesn't turn out right the first time. Many beginner bakers give up too easily. And remember, professionals have bad days, too.

Chances are, at some point in your life you have watched a cooking show on television. If so, you've seen the cook dumping bowls of this and that into the dish being prepared. Ingredients had been prepared ahead, making it possible to throw together several dishes in a short amount of time. If you follow the example of the cooking shows and premeasure everything (or in cooking terms, "prep" everything), you will have made baking the easiest thing in the world to do. Once you have your ingredients at your fingertips, ready to be mixed together, you may wonder why you ever felt intimidated by baking. Of course, you may dirty an additional bowl or two, but the payback in pleasure and ease of baking is worth the extra few seconds it takes to wash the bowl.

In Timing a Recipe, Use Your Common Sense

Kitchen Utensil
When you're trying to size up the amount of time it will take you to prepare a recipe, don't forget to allow for additional time for clean-up. For the most part, if you get started on the clean-up when the item goes into the oven, you will find you won't have much more than a pan or two to wash once you've finished baking.

Give yourself ample time to prepare baked goods. Each recipe in Part 6 of this book has prep times and cook times given, but not everyone works at the same rate, so allow yourself plenty of time. You'll find it much more relaxing when you don't play beat-the-clock. There are also times which are not included in the recipe, such as the 15 to 20 minutes it will take for a cake to cool enough to be handled. Or, if you want to frost the cake, you'll need even more time to allow the cake to cool and to frost it. What if you run out of an ingredient and have to run to the store? Allow for such things, and even if you don't need any additional time, you'll be better off having planned for it.

I have cooked under relaxed conditions and flustered conditions alike, and inevitably the conditions were reflected in my results. As you practice and become more proficient in the kitchen, it will take you less and less time to get a job done. Still, always give yourself more time than you think you'll need.

The Right Tool for the Job: Make Sure You Have It

When you read through a recipe, pay attention to the equipment that is called for. If you have to beat together butter and sugar, you will more than likely want to have a hand mixer available. If you are making rolled cookies, you'll need a rolling pin. The right tool makes baking so much easier and will save quite a bit of time.

Before starting a recipe, be sure that you have the correct pan that is called for in the recipe. If you use a larger or smaller pan size than what is called for, it will affect your finished product and you could run the risk of a burned cake or one that never cooks through. Certain pans can be fudged a little. Loaf pans, for example, can either be $8^1/_2 \times 4^1/_2$ or 9×5, and in most cases, either size can be used. If the recipe calls for a covered casserole, you can create a "cover" with aluminum foil.

Kitchen Utensil
In a pinch, you can sometimes improvise kitchen tools. Try using a wine bottle as a rolling pin, or a drinking glass as a cookie cutter.

Of course, much of baking can be done with just a few simple tools, so it doesn't mean you have to go out and stock your kitchen. Here is a list of what I would consider the essential tools for baking (check out Chapter 3 for more detailed descriptions):

Measuring cups/spoons

Wooden spoon

Rubber spatula

Pancake turner

Whisk

Oven thermometer

Mixing bowls (at least two sizes)

Cutting board

Knives (at least a large chef's knife and a paring knife)

Vegetable peeler

Box grater

Rolling pin (if you want to make pastry or rolled cookies)

Colander/strainer

Pots/skillet (at least a 1-quart saucepan, 2-quart saucepan, large stockpot, and 10-inch skillet)

Baking sheets

Cake/pie pans (8- or 9-inch)

Springform pan (if you like to make cheesecakes)

Cooling rack (two racks are a good start)

You probably already have many of these items. I baked for several years without any electrical appliances, so I'm a firm believer that you don't have to spend a lot of money to get into baking. Hand mixers, stand mixers, and food processors certainly make quick work of preparing and mixing ingredients together, so if you really start to enjoy baking, you may want to invest in one or more of those appliances. They really do make baking a breeze.

Clean as You Go

When I was a beginning baker, I was always amazed at the large mess I would end up with at the end. I seemed to dirty every single bowl, spoon, countertop, and article of clothing that came near me. When I began working for a caterer, there was a huge sign in the kitchen that read *Clean as you go*. Yes, of course, why

Kitchen Utensil

Recycle bowls and utensils as you bake. If you use a spatula to scrape the sides of the bowl when you are mixing, use it again to scrape the batter into pans. If a bowl had sugar in it and you need to beat eggs, either give the bowl a quick rinse or just use it as is. You might be amazed at how few utensils you really need.

Bakers Beware!
Flavors of food can be transferred just by sharing the same counter space, so it's important to keep counters and cutting boards clean. For instance, if you were chopping onions or garlic, be sure that the cutting board has been washed and dried (and even flipped over) before you use it to slice your strawberries. Otherwise, your berries might taste like onions.

didn't I think of that? And so I began that practice, and wow, what a difference it made! Not only did I use fewer utensils, but my mess was not nearly as large. Now I have one of the world's smallest kitchens. When I bake, I have no other choice but to clean as I go. It not only makes my life easier (I'm not saddled with a huge pile of dishes at the end), it also frees up space on my counters.

As soon as you are finished using measuring cups, pots, pans, spoons, and appliances (food processors, hand mixers, and so on), wash them and put them away. Make use of your "down time." If you have to mix dough for five minutes and you're using a stand mixer, take a look around and wash the bowls that held the ingredients for the dough. If things need chill time, wipe down the appliances you used and put them away if you won't be using them any more. I always find it convenient to have a container of hot, soapy, clean water ready in the sink to wipe down counters, rinse off utensils, or to soak things in.

Wash your hands often. Not only for sanitary purposes but also because you'll find that your hands will become dirty or sticky while you bake. If you don't wash them often (usually a quick rinse in the soapy water does the trick) you'll find batters and dough stuck on your refrigerator handle, on your appliances, all over your clothes, or on whatever else you touch (which means more cleaning for you later).

Wipe down your countertops often. As well as keeping them clean, a quick wipe every so often will help keep whatever you put on them clean, too. Always check to see if your garbage needs to be emptied before you begin baking. You might be amazed at the amount of trash you can produce, and you don't want to pile the garbage so high you run the risk of it spilling onto the floor or having to stop what you are doing to take out the trash.

Put away ingredients and equipment as soon as you finish using them. This will free up quite a bit of counter space, giving you room to work with dough or spread out pans.

Check Out the Number of Servings

As you are deciding what to make, be sure to take the number of servings into account. The following table gives approximate yields for some common baked goods.

Item	Number Served
8-inch layer cake	8–10
8-inch cheesecake	10
9-inch layer cake	10–12
9-inch cheesecake	12
9-inch pie	6–8

The richer the cake, the smaller the slices you will want to cut. Of course, take your guests into consideration when choosing a dessert. If you know someone has a particularly big sweet tooth, they might want seconds on dessert. I would always rather have too much than too little.

If you are attending a potluck or expecting a crowd for dessert, think about making a sheet cake or cupcakes to get a high yield. Almost all cake recipes can be made into sheet cakes or cupcakes, which will feed between 16 and 24 people. See if your recipe gives instructions for this type of conversion. Otherwise, just fill the pan $2/3$ full and check on its progress every 10 minutes or so.

The Least You Need to Know

➤ Select a recipe on a level that you feel comfortable with—over-challenging yourself might make you frustrated.

➤ Read and reread a recipe before beginning it to become familiar with what you'll be doing.

➤ Take stock of your ingredients before you start to eliminate trips to the grocery store.

➤ Don't let a mess get the best of you—clean up as you bake.

➤ Check your yield—will it make enough servings?

For Good Measure

In This Chapter

➤ Learn how to accurately measure everything from solids to liquids to fats

➤ Choose the right tool for your measuring needs

➤ A handy table for measurement equivalents

You probably know someone who bakes, and it seems she just tosses in a little bit of this and a little bit of that and presto, out come cookies or a pie or something else delicious. It's like magic, so you may wonder how important it is to be accurate in measuring. The answer is: VERY IMPORTANT. Proper measuring is critical to baking. Baking is a science, and when you are mixing ingredients together you are creating chemistry, albeit edible chemistry, so it's important to be precise. There is balance with flour, leaveners, fats, and liquids.

Extra salt or baking soda can ruin otherwise perfect cookies. Too much flour makes muffins taste dry and flavorless. No beginning cook should be nonchalant about measuring. The success of your recipe depends on it.

As you begin to feel more comfortable with baking, you may feel inclined to experiment a bit, maybe add some chocolate chips to peanut butter cookies or throw some nuts or dried cranberries into oatmeal cookies. That is all well and fine, but give it time. You are never too good or experienced to measure.

What Do I Measure With?

As I discussed in Chapter 3, measuring cups are essential baking tools. There are two types of measuring cups available: graduated and glass. Graduated cups range in sizes from ¹/₄ cup to 1 cup, and can range from 4 cups in a set to 6 cups in a set. Use graduated cups to measure dry ingredients and solid fats such as shortening and miscellaneous ingredients such as shredded coconut, nuts, and raisins. Glass cups are available in a wide range of sizes, the most common being 1-, 2-, and 4 cups. Use these cups for measuring liquids.

> **Kitchen Utensil**
> When measuring thick, sticky liquids such as honey, molasses, or corn syrup, spray the inside of the measuring glass with nonstick cooking spray or grease it a little with oil. The liquid will then be much easier to remove.

Used for measuring ingredients in small quantities (less than ¹/₄ cup), graduated measuring spoons usually come in sets of four or six, ranging from ¹/₄ teaspoon to 1 tablespoon. Sometimes sets will have ¹/₈ teaspoon and 1¹/₂ tablespoon, too. Use the measuring spoons for both dry and liquid measure.

Graduated and glass measuring cups.

Graduated measuring spoons.

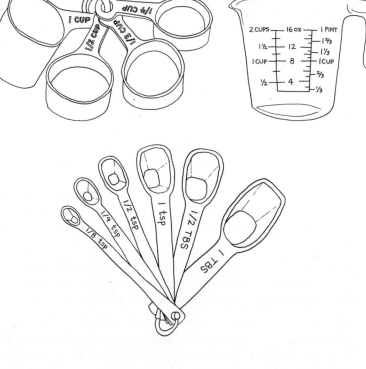

Using Measuring Spoons

When measuring liquids, fill the measuring spoon to the very top. For dry ingredients, pour or scoop into the spoon until it is full. Level off the spoon with the straight side of a spatula or knife.

For dry ingredients, pour or scoop into the spoon until it is full. Level off the spoon with the straight side of a spatula or knife.

Using Measuring Cups for Dry Ingredients

To measure flour, sugar, bread crumbs, and other dry ingredients, spoon ingredients lightly into the measuring cup. Then level off the cup with the straight side of a butter knife (do not use the cutting side). This will give you one level cup. If the recipe calls for a heaping cup, do not level off the cup. Instead, leave a small mounded top of ingredients. Never tap a measuring cup on the counter when measuring flour. The tapping will compact the flour and you will measure out too much.

Bakers Beware!
Never measure over the bowl of ingredients you are using for the recipe. If you overpour or level extra into those ingredients, your measurements will not be accurate.

To measure dry ingredients such as flour, pour or spoon ingredients lightly into the measuring cup. Then level off the cup with the straight side of a butter knife.

To sift or not to sift can be a bit of a dilemma for any beginning baker. All flour is presifted, so it's not mandatory to sift flour each time you bake something—just give the flour a stir before you measure it. However, sifting does aerate flour, and for some recipes, it is necessary. Sifting is also a good way to combine all of your dry ingredients, such as baking powder, spices, and flour. Also, pay attention to how the recipe is written. If the recipe calls for 1 cup of sifted flour, you should sift the flour before you measure it. If the recipe calls for 1 cup of flour, sifted, you need to measure out the flour, and then sift it. You won't do any harm to flour if you do sift it even if the recipe does not tell you to; however, if you don't sift when it is called for, the recipe may not turn out as expected.

To measure ingredients such as chopped nuts, shredded cheese, fresh herbs, or coconut, spoon the ingredients into the measuring cup and pack down lightly.

For dry ingredients such as fresh herbs or coconut, spoon the ingredients into the measuring cup and pack down lightly.

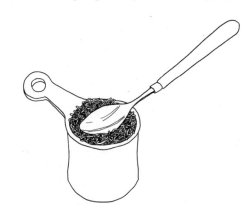

To measure brown sugar or shortening, spoon the ingredients into a cup and pack down firmly with a spoon or rubber spatula to eliminate any air holes.

Pack down shortening firmly with a spoon or rubber spatula to eliminate any air holes.

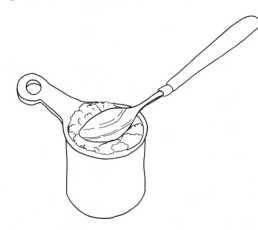

Using Measuring Cups for Liquids

You should always use a glass measuring cup, which is marked in fluid ounces, for measuring liquids, from milk and water to honey and molasses. For an accurate reading, always rest the cup on a level surface and read at eye level.

Always rest the cup on a level surface and read at eye level.

Equivalent Measurements

Sometimes you will need to double a recipe, or cut one in half, or a recipe may call for an amount in fluid ounces and you want to know how many cups that will be. The following list gives you some equivalent measurements, so instead of measuring out 16 table-spoons of something, you know it equals a cup.

Common Measurement Equivalents

Dash/Pinch	2 or 3 drops (liquid) or less than $1/8$ teaspoon (dry)
1 tablespoon	3 teaspoons or $1/2$ ounce
2 tablespoons	1 fluid ounce or $1/8$ cup
$1/4$ cup	4 tablespoons or 2 fluid ounces
$1/3$ cup	5 tablespoons plus 1 teaspoon
$1/2$ cup	8 tablespoons or 4 fluid ounces
$3/4$ cup	12 tablespoons or 6 fluid ounces
1 cup	16 tablespoons or 8 fluid ounces
1 pint	2 cups or 16 fluid ounces
1 quart	4 cups or 2 pints or 32 fluid ounces
1 gallon	4 quarts or 8 pints or 16 cups or 64 fluid ounces
1 pound	16 ounces

If a recipe calls for 3 pounds of apples, you may not know how many that is. Or maybe you need 2 cups of nuts and you're wondering how much you should buy at the store. The following table is a list of common equivalents that you can use as a guide when you need to know how much of an ingredient you need.

Common Food Equivalents

Almonds	1 pound	3 cups whole, 4 cups slivered
Apples	1 pound	3 medium, $2^3/_4$ cups sliced
Apricots, dried	1 pound	$2^3/_4$ cups, $5^1/_2$ cups cooked
Bananas, fresh	1 pound	3 to 4; $1^3/_4$ cups mashed, 2 cups sliced
Blueberries, fresh	1 pint	2 cups
Blueberries, frozen	10 ounces	$1^1/_2$ cups
Butter	1 pound	2 cups
Butter	1 stick	8 tablespoons, $^1/_2$ cup
Cherries, fresh	1 pound	$2^1/_2$ to 3 cups pitted
Chocolate wafers	18 wafers	1 cup crumbs
Chocolate chips	6 ounces	1 cup
Cranberries	1 pound	3 cups
Cream (sour, half-and-half, light)	$^1/_2$ pint	1 cup
Cream (heavy)	$^1/_2$ pint	2 cups whipped
Flour, all-purpose	1 pound	3 cups sifted
Flour, cake	1 pound	$4^1/_2$ to 5 cups sifted
Graham crackers	15	1 cup crumbs
Lemons	1 medium	3 tablespoons juice, 2 to 3 teaspoons zest
Maple syrup	16 fluid ounces	2 cups
Milk, whole	1 quart	4 cups
Oats, rolled	1 pound	5 cups
Oil	1 quart	5 cups
Peaches, fresh	1 pound	4 medium, $2^1/_2$ cups chopped
Peaches, frozen	10 ounces	$1^1/_8$ cups slices and juice
Pumpkin, fresh	1 pound	1 cup cooked and mashed
Raspberries	1 pint	scant $1^1/_2$ cups
Shortening	1 pound	2 cups

Strawberries	1 pint	$2^1/_2$ cups sliced
Sugar, brown	1 pound	$2^1/_4$ cups packed
Sugar, confectioners'	1 pound	$3^1/_2$ to 4 cups
Sugar, granulated	1 pound	2 cups
Vanilla wafers	22 wafers	1 cup crumbs
Walnuts	1 pound	$3^3/_4$ cups halves, $3^1/_2$ cups chopped
Yeast	$^1/_4$-ounce package	1 scant tablespoon

The Role of Tableware Spoons

Despite the fact that your kitchen cutlery shares the same names as your measuring utensils, you should never substitute the teaspoons and tablespoons you use for eating for your measuring spoons. There is no way to tell how much your tableware spoons will hold, and using them could have a serious effect on the outcome of your baked goods.

That said, when you are making cookies and the recipe calls for dropping the dough by the teaspoonful or tablespoonful onto a baking sheet, that is when you should use your tableware spoons, not measuring spoons.

The Least You Need to Know

➤ Accurate measuring is the key to successful recipes.

➤ Use graduated measuring cups for solids and glass measuring cups for liquids.

➤ Knowing measurement and food equivalents will help you in your baking.

Chapter 9

Basic Techniques

In This Chapter

➤ Easy-to-follow instructions for scalding milk, tempering chocolate, and more

➤ Quick tricks for preparing pans for baking

➤ Three different ways to separate an egg

➤ All you ever wanted to know about whipping egg whites

➤ Toasting nuts to bring out their flavor

When a recipe asks you to scald milk or temper chocolate without any further explanation, do you feel like throwing in the towel and going back to making brownies from a box? Don't give up yet. Understanding basic cooking techniques is essential for preparing successful recipes. By mastering the basics, you will find baking easier and much more enjoyable. In this chapter, I'll take you through these techniques, step by step, and soon you'll be scalding and tempering with the best of them.

That's "Scalding," Not "Scolding"

No, we're not talking about discipline here. To "scald" a liquid means to heat it to just below its boiling point. Milk is scalded in many baked-goods recipes to retard souring, especially if mixed with an acidic ingredient.

To scald milk, simply measure the milk into a heavy-bottomed saucepan and place it over medium heat. Stir the milk occasionally; as soon as the surface begins to bubble, remove the pan from the heat. If the milk does boil, it might form a thick film on top. Remove the film before using.

I learned a neat trick for scalding milk when I worked in the bakery. Rub some butter along the inside edge of the pan before heating the milk. Even if the milk does foam up when it is heated, it will stop when it reaches the butter.

Peeling Peaches

Peeling peaches can be a tricky business. If your peach is perfectly ripe, the skin will sometimes slip right off, without even so much as a knife, but as I'm sure you're aware, that is not always the case. The following method makes peeling peaches a snap, leaving the beautiful flesh unmarked.

Have ready a medium-size bowl of ice water. Fill a 2-quart pan with water and set it on the stove to boil. While you are waiting for the water to boil, lightly cut a small X on the bottom of the peach. Try not to cut into the flesh, but just the skin. When the water is boiling, gently drop the peach into the water. Wait about 30 seconds (you will see the cut skin start to loosen and flutter a bit in the water). Remove the peach from the water with a slotted spoon and plunge it into the ice water for 1 minute. The skin should slip right off. If not, return the peach to the hot water for 30 more seconds. This also works for almonds, plums, and tomatoes. And plum tomatoes, for that matter.

Zesting Citrus Fruits

The *zest* of citrus is the colored part of the skin that holds the essential oils. The *pith* is the bitter white membrane between the zest and the fruit. Your goal is to get the zest and not the pith. The most common citrus fruits used for zesting are lemons and oranges. Wash the fruits before you zest them.

There are two ways to zest any citrus. The first way is with a citrus zester, a kitchen tool that removes the zest of the fruit and leaves the pith behind. Hold the fruit in one hand and the citrus zester in the other and run the zester along the length of the fruit. The peel should come off in thin little strips. You can either dice the strips or use them whole (the recipe will call for one or the other).

The second way to zest a fruit is with the coarse, sharp-edged holes of a grater (not the large holes used to grate cheese). Gently rub the fruit against the sharp edges, rotating the fruit after a few rubs, until the peel grates off and the desired amount is grated. The peel will be reduced to tiny little particles, so it will not be necessary to dice it further. Be careful of your knuckles and fingers when using the grater because it's very sharp.

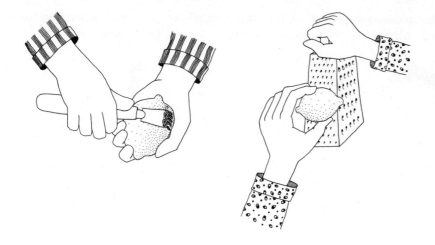

Two ways to zest citrus: using a hand-held zester (left) and using a box grater (right).

If your recipe does not specify grated or strips, read through the entire recipe to try and figure it out. If you are to remove the zest, from, say, a liquid, you can pretty much be sure the zest should be in easy-to-remove strips. If you are adding the zest to a frosting or batter, it's safe to assume that you will be grating up the lemon zest. As nice as lemon zest is for flavor, no one wants to bite into a big strip of it.

Sectioning Citrus Fruit

You probably won't come across too many instances when sectioned fruit is called for in a recipe, but this is a handy technique to know and sectioned fruit always makes a nice garnish.

Citrus fruits, particularly oranges and grapefruits, have a tough skin that can be difficult to chew. When you section a citrus fruit, you remove the fruit from the tough membrane, making it easier to eat.

Start by cutting off the top and bottom of the fruit. You should cut to the fruit and not leave any white pith. Lay the fruit on its cut end. Being careful not to cut too deeply, cut away the peel and the white pith, following the shape of the fruit. Hold the fruit in one hand or place it on the countertop. It will be juicy, so you will want to do this over a bowl. You will see the membranes that hold the fruit together. Make a cut parallel and right next to the membrane, cutting toward the center, to release the fruit. Once you get to the center, turn the knife and cut away, next to the other membrane, following the shape and size of the section of fruit. Continue cutting until the section of fruit is free. Let the fruit sections fall into the bowl underneath, along with all of the juice. Repeat until all the of the sections are free. Give the empty membrane a squeeze when you have finished to get all of the juice out. Remove any seeds from the sections before using.

Cut away the peel and the white pith.

Make a parallel cut along the membrane toward the center.

Turn the knife and cut away, next to the other membrane, following the shape and size of the section of fruit.

Melting and Tempering Chocolate

Never melt chocolate directly over a heat source. It burns very easily and must be melted over low heat. Since chocolate varies from brand to brand, each will melt slightly differently, so it's always best to follow manufacturer's instructions. If none are given, here are some guidelines.

Using a Double Boiler

The best pan to use for melting chocolate is a double boiler. A double boiler consists of two stacked saucepans, or a saucepan with a fitted bowl that sits on top. (For more information on double boilers, or a handy substitute if you don't have one, see Chapter 3.) Cut the chocolate into small pieces (about the size of chocolate chips; being exact here is not necessary, the pieces will be irregularly shaped). Place the chocolate pieces in the top part of the boiler and set it over simmering, not boiling, water. Stir the chocolate often and remove it from the heat when almost all of it has melted. Continue stirring until all the pieces have melted and it is smooth.

Nuke It!

The microwave is also a great tool for melting chocolate. Chocolate melts very easily, so set your temperature to medium-low, and follow the manufacturer's directions for time (usually 1 or 2 minutes). Check the chocolate after 1 minute. It will not melt the same way it does over a double boiler, so you will have to stir it and keep a close eye on it because it will burn easily. White or "vanilla" chocolate needs particularly close attention, a very low heat, and less time.

Temper, Temper

When you temper chocolate, you heat, cool, and reheat it to specific temperatures. Tempering chocolate is not necessary unless you will be using it for cake decorations or candy making. The process stabilizes the cocoa butter, which is present in all solid chocolate, so it will not "bloom." (Chocolate is said to bloom when the cocoa butter separates from the chocolate and the chocolate takes on a whitish appearance; even after chocolate blooms, you can still use it.)

To temper chocolate, you must have a double boiler with a snug-fitting top half so no steam escapes from the bottom pan. Finely chop the chocolate into small pieces and place two-thirds of the chopped chocolate into the top half of a double boiler placed over simmering water. Stir constantly, monitoring the temperature of the chocolate until it reaches 100° to 110°F. Don't let it go over this temperature (clip a candy thermometer onto the pot so you can read the chocolate's temerature). Remove the top part of the double boiler and stir the remaining one-third of chocolate into the melted mixture. Blend until smooth and the temperature reaches 89°F for semisweet or 86°F for milk chocolate or white "vanilla" chocolate. Maintain the temperature of the chocolate between 83° and 90°F while you work with it, otherwise you'll have to start all over again.

Candy thermometer.

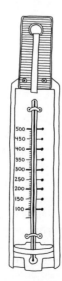

Bakers Beware!
Be sure to color enough frosting for your needs so you don't run out. It's difficult to match colors if you need to make more.

Kitchen Utensil
A simple, fun decoration for cakes and pies is tinted (colored) coconut. Place 1/4 cup of shredded coconut in a sealable plastic bag and add 3 to 5 drops of liquid food coloring. Seal the bag and shake like crazy to evenly distribute the color. If you want a deeper color, add 1 drop of food coloring at a time and shake. Keep adding drops until the desired color is achieved.

Tinting Frosting

It's not very difficult to tint frostings. The best frosting to color is a vanilla buttercream or basic frosting. There are two ways to tint frosting: with liquid food coloring or with food coloring paste, available at baking-supply shops. Liquid food coloring is the least expensive way to color frosting, and, like the paste, will last a lifetime (no kidding).

To use liquid food coloring, put several drops (no more than 5) into the frosting you plan on using. Mix thoroughly. Add 2 additional drops at a time until the desired color is achieved. To use a food coloring paste, dip the tip of a toothpick into the paste and then into the frosting you plan on using. Mix thoroughly. Dip the toothpick a second time, if necessary. Coloring paste is *highly* concentrated, so a very little bit goes a long way. Be sure you mix the frosting to a uniform color and there aren't any heavy color streaks.

If you have colored your frosting too dark, hopefully you have some additional white frosting and you can mix the *colored* frosting, bit by bit, into the *uncolored* frosting until the right color is achieved. (If you mix the uncolored frosting into the colored frosting, you may find the frosting never changes color.) If you don't have any leftover white frosting, you can mix up another batch (or half-batch) of frosting and mix in the colored frosting, little by little, until you get the desired shade. If you have made a simple buttercream frosting, you can freeze the leftover frosting for another use.

Separating an Egg

The most important thing to know about separating eggs is that you don't want to have any egg yolk in the whites (but it's okay if the whites get mixed into the yolks).

Kitchen Utensil
Eggs separate best when they are cold, so keep yours in the refrigerator until you're ready to use them.

When working with raw eggs, be aware that a bacteria may be present in the porous shells of the eggs that can cause salmonella poisoning. While this is rare indeed, it is helpful to know that nearly every carton of eggs sold in the United States has a toll-free number on it, as well as an expiration date for the eggs, and you can call the supplier to see if there have been any cases of salmonella. You'll find more tips on buying and storing eggs in Chapter 5. That said, you can choose how you want to separate your eggs. I will suggest three different ways to separate an egg.

The most common practice is to crack the egg cleanly in half over a bowl and pass the yolk from one shell to the other, allowing the white to gradually fall into the bowl below. This can be a bit messy, and you run the risk of the yolk getting punctured. It's important that you not let any yolk contaminate the whites because egg yolk will prevent the whites from whipping to their full volume. Another disadvantage to this method is that some whites will be lost to the shell.

Separating an egg by passing the yolk from shell to shell.

My favorite method is to separate an egg in my hand. Crack the egg without splitting it. Then hold the egg upright, over a bowl, and gently pry off just the top half of the shell (some egg white will spill into the bowl, but the bottom half will contain the yolk and more white. Carefully dump the egg into your cupped hand held over a bowl. Gently relax your fingers, allowing the white to spill through and drop into the bowl below. Once all the white has fallen into the bowl, you will be left with a perfect, round yolk which you can neatly deposit into another bowl. Wash your hands thoroughly before and after using this method.

Separating an egg using the cupped-hand method.

The third way to separate an egg is to use an egg separator. An egg separator is a small plastic gadget that has a suspended bowl with a handle and a small hook to fit onto a cup (you can find them at any kitchen supply store). Place the egg separator over a small bowl or glass. Crack the egg open and let it fall into the center of the separator. The whites will slip through the slots of the separator into the bowl and the yolk will stay in the separator. It can then be easily transferred into another bowl.

Separating an egg using an egg separator.

Whipping Egg Whites

The purpose of whipping egg whites is to incorporate as much air as possible into them, which will give good lift to your cakes or meringues. You also want them to be stable, so they hold their shape when you use them. If you have good arm strength, the best method is a copper bowl and a whisk with a large balloon. The most common method of whipping egg whites is with a mixer with the whisk attachment. A pinch of salt helps break up the gelatinous texture of the egg whites; a pinch of cream of tartar helps to stabilize them. If you use a copper bowl, you do not need the cream of tartar or salt since the copper of the bowl helps stabilize the egg whites naturally. Even if the recipe does not call for it, you can add a pinch of salt or cream of tartar when whipping egg whites, if you like.

Egg whites increase their volume best if they come to room temperature first (20 minutes, and no longer than 40 minutes). Remember that egg whites can expand up to six times their natural volume, so make sure the bowl you choose can accommodate them.

Be sure the bowl and whisk you are using are perfectly dry and clean; any amount of moisture or egg yolk or other debris will prevent the egg white from whipping up properly.

Some recipes call for egg whites to be beaten to soft peaks, while other recipes call for them to be "stiff but not dry." Beating whites to soft peaks means the whites will flop over gently when the beater is removed. Stiff peaks will hold their shape when the whisk is lifted and be somewhat glossy. You will also be able to turn the bowl upside down without the whites budging. Be careful not to overbeat the egg whites, or else they will become dry. If you're nervous about overbeating egg whites, you can always stop using the electric mixer when the whites reach soft peaks and finish beating

Kitchen Utensil

If you have overbeaten your egg whites—they slip around in the bowl and there is water released by the whites, or they clump and are no longer smooth—don't despair. Try to rescue your egg whites by using an unbeaten egg white for every four whites you have in your bowl. Stir in the unbeaten white, then whip the whites by hand with a wire whisk very gently for about 30 seconds.

them by hand with a wire whisk. Also, be sure not to beat the egg whites until you are ready to use them. If you let them stand around, they will deflate.

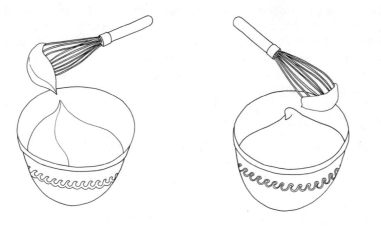

Egg whites beaten to stiff peaks will hold their shape (left), while egg whites beaten to soft peaks will gently flop over (right).

If you're adding egg whites to a heavier batter, mix about $^1/_4$ of the beaten egg whites into the batter beforehand to lighten up the batter. Then fold in the remaining beaten egg whites. The beaten egg whites should always be added to the heavier batter; never add the batter to the beaten egg whites.

You can freeze egg whites and egg yolks for several months. Place the whites in a small plastic sealable container, make sure to mark on it how many egg whites it contains, and freeze it. Just defrost them before using. To freeze egg yolks, first beat them with a pinch of salt or sugar per egg and then freeze them, making sure you mark how many yolks are in a container. You can freeze whole (unseparated) eggs too, by lightly beating them with a pinch of sugar or salt per egg. (Do not freeze eggs in their shells.) Defrost eggs in the refrigerator overnight (never at room temperature) and never refreeze eggs which you have frozen.

Preparing Your Pans

Often, a recipe calls for greasing and flouring a pan. A pan is greased and lightly floured to prevent the cake or bread from sticking to the pan. Although a pan's nonstick coating can eliminate sticking for the most part, these coatings can wear off over time and are not always 100 percent reliable. Always prepare the pans before you embark on the recipe, so the pans will be ready when you have finished mixing the batter.

If your recipe only calls for greasing the pans, I think the absolute best tool for the job is nonstick cooking spray. This will do the greasing job in half the time or less than using shortening or butter, and adds less fat to your recipe. This is an especially good tool for greasing bundt pans, because they have so many cracks and crevices. If you don't have nonstick cooking spray, just scoop up about a teaspoon of shortening or softened stick butter or margarine and smear it around the cake pan or loaf, making sure you grease the sides and well into the corners of the baking pan. You should leave a film of grease around the pan and not leave chunks of shortening on the pan itself. I always use my fingers to do the smearing, but you can also use a crumpled-up paper towel or piece of waxed paper.

If the recipe calls for flouring the pan, sprinkle about a tablespoon of flour into the greased pan. Tap the flour into the corners, then tilt the pan slightly and shake the flour carefully onto the sides. Do this part over the sink or trash can. If you are flouring two pans, tap the excess into the second pan. You can tap the excess flour into the trash when you are finished dusting. If you have to flour the pans, don't use cooking spray as your grease because the flour does not stick to it as well as it will to shortening. If you are into "spraying stuff," there is a nonstick spray called Baker's Joy that will both grease and flour your pans. It's available in the baking supply section of the supermarket.

Occasionally, a pan will have to be lined with parchment or waxed paper to prevent the cake from sticking to the pan. The simplest and most common form of lining is that used for cupcakes or muffins. You can purchase muffin cup liners at the grocery store to fit the cup, then you can pour the batter directly into the paper cup.

Kitchen Utensil
To prevent paper liners from slipping out of place, grease the pan with shortening or butter and the paper will stick in place.

To cut a liner to fit a round pan, place the pan on the sheet of parchment or waxed paper and trace the shape of the pan onto the paper. Cut out the circle and place it in the pan. You can grease and flour the paper and the sides of the pan, too, to ensure it will not stick to the cake once it is baked. Just remove the paper from the cake while it is still hot. Otherwise, the paper will adhere to the cake and pull the cake off with it.

Trace the shape of the pan onto the paper. Cut out the circle and place it in the pan.

To cut a liner to fit a loaf pan, take two long pieces of parchment or waxed paper. Cut one piece to fit the length of the pan and the second to fit the width of the pan. Grease the pan, then fit both pieces of paper (they will overlap and there should be some overhang).

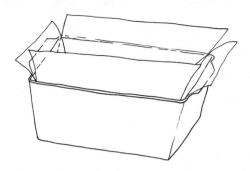

Cut one piece to fit the length of the pan and the second to fit the width of the pan. There will be some overlap and there should be some overhang.

To line a jelly roll pan, trace the pan size onto a piece of waxed or parchment paper. Secure the paper onto the jelly roll pan by greasing it first, then flatten the liner onto the pan to fit. Again, remove the paper liner from the cake or bread while it's still hot.

Toasting Nuts

Toasting nuts helps bring out their wonderful flavor and removes some of their "raw" taste. To toast nuts, place them in a shallow baking dish and bake in a 350°F oven, stirring often, until they are golden brown, 5 to 10 minutes, depending on the nut (pine nuts will take the least amount of time; almonds or hazelnuts will take a bit longer). Don't overbake them or their flavor will become bitter.

You can also toast nuts in a dry skillet over medium heat. Stir the nuts frequently until they become golden brown and smell toasted, about 5 to 10 minutes, depending on the nut. If I have a small amount of nuts to toast, I use my toaster oven. I spread out the nuts on the small tray and set the toaster to the lowest setting. After the nuts finish toasting, I let them sit for a few minutes and then check to see if they are golden brown. If not, I just push down the toaster button again. The second time around, I closely monitor them to make sure they don't brown too much. If you have burned your nuts, discard them—they will ruin the flavor of your baked item.

The Least You Need to Know

- ➤ If you are unfamiliar with a technique, be sure you look up how to do it so that you feel comfortable before proceeding with a recipe.
- ➤ Always use a double boiler to melt chocolate.
- ➤ When whipping egg whites, make sure that all of your equipment is clean and dry.
- ➤ Grease and flour your pans before you start the recipe.

Part 4
Now You're Baking!

Okay, you know you want to make a cake, a pie, a batch of cookies, or maybe some bread. What now?

This section explores the makeup of all varieties of baked goods and how to make the type you choose the best ever. It explains the processes and ingredients involved in the preparation of cakes, frostings, pies, cookies, and more. It presents fundamental information for each of the different categories in baking so you'll have a good foundation to work from when you're in the kitchen or shopping for baking ingredients.

Creating Great Cakes

In This Chapter

➤ A complete breakdown of the different types of cakes

➤ How does a cake bake?

➤ How to bake great-looking cheesecakes

➤ How to cool a cake properly

Anyone can bake cakes. There's no magic to it, although it may seem that there is when you watch a simple mixture of eggs, butter, flour, and sugar turn into a thick, creamy batter, then bake into a yummy treat that melts in your mouth. While there is no magic per se, there is chemistry and there is technique. Both can be explained, taught, and learned. If you are feeling at all apprehensive about making a cake, don't. You can feel like a complete klutz in the kitchen and still turn out a respectable cake. My premise is everyone can, and should, bake cakes.

Once you've decided to bake a cake, you need to choose the kind of cake you want to make. In this chapter I'll introduce the categories of cakes so that you can size them up for yourself. Whichever you choose, I've included lots of tips and hints to help you bake a great cake.

The Magic of Butter Cakes

The most popular and best-known type of cake is the butter or shortening cake. These are our classic layer cakes, the cakes we associate with birthday parties and festive occasions, loved for their moist sweetness and high-stacking layers filled with delicious frostings and topped with decorations.

A finished butter cake.

Information Station

Birthday cakes have a long history. The Roman emperors celebrated their birthdays with offerings of cakes to the gods and to the common people. In the Middle Ages, people celebrated with a cake on the feast day of their name saint instead of their birthday.

It is believed that the first birthday cake candles were used in Germany during the Middle Ages as symbols of earlier religious votive candles. The candle in the center of the cake was called the *Lebenslicht*, or "light of life"; today we call this the "one to grow on."

What makes butter or shortening cakes different from other varieties of cakes is they have a lot of fat (butter, shortening, or oil) in relation to the number of eggs used. It's not hard to make a good butter cake, but you do need to know how to correctly mix the ingredients together to produce a smooth batter that includes the right amount of air. Butter cakes rise from the air whipped into the batter as well as from the addition of baking powder or soda. The exception to this rule is the true pound cake; these dense cakes don't use baking powder or soda.

Because the fat is the essential ingredient here, it is critical that you select the best one for your purposes. Many professionals say unsalted butter is the best choice. Salt was originally added to butter as a preservative; with modern refrigeration we no longer really need the salt. If you bake without it you have more control over the salt content of your foods, if that is a concern. If, however, you have only salted butter on hand, don't worry; it won't affect the flavor of your cake.

An often forgotten ingredient in good butter or shortening cakes is air. Solid vegetable shortening is great for incorporating air into the batter, which gives added volume to cakes and makes them softer and spongier. Solid vegetable shortening is the most dense and will cream the best of all your choices of fat. Unfortunately, the flavor is not as rich as if you were to use butter (or even margarine), which can be disappointing. In all the butter/shortening recipes, feel free to substitute half shortening and half butter to get the best of both ingredients. For more on this, see the section "Fats, the Good Guys With a Bad Rap" in Chapter 5.

A well-prepared butter cake is moist and has a tender crumb. For the best results, make sure the fat you choose is softened. Shortening is ready to go from the can, but if you choose butter, you will have let it soften. If the butter yields slightly to your touch, but is still solid and not melted, it is just right. If you have to press hard, it is still too cold. Let it sit out for 15 more minutes and test again. If the butter is melting inside of the wrapper, it is too soft; pop it in the fridge for about 15 minutes to harden slightly before using. Butter taken directly out of the refrigerator should be ready to use in 20 to 30 minutes. Cream the butter or butter/shortening blend with the sugar until light and smooth. Begin on medium-low speed, then increase to medium speed. This will allow air to be incorporated into the fat without overheating and melting it, an important thing to keep in mind when working with all-butter cakes. Then add the eggs, followed by the dry ingredients, oftentimes alternated with the liquids to keep the batter creamy and smooth. Bake, and violà! Perfect cakes!

Pound Cakes, the Heavyweight of the Butter Cakes

The pound cake got its name because it traditionally contained one pound each of flour, butter, eggs, and sugar. It is a staple for bakers because it's easy to make, reliable, delicious, and keeps for a long time. Today's pound cakes are not restricted by the original recipe and can be glamorized with bits of chocolate, poppy seeds, fruits, and raisins, just to name a few additions. The old-fashioned plain pound cake is still a classic, though.

For a truly dense cake, mix the batter by hand. For a lighter texture, use an electric mixer to cream the butter and sugar, then finish mixing by hand. This is supposed to be a dense cake, so be careful not to overmix the batter by beating it too long with the mixer, otherwise it might come pouring over the sides of the pan when it bakes.

Don't fret if the top of the cake splits—this is normal, caused by steam escaping during baking.

Kitchen Utensil
Bake pound cakes in loaf, tube, or bundt pans, preferably of shiny metal rather than dark steel. Dark pans cause the outside of the cake to brown before the inside is baked through.

A finished pound cake.

Cupcakes, Just a Smaller Version

Like pound cakes, which originally contained a pound of each ingredient, cupcakes are so-called because all ingredients were originally measured out by the cup: 1 cup of butter, 2 cups of sugar, 3 cups of flour, and 4 eggs. The individual tins came later, so the name was really derived from the recipe, not from the baking pans.

Any recipe for layer, butter, or pound cake makes a fine cupcake; coffee cake recipes can also be used, as can recipes for fruit cakes, nut cakes, and tea cakes. Cupcakes are baked in muffin pans. As a general rule, the pans are prepared for baking by spreading them with shortening or spraying them with nonstick coating. They can also be lined with paper or foil baking cups, which ensure that the cakes won't stick to the pan, making clean-up a snap. The liners also help keep moisture in the cakes, keeping them fresher longer.

Flat-bottomed, cake-type ice cream cones can also be used as baking containers for cupcake batter. Children are particularly fond of them. To make them, fill the cones $^2/_3$ full with batter (about 2 generous tablespoons). Place the filled cones on a flat baking sheet or in muffin tins and bake for about 25 minutes, or until a cake tester inserted in the center of the cupcake comes out clean. Eat the cake and its container.

Cupcakes are great for any occasion.

Lighter Than Air: Sponge and Angel Food Cakes

Sponge cakes are light and airy. The primary reason they rise so high is the air beaten into egg whites. Sponge cakes are both lighter and drier than butter cakes. They are drier (in a good way, not like an overbaked cake) because they don't have the fat that adds to the moistness of butter cakes. Butter cakes cut sugar into the fat to make the air pockets. In contrast, sponge cakes whip the eggs with sugar until light in color (lemon-colored, if you will), thick, and at the ribbon stage (when the batter forms a flat ribbon falling back upon itself when the beater is lifted). At this stage, a line drawn with your finger through the batter will remain visible for at least a couple of seconds. Whisk-type beaters, not paddles, are always used to make sponge cakes. The air whipped into the egg-sugar mixture at this stage contributes to the rising of the sponge.

When the cake is placed in the oven to bake, the second essential factor is the heat of the oven. Basically, what happens is this: The liquid in the batter becomes steam, which rises and escapes through the foamy batter. The heat also causes the air in these bubbles to expand, which contributes to the rise.

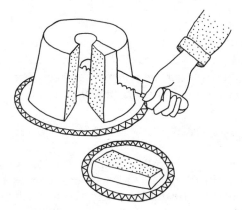

A finished angel food cake.

An angel food cake is a light, fluffy, high-rising cake that is basically a sponge cake without egg yolks or fat. To make a good angel food cake, you just need to know some basic tricks:

➤ *Whip the egg whites properly.* An angel food cake is made with a large quantity of egg whites, which are whipped into a foam; this foam provides all of the cakes leavening (see "Whipping Egg Whites" in Chapter 9).

➤ *Don't grease the cake pan.* The rising batter must cling to the pan sides and hold itself up. The sides of a greased pan will be too slippery for the cake to rise.

➤ *Preheat the oven.* The cake should not be sitting around waiting to rise, allowing the air cells to deflate. The oven must also be the correct heat: 325° is the ideal temperature.

➤ *Test for doneness.* Use something long and thin to test the cake for doneness, such as a clean broom straw, a long thin knife, or a thin bamboo skewer.

➤ *Invert the pan.* As soon as the cake is done baking, turn the pan upside down and stand it on its feet or hang it upside own over the neck of a bottle or tall funnel. What you want to do is invert the cake until it has completely cooled to ensure it will be firm enough to hold its rise.

When the cake is done, turn the pan upside down over the neck of a bottle or tall funnel to cool.

➤ *Saw, don't cut.* To cut angel food cake, use a sawing motion with a serrated knife or a pronged angel-food cutter (this looks like a row of thin nails attached to a bar). Just remember that if you try to cut the cake with a regular straight-blade knife, you will end up pushing down on the cake, which will flatten it.

Rolling With the Jelly Rolls

The jelly roll is simply a thin sponge cake baked in a broad flat pan, then rolled up around a filling. Typically, the fillings include jelly or preserves, custard, or mousse. The ever-popular Christmastime treat is the Bûche de Noël: a jelly roll filled with a buttercream frosting and coated in chocolate. Another delicious idea: Fill the jelly roll with whipped cream and fresh berries, then top with more whipped cream or dust with confectioners' sugar.

You want a jelly roll cake to be light and fine-grained, but it should also be a bit elastic and flexible so it can roll without cracking. I recommend using a sponge cake recipe—just bake it in a jelly roll pan. The texture of the angel food cake is light and flexible enough to make a delicious roll. To ensure that the jelly roll will come neatly out of the pan, spread butter or margarine on the bottom and sides of a pan. Line the bottom of the pan with waxed paper or baking parchment.

To assemble a jelly roll, as soon as the cake comes out of the oven to cool, invert the pan over a clean kitchen towel sprinkled with granulated sugar. Lift off the pan and carefully peel off the paper. With a serrated knife, carefully slice off an $1/8$-inch strip of the crisp side, which will make rolling the cake easier and prevent cracking. Fold one short end of the towel over the end of the cake, then roll up the cake. Place the cake seam side down to cool. The cake can be left to cool for several hours or even overnight before unrolling and filling it. Once filled, cut the jelly roll with a serrated knife, using a sawing motion. Otherwise, you might press down too hard on the roll and squeeze out the filling.

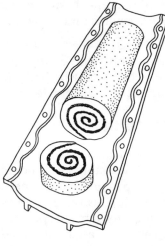

A finished jelly roll cake.

Say Cheesecake!

Who can resist the appeal of a rich, creamy, satin-smooth cheesecake? Since this is one luxury that is well within reach, easy to make, and which freezes well, it is worth preparing for any occasion.

A finished cheesecake.

For a cheesecake to taste smooth and creamy, the batter must be smooth and creamy at all times. The best way to do this is to have all ingredients at room temperature. Using a mixer with a paddle attachment, beat the cream cheese until it's smooth and soft before adding the other ingredients. If you use a hand-held mixer, use it on a low speed so you don't incorporate too much air into the batter, which can cause your cheesecake to crack.

Another popular method is to dump all the ingredients into a blender and give it a whiz for a minute or so, then just pour and bake. This can incorporate a bit too much air, so if you use this method, remove the blender from the motor base and thunk it on the countertop a few times. (But don't thunk too hard—you don't want to break anything. It should sound like someone is knocking on your door.) This will encourage the air bubbles to rise to the surface and escape now instead of during baking, which will prevent your cheesecake from looking like the San Andreas fault is running across it.

Whichever method you choose to mix the batter, stop several times and scrape the sides and the bottom of the container to be sure your batter is lump-free and that no ingredients are stuck to the bottom or sides. Woe to the baker who has poured the batter into the pan, only to realize half the ingredients are still clinging to the walls of the bowl.

Baking a Great-Looking Cheesecake

A cheesecake is baked in a springform pan. It's a good idea to place the springform on a baking sheet with a lip. A springform pan can sometimes leak, despite your best attempt to make sure it is tightly fastened. Placing the pan on a baking sheet will prevent a leaky springform from making a mess in your oven. It is also an easy and safer way to take the cheesecake in and out of the oven, preventing any surprise openings of the springform. If you don't have a baking sheet with a lip, you can wrap the bottom of the springform pan in aluminum foil to seal off any potential leaky cracks.

To tell if your cheesecake is done, observe the top surface carefully. For most cheesecakes, the edges of the cake puff up slightly and might turn faintly golden (a golden brown cheesecake is undesirable). The top should also be dull, not shiny, and when you tap the sides they should move, but not have the jiggle of liquid. Don't use a knife or cake tester to determine doneness, since the cheesecake will normally be moist in the middle. It's normal for the center to be softer than the edges, and the cake will rise slightly during baking, but when it cools it will settle and solidify. If any cracks appear, they will get smaller as the cake cools and sinks down.

Kitchen Utensil
A great trick for cutting a cheesecake is to use dental floss or heavy thread. Cut a piece of floss the length of the diameter of the cake, plus enough to wrap around your fingers. Simply pull the thread taut between your hands, then press it down all the way through the cake. Release the thread in one hand and pull it out with the other. Repeat, cutting the cake like the spokes of a wheel. It makes a great conversation piece for your guests.

You can cool your cheesecake by removing it from the oven, or you can just turn off the oven and crack the oven door. Let the cheesecake cool to room temperature before chilling it in the refrigerator at least 3 to 4 hours, or preferably overnight, before serving.

Cutting the Cheesecake

Cutting a cheesecake can sometimes be messy. The cake has a tendency to cling to the knife, so making neat slices can be quite a challenge. One solution is to run the knife under hot water after each slice is made. This keeps the knife clean, and the warm knife slices neatly through each piece. Of course, if you are cutting the cheesecake at the table, this method is out. Instead, use two knives: one to cut the cheesecake and the other to scrape the knife clean after each slice.

Coping With Cracks

Cracks in a cheesecake, whether they happen during baking or cooling, can be caused by several different factors: extreme temperature changes, too high an oven temperature, too much air in the batter, baked for too long a time, or being placed in a drafty place to cool. Sometimes cracks just happen, despite your best efforts. But, worry not, the taste of the cake will not be affected. If you are serving the cheesecake to guests and appearance is important, here are a few tips to help disguise those cracks:

➤ Top the cheesecake with sliced fruit. Strawberries are great in the summertime, kiwi fruit in the winter makes a nice presentation, but any fresh fruit will do. If you use bananas or peaches, remember to toss them in a bit of lemon juice to prevent them from browning before serving.

➤ Spread the top with a thin layer of sour cream; it will add to the richness of the cheesecake and conceal any imperfections.

➤ Drizzle melted chocolate on top. Dip a fork in melted chocolate (see "Melting and Tempering Chocolate" in Chapter 9) and drizzle a pattern on top of the cheesecake. It will give the cheesecake a new look. When didn't chocolate make everything a little bit better?

What Happens When a Cake Bakes?

There are several great mysteries of life: Why are we here? Who or what created the world? How does the NFL scheduling system work? How exactly does a cake bake? I have finally figured out the answer to one of these. It seems like magic when the heat of the oven causes chemical reactions to take place that transform liquid into a cake with a light texture and wonderful flavor. Don't worry, you don't have to go back to your high school chemistry lab to understand what's going on.

Oven heat causes flour and other starches to absorb moisture from the batter and begin to swell. Proteins in the flour, starch, eggs, and milk coagulate and set, which gives the cake its texture. The heat also causes the liquids in the batter to evaporate and make steam, which expands, causing the cake to rise. The air bubbles beaten into the fats also expand, as does air in the egg foam or stiffly beaten egg whites. With all of these elements expanding, the cake has nowhere to go but up. Also, the moisture and heat cause chemical

Bakers Beware!
Always preheat the oven and position the rack in the center of the oven before baking. A cold oven or an uncentered rack will cause a cake to bake unevenly. Also, make sure the racks are level.

leaveners such as the baking soda and powder to release carbon dioxide gas, which also gives the cake an additional push upwards. After a bit, the risen batter sets into a firm shape while the sugars continue to cook and darken the color of the cake's surface. So, there you go; it all makes perfect sense now.

Most cakes are baked at a temperature between 325°F and 375°F, with the most common temperature being 350°F. At these temperatures, the steam and gas in the batter expands and rises quickly, and the batter can set, holding the rise, without drying out. At a cooler temperature, the heat of the batter takes place too slowly, the rise is incomplete, and the cake dries out because it takes a long time to bake through. In a hot oven, the gases are released too quickly and the cake may rise unevenly. Also, the top and bottom of the cake will bake too quickly, leaving the middle still raw.

Testing for Doneness

There are several things you can do to make sure that your cake is thoroughly baked. If the cake is done, the color of the top should be golden brown, the edges should just be beginning to pull away from the pan, and the cake should appear to be firm, and not jiggle when lightly shaken. Touch the top surface lightly with your finger; the cake should spring back and your finger should not make a dent. To be absolutely sure your cake is done, insert a cake tester into the center of the cake. There is actually a product called a cake tester, but save your money. A toothpick, thin wooden skewer, or butter knife will do nicely. The tester should come out clean and dry, indicating that the cake is done. If the tester comes out wet and covered in batter, bake the cake for a couple more minutes, then retest.

Be sure you set your timer to the minimum baking time given and try not to peek while the cake is baking. As exciting as it is to watch, you are adjusting the oven temperature each time you open the door and that could affect the way the cake bakes—the worst case being it could fall. The only exception to the cake-test rule is the cheesecake, which has its own set of rules (see the earlier section, "Baking a Great-Looking Cheesecake").

Testing a cake for doneness.

Cooling a Cake

It's important that cakes are cooled properly before they are handled. If a cake has not cooled enough, it will be quite reluctant to leave the pan—some might stick or half will come out and the other half will stay attached. Wire racks are perfect for cooling cakes to cool on once removed from the baking pans because they allow air to circulate all around the cake while it cools. Following are cooling guidelines for the types of cakes I've discussed in this chapter.

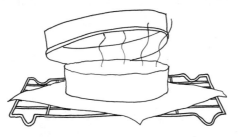

Cooling a layer cake.

➤ *Butter/Shortening cake.* As a general rule, baked cakes should be left in their pans and set on a wire rack for about 5 to 10 minutes after coming from the oven. Then run a thin knife (such as a paring knife or butter knife) around the sides of the pan to loosen the cake. Place another wire rack upside-down on top of the cake pan. Take hold of both racks, with the cake pan sandwiched in the middle, and gently turn it over. The cake should gently plop out of the pan. If it is reluctant, give the bottom of the pan a few taps to encourage the cake to leave. If it still won't go, just re-flip the whole ensemble and give it 5 more minutes before you try again.

➤ *Cheesecake.* It's important to allow the cheesecake to fully set before removing the springform pan. Cool the cheesecake to room temperature. Then cover the top of the pan with plastic wrap and place it in the refrigerator to set for at least 4 hours; overnight is ideal. Once completely chilled, run a butter knife between the cake and the edge of the pan and gently release the springform ring, bringing it over the top of cake.

➤ *Sponge/Angel food cake.* Sponge and angel food cakes are leavened with air, so they have to cool hanging upside down or they will collapse into themselves. The easiest way is to use a pan that has "feet" attached to the pan. Just flip around the feet, and turn the cake upside-down. If your pan doesn't have feet, just turn the pan over onto the neck of a wine bottle or long funnel. If those are not handy, balance the edges of the pan on inverted mugs or cups. Allow the cake to completely cool for several hours. Then remove the pan from the bottle and slide a sharp knife with a long, thin blade between the cake and side of the pan to free any sticking crumbs. Place a plate over the top of the tube pan, flip it over, and remove the pan.

The Least You Need to Know

➤ Always follow the recipe precisely.

➤ Different types of cakes require different baking methods. Familiarizing yourself with these types will ensure your success.

➤ Proper combining of ingredients makes the difference between a good cake and a great cake.

➤ Cool your cakes completely before you frost or refrigerate them.

Chapter 11

Frosting Fundamentals

In This Chapter

➤ Learning about the different types of frostings

➤ Guidelines for proper frosting amounts

➤ Easy-to-follow instructions for frosting cakes

➤ Helpful hints for decorating with a pastry bag

For some people, cake is just a vehicle for frosting. Never can the frosting be too rich, thick, sweet, or chocolatey. I prefer my frostings to enhance, not overwhelm, the cake I am eating, but I am sure I'm not in the majority of cake eaters out there. Whether you like a lot or a little, when you dress a cake, you generally say you are "frosting" it. In this chapter you'll learn about the different types of frostings, how to frost a basic cake, and even some advice for making it look great without a lot of fuss.

Tips on Toppings

There are actually several different types of frostings: buttercream frostings, icings, toppings, glazes, and fillings (which aren't really frostings, but we can lump them in here, anyway). These types fall into two categories: quick frostings (meaning you just throw all the ingredients in a bowl and beat until smooth), and cooked frostings (while these can be quick, too, they usually require melting something).

Quick frostings are self-explanatory—you just follow the recipe, making sure all your ingredients are sifted for the smoothest finish. Cooked frostings, also called glazes, icings, or ganaches, need a bit more attention. The blend of sugar, cream, butter, and/or chocolate needs to be carefully monitored. Never cook frostings over high heat; for best results, use very low heat or a double boiler placed over simmering water. And follow the recipe carefully.

Kitchen Utensil
If the recipe calls for confectioners' sugar, be sure to sift it before incorporating it into the frosting. Even the tiniest lumps will cause the frosting to have a grainy appearance.

A good frosting has a smooth consistency and a silky appearance. The texture should be spreadable but not runny (unless it's a glaze). If you find that the frosting you have made is too thick, add a few drops of milk or water to thin it. A small amount of liquid makes a big difference in consistency, so go slow when adding. Use butter or margarine (not a vegetable spread or shortening) when preparing frostings for the best flavor and most spreadable consistency. Always let your butter soften to room temperature before creaming, otherwise your frosting will be lumpy.

Frosting Amounts

How many times have you been halfway though frosting a cake when you realize that you are running out of frosting? Panic sets in and you start scraping bits from here or there, spreading it out thinner in spots, or—in moments of sheer desperation—taking off the top layer and scraping out the frosting center. Well, worry no more. In the following table, I give you guidelines for the amount of frosting you'll need to adequately cover your cakes. As a general rule, the fluffier the frosting, the more you will need.

Type of Cake	Amount of Frosting Needed
8-inch layer cake	$2^{1}/_{2}$ cups
9-inch layer cake	3 cups
Bundt, tube, or sheet cake	1 cup glaze; 3 cups frosting
16 large cupcakes	$2–2^{1}/_{2}$ cups

Preparing to Frost

Preparing a cake for frosting is quite easy. First, inspect the cake layers carefully. You want the cakes' surfaces to be as flat as possible, since you will have to balance one on top of the other. A quick and easy solution for a flat surface is to place the bottom layer upside-down, so the rounded side is on the serving plate, leaving you with a perfectly flat frosting surface. The top layer will be placed rounded side up, so the two flat layers are together with the frosting in between.

Another solution is to even out the layers by cutting the domed tops off of the cakes. Hold a serrated knife parallel to the top of the cake and gently saw off the domed top. Do this at eye level to be sure you are cutting straight, and not downward, to ensure a flat top. If you have cut your layers, the cut side should always be up.

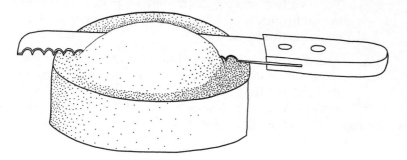

To even out cake layers, hold a serrated knife parallel to the top of the cake and gently saw off the domed top.

Once your cakes are level, find a serving plate or a cake round. If you're using a serving plate, place four 5-inch-wide strips of waxed paper around the edge of the plate. This will make it easy to frost the cake without dirtying the serving plate. Place the cooled cake layer on top of the waxed paper strips in the center of the serving plate. Brush off any crumbs on or around the cake.

Frosting a Cake

The best utensil for frosting cakes is a thin, metal spatula with a rounded tip or a firm but flexible plastic spatula.

Spread between $^1/_2$ cup and $^3/_4$ cup of frosting (depending on how heavy you like to frost your cake) on top of the bottom layer. Don't spread the frosting with hard, downward strokes as if you were buttering bread. This will pick up crumbs on the cake's surface and mix them into the frosting, giving you an unevenly textured cake. Instead, gently use the knife or spatula to push the frosting where you want it to go. The frosting should be soft and creamy enough to do this easily. If the frosting is too stiff, thin it out with just a few drops of water or milk.

Kitchen Utensil

Cake rounds are a busy baker's dream. These thick cardboard circles are available in most kitchen supply stores in a variety of sizes. They hold your cake layers while you're frosting and transporting them from work area to refrigerator to serving plate. If you can't find cake rounds, just trace a circle, using your cake pan as a size guide, on any heavy, corrugated cardboard and cut it out. Cover them with aluminum foil and they are reusable.

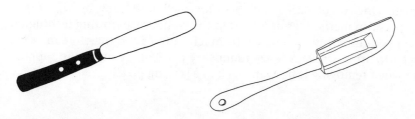

Metal spatula (left) and plastic spatula (right).

Kitchen Utensil
To keep the top of the cake from looking domed or sloped, make a rim of frosting around the edge, about ¹/₄ inch above the top of the cake. Spread the frosting over the top of the cake to this rim to give a flat-shaped top.

Place the second layer on top of the first, cut side down or domed side up, and brush off any crumbs. Frost the sides of the cake with another ¹/₂ or ³/₄ cup of frosting, or to taste. Begin with a thin layer of frosting to seal in any crumbs. Then, with smooth, back-and-forth strokes, frost the sides. Spread frosting on the top last, using smooth gliding strokes across the cake.

Rather than dumping the whole blob of frosting on the top layer of the cake, place three or four smaller portions on the surface, then smooth them out using a gentle pushing motion. Add more frosting as needed. This is particularly good for delicate cakes because it keeps the cake surface from lifting and crumbing up the frosting.

Frost the sides of the cake; then, with smooth back-and-forth strokes, frost the top.

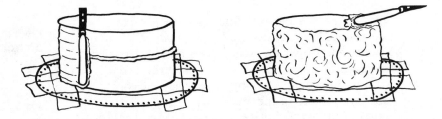

Once your cake is frosted, gently pull the waxed paper strips out from underneath the cake (you might have to give them a gentle tug to get them started). Any frosting on the strips will gently slide onto the frosted cake, leaving you with a perfectly clean serving plate.

Glazing

Glazing a cake requires a slightly different technique since the glaze is runny, not smooth and spreadable. Begin by positioning the completely cooled cake on a wire rack over aluminum foil or a baking sheet (to catch the drips). Spoon or pour the glaze, a little at a time, over the top of the cake. With a metal spatula or the back of a spoon, spread the glaze into thin areas and to the edge of the cake, allowing some to drizzle over the side. Don't continue spreading the glaze once it begins to set, or the smooth finish will be lost (don't panic, you will have several minutes before this happens). Repeat until the cake is well coated and the desired look is achieved. Once the glaze is set, carefully transfer the cake to a serving plate. One cup of glaze is sufficient for one bundt, tube, or angel food cake. The waxed-paper-strip method (as described in the earlier cake frosting technique) can also be used, but because the glaze tends to be much runnier and therefore messier than frosting, I prefer to use a wire rack. Cake rounds are particularly helpful in supporting the glazed cake when removing it from the rack to a serving plate.

Glazing a cake.

If possible, allow the cake to sit for at least 30 minutes to allow the frosting to set. If it is more than four hours before serving time, refrigerate the cake. Cover the cake with either a cake dome or an inverted mixing bowl. Make sure the bowl will leave enough space between the sides and top of the cake so you won't end up smashing your lovely cake.

Using a Decorating (Pastry) Bag

Some occasions require a slightly fancier-looking cake. For decorating with frosting or whipped cream in a pattern, use a decorating bag. Decorating bags, also called pastry bags, are plastic-coated, reusable nylon bags. The frosting is spooned into the bag, and then squeezed out through the tip. The type of tip you choose determines the decoration you make.

There are three types of pastry bags available—two are bags and one is a syringe-type of metal tube. I find the decorating bags the easiest to use. When selecting your bag, there are two varieties: one in which the tip is dropped through the bag and comes out the narrow end, and one in which a tube (called a coupler) is inserted and the tips are screwed on the outside of the narrow end. I recommend the second, the coupler assembly, if you want to purchase a decorating bag. With the coupler, you can change the tips (which are usually included in the purchase of the bag) without having to empty the bag of the frosting. There are inexpensive kits available that come with a variety of tips included. With the drop-in tips, you are committed to the tip you have inserted in the bag. If you need to change tips, you must empty out the frosting, wash the bag, and then reinsert the new tip, unless you purchase several bags. It can become very messy.

The third type of decorating bag is a metal syringe-type tube. Although this choice is fine for writing, I prefer the first two choices because they give me more control over the amount of frosting I use and how I decorate. No matter what your choice is, before you use your bag, be sure to wash it out with hot, soapy water and let it dry completely before filling it. Be sure to wash your tips and bag with hot, soapy water immediately after use so that frosting won't dry and clog in the tips or bag.

Three types of pastry bags: without a tip (left), with a coupler (middle), and with a drop-in tip (right).

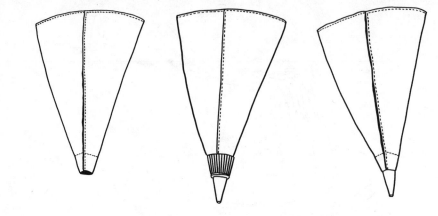

Pastry bags come in many sizes. For all-purpose use, select a 12- or 16-inch bag. If you're unsure of what size you want, remember it's always better to choose a bigger bag than smaller.

Using Your Decorating Bag

To fill your decorating bag, place the empty bag (with tip in place) in a tall, narrow glass. Fold back about 5 inches to form a cuff over the sides of the glass. Using a spatula, fill the decorating bag no more than halfway full with icing. It's important not to fill the bag more than this, or the frosting might back up out of the bag. To close the bag, unfold the cuff and gently press all the frosting down toward the tip. Don't press so hard that frosting starts to come out. You just want to get the air pockets out of the bag. Once the frosting is pressed down, twist the top of the bag. Continue twisting as you decorate. Don't squeeze it as if it were a tube of toothpaste.

To fill your decorating bag, place the empty bag (with tip in place) in a tall, narrow glass.

To close the bag, unfold the cuff and gently press all the frosting down toward the tip.

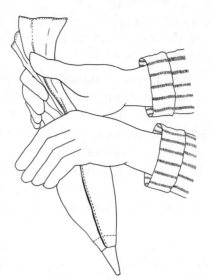

The amount of pressure on the decorating bag, the size of the tip, and the consistency of the icing will determine the amount of icing that flows out of the bag. By increasing the pressure and moving the bag slowly, you can increase the size of the line being piped out.

If the tip gets clogged while frosting, give the bag a little extra squeeze over a piece of waxed paper. Avoid doing this over the cake; you might end up with a big splotch of icing where you don't want it. If this method doesn't work, take a toothpick and poke it into the tip to release the blockage.

Kitchen Utensil
Practice your decorations on waxed paper before decorating the cake. This will help you determine the type of decoration you'll be making.

Last but not least, a turntable or lazy Susan is a cake decorator's best friend. It makes it easier and faster to frost and decorate cakes.

After decorating the cake, be sure you clean the tips well in hot, soapy water. Pick out the icing in the hard-to-clean cracks with a toothpick. Always wash your pastry bag and tips by hand. A dishwasher will send your tips flying and they may become crushed, ruining the delicate tip forever.

If you're not feeling adventurous enough to try using a decorative bag, see "Quick, Spiffy Garnishes" (in Chapter 18) to add some pizzazz to your cakes without adding stress to your life.

Tips on Tips

There are hundreds of tips in all sizes and numbers available for cake decorating. The most important thing is to make sure the tip fits your pastry bag, so try and buy them together or know what kind of bag you need to fit. If you're not sure, bring the pastry bag to the store with you and try out the tips there. Also, be sure to choose the correct tip for the decoration you want to do. Here are five of the most popular styles of tips available:

➤ *Shell tips.* These tips make the easiest flowers or shells for the beginning cake decorator. The flowers are dropped directly onto the cake, either just dropped on or swirled. Popular sizes include 107, 129, 190, 217, and 255.

➤ *Leaf tips.* The opening forms the pointed end of the leaf. Leaf tips can make plain, ruffled, or even stand-up leaves. String the leaves together to make an attractive border. Popular sizes include 65, 67, and 352.

➤ *Petal tips.* These tips are used by more advanced decorators to make roses, violets, carnations, and other flower shapes. This tip is also used for making ribbons, bows, swags, and ruffles. Popular sizes include 101, 102, 103, and 104.

➤ *Star tips.* If you were going to get just one decorative tip, I would recommend buying a star tip. This tip enables you to make rosettes, drop flowers, stars, scalloped borders, rope borders, and shells. Popular sizes range from 13 to 22; the larger sizes include 32 and 43.

➤ *Writing or line tips.* Writing tips are plain, round tips. In addition to writing, you can also make polka dots, stems, vines, or just smooth lines for decoration. Popular sizes include 1–4 (small), 5–12 (medium), and 1A and 2A (large).

Decorating tips.

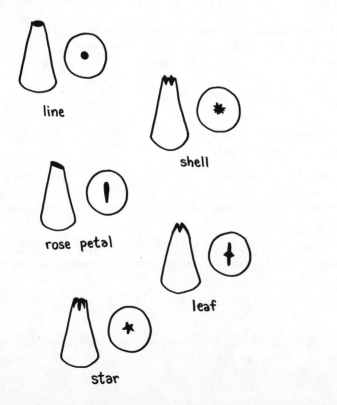

line

shell

rose petal

leaf

star

Technique Tips

Most designs are made by holding the decorating bag at a 45-degree angle to the surface of the cake. Support the bottom of the bag with one hand and twist the top with the other. Always begin with just a slight twisting pressure on the bag. Don't jerk the bag around too much; let the frosting glide out and fall onto the cake.

Before making a design or writing a message on the cake, lightly outline the design with a toothpick to use as a guide. Small strips of sewing thread or dental floss gently placed on top of the cake can serve as straight lines on which to write.

If you make a mistake while decorating, don't panic—everyone has done it. The easiest thing to do is to get a metal frosting spatula with a rounded tip and gently lift off the mistake and scrape away any additional coloring. With the tip of the spatula, gently smooth out the area and start over again.

> **Kitchen Utensil**
>
> Before decorating, pop the frosted cake in the freezer or refrigerator for several hours to allow the frosting to harden. Then, if you make a mistake while decorating, the decoration will be easy to lift off the hardened frosting and you can start over again without having ruined the frosted cake.

If you're going to color your frosting, remember that colors will darken as the frosting hardens. To color frosting, you can use food coloring or paste food coloring, which is available in kitchen supply stores. BE VERY CAREFUL WHEN USING THE PASTE. A tiny amount will vividly color your frosting. When I used these pastes in the bakery, I would dip the tip of a toothpick into the paste and then dip that into the frosting. It usually was the right amount of color for a large bag of frosting.

If you don't want to deal with pastry bags and tips but still want to add a little something special to your homemade cake, check out the tube frostings sold in grocery stores in the baking aisle. You can have your pick of colors, and they come in handy tubes. Look for gels with a writing tip, so you can write a message on the cake if you like. One tube has adequate frosting for scrawling out a "Happy Birthday" message.

The Least You Need to Know

➤ Make sure all your ingredients are at room temperature and the sugar is sifted.

➤ Frost the sides of the cake first, then the top.

➤ If you want to decorate your cake, use a pastry bag or a ready-made tube frosting.

➤ Practice your cake decoration on waxed paper before decorating the cake.

➤ Choose the right tip for the design.

➤ Be careful when coloring frostings; a little color goes a long way.

Chapter 12

A Piece on Pies

In This Chapter

➤ Hints for perfecting a flaky pie crust

➤ Ideas for top-crust pies

➤ Easy instructions for making decorative crusts

➤ Troubleshooting, and how to fix what went wrong

Everyone loves pies, and there is nothing more American than a warm pie cooling on the windowsill. Whether that pie is filled with sweet summertime berries, hearty slices of tart apples, or thick pureéd pumpkin kissed with brown sugar and cinnamon, pies are satisfying fare. Nevertheless, many bakers shudder at the thought of making the crusts that hold the delectable fillings. Have you turned to frozen or refrigerated pie crusts to make your baking fuss-free? If so, you've probably found that those crusts can be flavorless and thin. But fret no more. In just a few easy lessons, you will have the confidence to make your own dough for incredibly flaky crust.

Pie doughs have simple ingredients: flour, fat (butter or shortening), and a liquid (water or milk) to bring everything together. It's the *technique* you have to master if you want tender, flaky crusts. The best method for achieving perfect pie dough is practice, practice, practice. Before long, you'll wonder why you ever hesitated to make your own.

Kitchen Utensil
If you want to know how many cups your pie plate will hold, fill it with water, then pour the water into a measuring cup.

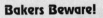

Bakers Beware!
Never use a shiny pan for pie baking. The pan will reflect heat and the pie will have a soggy bottom crust. Use heat-resistant glass or dull-finished metal pie plates for good browning.

Pick the Proper Pie Plate

Get off to a good start by picking the right pie plate. The most common pie size is 9 inches. But even though a pie plate may be 9 inches, the amount of filling it can hold can vary dramatically. A shallow pie plate will hold less filling; a deeper pie plate will hold more. Make sure your pie plate can hold the amount of filling that's called for. Keep in mind fruit fillings will shrink as they bake, so always be generous.

Be careful if you use a nonstick pie plate. The Teflon coating does not hold the dough in place while it cooks (and the dough contracts), and if your crust is not secured over the edge of the pie plate, your dough might shrink up quite a bit in the oven.

Because crusts have plenty of butter or shortening in them, do not grease the pie plate.

Tips for Perfect Pie Crusts

There is not much to making a pie crust. You begin with flour, maybe add a pinch of salt, cut in the shortening, and then add a few drops of water and chill (not you, the dough). You now have little bits of butter mixed with flour and held together with water. When you roll out the dough, you will flatten the butter even more, and when you bake the crust, the butter will melt into the flour, flavoring it and leaving behind little pockets of air where it had once been. That is how a flaky pie crust is born.

Knowing this, you can now understand why overmixing the dough is so bad for a pie crust. It will incorporate the butter into the flour before the oven has a chance to melt it. Kneading the flour too much will also form gluten, which will toughen the dough. If you have not heard it before, you will hear it now: The secret to flaky pie crusts is less, not more, handling.

If you use your fingers to incorporate the butter into the flour you run the risk of melting it (butter melts around 95°F. and our body temp is 98.6°F.) A pastry blender is handy to help cut shortening evenly into the flour. If you don't have one, you can also use two knives, cutting parallel with one another, to cut in the butter. Another choice is a fork.

Many bakers swear by shortening for a flaky crust. It doesn't melt at the low temperature that butter does, and it's easier to cut into the flour, which means you can handle it less. I find shortening falls short when it comes to flavor. But, if the pie has good flavor, this can be compensated for. You can also use a mix of half butter and half shortening for the qualities of shortening and the flavor of butter.

Chilling the dough is another important step in preparing pie pastry. After the butter or shortening is cut in, the dough needs to return to the refrigerator, well wrapped, for an hour or so, so that the butter can harden again and the dough can relax, making it easier to handle. If you have made a dough for a double-crust pie, split the dough in half, flatten the pieces into disks, wrap them tightly in plastic wrap, then refrigerate. Skimping on this step could have undesirable effects on your finished pastry, so plan accordingly. Pie dough will keep in the refrigerator for up to one week and in the freezer up to one month.

Rolling Out, Not In, the Dough

Once you have chilled your dough, remove it from the refrigerator and set it at room temperature for about five minutes to let the chill come off of it. A pastry cloth, kitchen towel (not terry-cloth), or rolling stocking (a mesh or cloth casing which is slipped over the rolling pin and gently rubbed with flour) is handy to have because it practically eliminates sticking and a minimum of additional flour is needed. But rubbing flour into your rolling pin and onto your work surface also works fine; just don't use too much. Two table-spoons of additional flour is all you should need. Roll your dough out on a clean, cool, smooth countertop. The work surface I like best is a large wooden board, at least 14 × 14 inches. It's flat and hard and gives me plenty of room to spread out. Or, if you have access to one, a large slab of marble is the perfect surface because it stays so cool.

Kitchen Utensil
I like to use a food processor to make the dough. I chill the metal blade and precut my butter into 10 to 12 pieces before adding it to the flour. In just a few quick pulses, the butter is incorporated into the flour and I haven't touched a thing. I like to add the water by hand, though, as the food processor can overwork the dough.

Kitchen Utensil
When rolling out pastry for sweet pies, instead of using just flour for dusting the work surface, use a combination of granulated sugar and flour. The sugar acts like little grains of sand and isn't as easily absorbed into the dough as the flour. It is a marvelous trick for keeping pastry dough from sticking to the work surface and it won't toughen the dough.

Begin rolling from the center of the dough outwards (don't roll back in or push the rolling pin back and forth), lifting and turning the pastry occasionally to make sure the dough is not sticking to the countertop. Also, don't press down hard when rolling out the dough; the weight of the rolling pin is all the pressure you need. Roll the dough out to $1/8$ inch or less; it should be at least 2 inches larger than the pie dimensions (if you have a 9-inch pie plate, the dough should be 11 inches across). If the dough rips while you are rolling it, don't worry, you can repair it by pressing the two torn sides together. If the dough begins to stick, rub more flour into the work surface and on the rolling pin.

Roll pastry from the center to the outside edge in all directions, rotating the dough a quarter-turn occasionally.

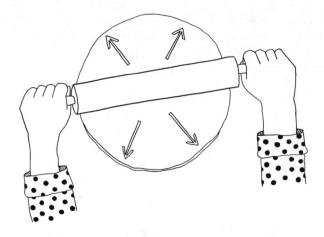

Bakers Beware!

If your pie crust tears either while you are rolling it out or when you are transferring it, don't ball it back up and reroll it. Instead, moisten the edges of the torn pastry and gently press them back together again. If you reroll the dough, you will overwork and toughen it.

Fold the pastry in half and then in half again. Gently transfer the crust onto the pie plate. Unfold and ease gently onto the plate.

To transfer the dough to the pie plate, gently loosen the pastry from the work surface and fold it in half and then in half again. Place the pie plate right next to the pastry and gently slide the folded pastry onto the pie plate. Next, carefully unfold it. Ease the dough gently onto the pie plate and press it against the side of the pie plate so there will be no air left between the dough and the plate, which can cause the crust to blister up while baking. Trim off the excess crust with a knife or kitchen shears and crimp the edges with your fingers.

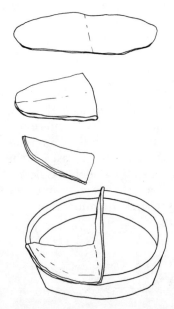

Double-Crust Pie Ideas

If you are preparing a pie with a top crust, roll out the top crust as directed earlier. Use the top crust of your choice:

➤ *Solid top crust.* Fold the crust in half and make several cuts along the fold, about 1 inch apart. This will allow steam to escape while the pie is baking. You can also cut slits into the top crust after it's positioned on top of the filling. Gently transfer the folded crust to the pie plate, unfold the crust on top of the filled pie, and trim the top crust to have a 1-inch overhang. Gently press the top crust over the filling, tucking the extra top crust under the bottom crust, and flute the edges. *Fluting* or pinching the edges of the pastry with your fingers makes a decorative crust. It also extends the height of the crust edge, to better hold in juicy pie fillings.

A double-crust pie.

➤ *Lattice crust.* Using a thin, sharp knife, pizza cutter, or a straight- or crinkled-edge pastry wheel, cut 10 to 14 $1/2$-inch strips from the top crust pastry. Place 5 to 7 strips on the filling, about $3/4$-inch apart. Fold back every other strip halfway and place a strip perpendicular over the unfolded strips. Unfold the strip. Fold back the alternate strips, and place another strip $3/4$-inch apart from the first. Repeat until all the strips are used up.

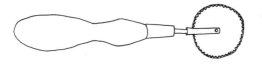

Use a pastry wheel to cut the lattice strips.

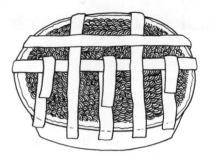

Step 1: Place 5 to 7 vertical strips on the filling, about 3/4-inch apart. Fold every other strip halfway back and place a horizontal strip over the unfolded strips.

Step 2: Fold back the alternate strips and place another strip 3/4-inch away from the first.

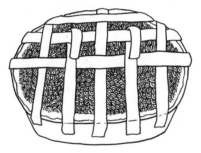

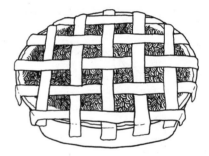

Step 3: Repeat step 1.

Step 4: Repeat steps 1 to 3 until all the strips are used.

When the whole pie is latticed, attach the strips loosely to the pie edge by moistening the ends with a little water or milk and pressing down slightly into the bottom crust edge (do not pull the strips taut, but instead allow for some shrinkage during baking). Cut off any excess from the strips and flute the edges.

Here's a tip for an easy lattice top. Just place 5 to 7 strips over the filling, about 3/4-inch apart. Turn the pie plate a quarter-turn and place the remaining strips at right angles to the first set of strips, about 3/4-inch apart. Do not weave the strips.

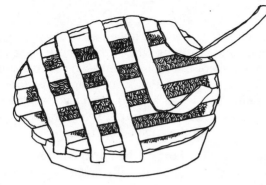

An easy lattice top.

➤ *Cutout top crust.* Using a small cookie cutter, no bigger than 1 inch across, make a pattern from the center of the pastry to within 1 inch from the pastry edge (make sure the pastry is not sticking to the work surface). Gently roll the cutout pastry onto a floured rolling pin and carefully transfer the cutout top over the pie filling. By gently rolling the pastry onto the rolling pin, there is less chance of it ripping while you transfer the pastry. Flute the edges of the bottom pastry. Some cutout ideas include hearts, leaves, stars, and holiday shapes.

Gently roll the cutout pastry onto the rolling pin while you transfer the pastry.

You can also use a larger cookie cutter to cut the top pastry. Place the large cutout on top of the filling. Flute the edges of the bottom pastry.

Use a larger cookie cutter to cut the shapes you want and place the cutouts on the filling.

139

Prebaking Pie Crusts

If the pie shell is to be baked without filling, prick the dough all over with a fork. To prevent the pie shell from puffing up and blistering while it bakes, place a sheet of aluminum foil, parchment, or waxed paper on top of the unbaked pie crust and weigh it down with rice, dried beans, or pie weights (small, flat, stone-shaped instruments used by bakers to keep pie crusts from puffing up when baking), then bake according to the recipe. Remove the weights from the pie shell a few minutes before the baking time is finished so the bottom will brown a bit. Cool the crust before filling.

Before baking, be sure you have preheated your oven. The initial contrast in temperature aids in the flakiness of your dough. Crusts that are generally prebaked are crusts for cream pies or those that have chilled fillings.

Simple Pastry Edges and Decoration

To *flute* the edges of the pastry crust means to squeeze the edges of the pastry all along the pie plate to make a finished, decorative edge. This can be done several ways:

➤ *Pinch or crimped edge.* This is the most classic pie edge decoration. Place the index finger on the outside of the pastry and pinch your thumb and index finger of your other hand to form a "V" shape on the inside of the pastry. Push the pastry into the "V" shape with your index finger, along the entire edge or rim of the pie plate. Once finished, go around and pinch again to sharpen the edges. When the crusts bakes, the "V" shapes will relax, so you will want them as sharp as possible.

A pinch edge.

➤ *Fork edge.* This edge is the best for beginner bakers. Just flatten the pastry evenly along the rim of the plate with the tines of a fork. To prevent the fork from sticking to the pastry, dip it lightly in flour.

A fork edge.

➤ *Cutout edge.* Trim the overhang to the rim of the pie plate. With a tiny cookie cutter, thimble, or bottle cap, cut out decorations from the scraps of pastry. Moisten the edge of the pastry and the bottoms of the cutout with water and press them into place.

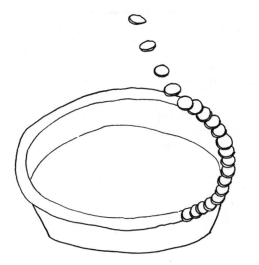

A cutout edge.

➤ *Twisted edge.* Trim the overhang to the rim of the pie plate. Twist two $1/4$-inch strips around each other, making the twist long enough to fit around the edge of the plate. Moisten the rim of the pie plate and the bottom of the twist and gently lay it on top. Press it lightly into place. Or, you can loosely braid three $1/4$-inch strips and lay the braid around the edge.

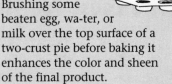

Kitchen Utensil
Brushing some beaten egg, wa-ter, or milk over the top surface of a two-crust pie before baking it enhances the color and sheen of the final product.

A twisted edge.

Troubleshooting

Despite our best efforts, sometimes pie crusts just don't live up to our expectations. Here's a quick explanation of what might have happened, why it did, and how to prevent it from happening next time.

Problem	Possible Reason	Solution
Pale color	Undercooked	Increase baking time by 3-minute increments.
	Baked in a shiny pan	Choose a dull finish or glass pie pan next time.
Bottom crust is soggy	Baked at too low a temperature	Increase temperature by 25°.
	Did not seal with egg white or melted butter	Seal the bottom next time before filling.
Tough, not tender	Overmixed	Try handling the dough less.
	Too much flour	Use less flour when rolling out the dough.
Too tender	Too much shortening	Decrease the shortening by $1/2$ tablespoon.
Not flaky	Too little water	Increase water by 1 teaspoon.
	Overworked	Handle the dough less.
	The butter was cut in too much	Stop cutting when the dough resembles coarse crumbs.

The Least You Need to Know

➤ Less handling, not more, is the secret to flaky pie crusts.

➤ Keep all your ingredients cold.

➤ Don't use a lot of flour when rolling out your pastry.

➤ If you're making a double-crust pie, try some of the double-crust ideas.

➤ Remember, practice makes perfect. Don't be discouraged if you don't succeed on your first try.

Chapter 13

All About Cookies

In This Chapter

➤ Everything you need to know about baking just about every kind of cookie

➤ A complete rundown on drop, shaped, rolled, and bar cookies

➤ Great tips for dressing up and serving your cookie creations

It would be difficult to find someone who didn't like cookies in some form or another. They come in any shape or size and they go well with just about every event. They can be dressed up or eaten plain, dunked in milk, or quietly accompany a cup of tea. Cookies are great, and most are easy to make even for the most apprehensive baker. You don't need much equipment, they have a relatively high yield (as long as not too much dough is snacked on for quality control), and the ingredients are easy to have on hand. Some people like thin, crunchy cookies, some like softer cookies. Some like a crispy, drier cookie, while others prefer them to be soft and gooey. No matter which type you like, there's a recipe for you.

Despite the average cookie's simplicity, there are some basics you should know so you get the most from your cookie baking. Because you are baking such small amounts of batter, it's easy to see when the dough is just not quite right—maybe it spreads too much or too little, or maybe the cookies are too crunchy. So, it's important to familiarize yourself with the fundamentals of what makes your cookies crumble.

Making the Cookie Connection

Always measure your ingredients carefully when making cookies. Too much or too little of just one ingredient will affect the outcome of your cookie.

You can use butter, margarine, or shortening that comes in sticks interchangeably when you make cookies. Only use vegetable oil when it is called for in the recipe. Cookies baked with butter or margarine will flatten out more than cookies baked with shortening, but will have a richer taste. Cookies made with shortening are crispier, with a nice crunch to them, and hold a shape a bit better. Sometimes I use half butter and half shortening when I want a round cookie with good flavor.

If you like your cookies dense, mix the dough by hand. An electric mixer will incorporate more air into your cookie dough, giving it a lighter and crispier texture. Either way, be sure not to mix the cookie dough too much; it will toughen the cookies.

Nonstick coatings are a boon for any cook, but you may find they brown your cookies on the bottom a bit faster than desired. If this is happening to your cookies, lower the oven temperature by 25°F and bake as instructed. If your cookies are still browning too quickly on the bottom, use two cookie sheets (one on top of the other) to create an insulated cookie sheet.

If a recipe calls for a greased cookie sheet, don't grease with butter or margarine. Use shortening instead. Otherwise, the area in between the cookies will burn onto the sheet and it will be next to impossible to clean.

Information Station

When I worked in the bakery, we used parchment paper to line our large, industrial baking sheets. Parchment paper, available in many sizes in baking-supply stores and in some supermarkets, is a wonderful tool in the kitchen. It does not burn or smoke like waxed paper sometimes can, and it comes in either precut sheets or in a roll. Cut the sheet to fit your pan and scoop the cookies onto it. When the cookies are done baking, you can slide the whole sheet of parchment paper (with the cookies on them) onto a cooling rack. Parchment paper is wonderful because it keeps your baking sheets clean and mess-free. It also eliminates greasing cookie sheets and can be reused several times.

When placing cookies on the baking sheets, be sure to leave enough room for them to spread. Most recipes will tell you the amount of space to leave. If not, use 2 inches as your general rule. This includes space from the edge of the sheet, too.

All the cookies on one tray should be the same size and shape to ensure even baking. Otherwise, the smaller cookies will burn while the larger cookies are still uncooked.

Make sure your cookie sheets fit into your oven. You want to be able to leave at least 2 inches on all sides to ensure proper heat distribution while baking. If the cookie sheet is too big, you may find the cookies on the end of the sheet are burning, while the cookies toward the middle are too raw.

I always bake one sheet of cookies at a time and I recommend you do the same. Baking one tray at a time lets all the cookies cook evenly. If you are pressed for time and need to bake two sheets at once, make sure you turn the sheets halfway around and switch rack placements halfway through baking.

Be sure you have at least two sheets, so you can prepare one sheet while another batch bakes. If you only have one sheet, be sure you let it cool between batches (at least 10 minutes) to prevent the cookie dough from spreading too quickly. Cookie dough placed on a hot sheet will begin to melt immediately, resulting in very flat cookies.

Always bake a test cookie. A test cookie will let you see what an entire batch of cookies will turn out like before they are baked. That way, if you want to make any adjustments, you will not waste a whole batch of cookie dough in the process. If you find your test cookie has spread too much during baking, add 2 tablespoons of flour and bake another test cookie (also try chilling the dough before baking for at least 30 minutes, it really works wonders). If you find your cookie is too dry, add 2 tablespoons of milk or water to the dough and test again.

Drop Cookies

As their name suggests, drop cookies are formed by dropping the dough onto the baking sheet. You should use a regular tableware spoon, not a measuring spoon, to drop the cookies onto the sheet. Usually the teaspoons in your silverware drawer are perfect. Use two, one to scoop up the dough and the second to push the dough onto the baking sheet.

When I worked in the bakery, we used spring-handle ice cream scoops to make cookies all the same size and shape. You can use this trick at home. Some ice cream scoops are sold by number; this number corresponds to the number of level scoops you will get out of a quart of ice cream. I suggest choosing a #70 scoop if your recipe calls for dropping the dough by rounded teaspoonfuls. It's a pretty small scoop, but you will discover how easy it makes scooping out cookies.

If you like rounded cookies and you find your dough is spreading too much in baking, try chilling the dough for an hour or so. To speed this process, you can also scoop out the dough onto the baking sheet and place it in the refrigerator to chill for at least 30 minutes.

Always check the cookies after the minimum amount of baking time given. Also, you should remove cookies from the baking sheets to the cooling rack with a wide spatula once they are done baking, unless the instructions say otherwise. Don't let cookies cool on their sheets for more than a couple of minutes—they become harder to remove.

Shaped Cookies

Shaped cookies can be as simple as peanut-butter cookies, with the criss-cross pattern on top, or as fancy as candy-cane cookies. The dough for shaped cookies is usually richer and softer than drop cookie dough, so it's helpful to chill the dough before working with it. If it's still too soft after chilling, mix in 2 tablespoons of flour. If it's too soft and crumbly, add 2 tablespoons of water.

The dough for shaped cookies can be rolled out and slid onto a baking sheet and refrigerated, then cut. Or it can be shaped into a log, wrapped in plastic wrap, then refrigerated. Use a thin, sharp knife to slice the dough.

If you are forming the dough into different shapes, make sure all the cookies are the same shape and size to ensure even baking.

Information Station

It's easy to make your own slice-and-bake cookies. Shape chocolate-chip, peanut-butter, sugar-cookie, or gingerbread cookie dough into a log (3 inches in diameter and between 9 to 12 inches long). Wrap tightly in plastic wrap, with the ends tightly twisted, and refrigerate for at least two hours and up to 24 (or freeze for several weeks). When you're ready to bake, bring the dough to room temperature (it should be workable, but not too soft or rock-hard) and slice the dough into rounds about $1/4$-inch thick. Place the rounds onto the baking sheet and bake according to instructions.

Rolled Cookies

Making rolled cookies is much like making pastry dough, and it follows many of the same baking principles. The cookie dough usually requires some chilling time to reharden the butter and to let the dough rest so it's easier to roll out. Keep in mind when you are rolling out the cookies that the dough will toughen up if you roll it out too many times. That is why you want to cut out as many cookies as possible the first time, then gather up all of the scraps and roll it all out again. When you chill the dough, divide it in half or in thirds. Take out one piece of the dough at a time, leaving the remaining pieces in the refrigerator. Lightly dust the work surface with flour (I like to use a large, flat, nick-free, odor-free wooden cutting board, but any countertop is fine). You can also lightly dust the work surface with flour and granulated sugar. The granulated sugar does a great job of preventing the dough from sticking and it won't toughen your cookies the way too much flour will. Don't be too generous with either ingredient when dusting.

To make sure your cookies will bake evenly, make sure you roll out the dough to an even thickness. When you're ready to cut out the shapes, dip your cutter in flour, granulated sugar, or powdered sugar to prevent the dough from sticking to the cutter. Make sure you tap off any excess before cutting the dough. When you cut through the dough, give the cookie cutter a tiny twist to be sure you have cut all the way through the dough. The twist should be subtle, just a fraction of an inch.

Be economical when cutting out cookies; try and cut as many as possible out of one sheet of dough. Sometimes flipping the cookie cutter around on every other cookie will enable you to cut out more cookies.

Once you have cut out all of your cookies, carefully lift up the scrap dough and put it aside. On your work surface, you will have all your cutout cookies. Use a pancake turner or metal spatula to transfer your cookies to a baking sheet. The dough is quite delicate and you wouldn't want to stretch it or tear it by transferring the cookies by hand.

Kitchen Utensil
Cookie cutters make a great gift. You can find them in just about every shape and size and for just about every occasion. Check out your local baking-supply or kitchenware store to come up with ideas for great cutout cookies.

Sticky Business

Do you find yourself continually frustrated by your cookies sticking to the countertop as you attempt to transfer them to the baking sheet after you cut them out? Instead of giving up on rolled cookies, try these easy tips to keep your dough in line. First, after you finish rolling out your dough but before you cut into it, give the dough a half-turn. If the dough is sticking to the counter, unstick it and toss a dusting of granulated sugar on your rolling surface. Give it another half-turn and make sure the dough moves easily. Then cut out your cookies and transfer them onto the baking sheets. They should cooperate beautifully.

Save all the scraps from each section of dough, then gather all the scraps together to reroll. This will eliminate excessive rerolling. After you have rolled out the dough twice, you might want to consider discarding the scraps, since the dough will toughen considerably.

If you don't have a rolling pin or you don't want to bother rolling out the cookie dough, you can "unroll" cookies. Scoop out a heaping tablespoon of cookie dough and roll it into a ball. Place the ball onto a cookie sheet. Dip the bottom of a drinking glass (2-inch diameter) into granulated or confectioners' sugar and gently press down the dough into a $1/4$-inch-thick round. Repeat until you have filled the tray (9 to 12 cookies) and then bake as directed.

Kitchen Utensil
Choose your cookie cutters wisely. Choose big, basic-shaped, well-made cookies cutters that will free your dough easily. Cookie cutters that have lots of angles or make thin shapes (thin animal legs and tails, for example, or tiny arms and legs) often create cookies that will break or tear easily or get stuck in the cookie cutter.

Once your cookies have baked, let them cool for a few minutes on the cookie sheet before removing them to a cooling rack. This will let delicate shapes harden, so gingerbread people won't leave any limbs stuck onto the baking sheet.

Brownies and Bar Cookies

Brownies and bar cookies are different from other cookies because they are baked in one pan, then cut into squares or whatever shape you desire.

Always use the correct pan size. If you substitute a larger pan, your brownies or bars will be too thin and might dry out when you bake them. If the pan is too small, it will take a much longer time to bake your brownies or bars, and the inside might still be raw when the outside is done cooking.

If you use a glass baking pan instead of metal, reduce the baking temperature by 25°F.

Be sure that you cut your bar cookies into their shapes after they have cooled completely, unless otherwise instructed. If you cut them when they are too warm, they will be difficult to cut cleanly and might crumble much easier than when they have cooled completely.

Kitchen Utensil
An incredibly easy way to slice up bar cookies is to use a pizza cutter instead of a knife.

A great trick for cutting brownies and bars evenly and eliminating dirty pans is to line the baking pan with aluminum foil. When the brownies have cooled completely, just lift out the aluminum foil and place them onto a cutting board and remove the foil. You can then cut the bars and place them on a serving plate or even back into the pan.

Storing Cookies

Cookies can be stored at room temperature if they will be eaten within a few days, in the refrigerator if they will be eaten within a week, or in the freezer for several months (always a good idea when you want to have cookies on hand). Some cookies (usually those with frosting) need to be refrigerated once they are cooled. This will be indicated in the recipes.

It is very important that cookies be allowed to cool completely before they are stored. If cookies are stored in an airtight container while they are still warm, they will give off heat, create condensation, and become soggy.

Crisp, thin cookies actually do better if they are wrapped in an airtight container. If your crisp cookies soften a bit, recrisp them by placing them on a baking sheet and popping them into the 250°F oven for 5 to 7 minutes. Freezing crispy cookies, then defrosting them before eating, also helps them retain their crispiness.

Soft, moist cookies should also be stored in an airtight container. You can also put in a slice of bread (a trick I learned from my friend Martha) or a slice of apple (which you need to change daily) to help your cookies stay moist and chewy.

Frosted cookies should be stored in a single layer or with a sheet of waxed paper between layers, depending on how soft the frosting is. Also, if you have delicate-shaped or rolled cookies, consider storing them in single layers or with waxed paper between the layers.

Bar cookies are easy to store because you can wrap the top of the baking pan with aluminum foil or plastic wrap and you're done. They can also be removed from the pan and placed in a container or on a serving plate. Just be sure to seal the container or wrap the plate with aluminum foil or plastic wrap, and your brownies or bar cookies will stay fresh.

Kitchen Utensil

When I make a big batch of cookies, I like to store them in a large plastic cake saver, turned upside down. I can always fit the entire batch of cookies, it has an airtight seal, and it doesn't take up much room on the counter.

Quick Tips for Making Your Cookies Mag-ni-fique

Cookies are a great thing to fancy up a bit and decorate. You can either decorate each cookie individually or you can jazz up the container in which you present your cookies.

➤ If you're going to a picnic and decide to bring cookies for a portable dessert or snack (which is always a good idea), jazz up the presentation by lining the container with clean linen napkins or bandannas.

➤ Personalize your basic sugar cookie or gingerbread cookie recipe by decorating the dough with cinnamon hearts, chocolate chips, colorful candy-coated chocolates, chopped nuts, or raisins (or even chocolate-coated raisins!) before baking.

➤ Melt some semisweet or milk chocolate and dip half the cookie into it. Set the cookie on a cooling rack until the chocolate hardens. You can even sprinkle some colored sprinkles or finely chopped nuts on top of the chocolate before it hardens.

➤ Sandwich a scoop of ice cream between two homemade cookies and watch them disappear. Who doesn't like ice cream sandwiches?

➤ Buy some tubes of frosting in the baking aisle of the supermarket. Decorate your cookies to match a party theme or make them fancy. Any cookie looks good wearing a bit of frosting. You can even cut cookies into squares, decorate them with frosting, write each of the guests' names on a cookie, and use them as place cards for the party.

➤ Press your thumb into the center of each drop cookie to make a little depression. Fill it with chocolate chips or jam before baking.

➤ Decorate the plates or trays you serve the cookies on with colorful napkins or pretty doilies.

➤ Paint your cookies! Blend 1 egg yolk with 4 drops of water. Divide the mixture into several small cups. Tint each cup with a drop or two of food coloring and paint onto

149

a basic sugar cookie before baking. If the paint thickens too much, thin it with a few more drops of water. If you prefer, you can use a tablespoon or two of evaporated milk for paint instead of the egg.

➤ Instead of chocolate chips, stir in the following (either alone or a combination to equal the amount of chocolate called for in the recipe): trail nut mix, chopped chocolate toffee bars, crushed chocolate mint wafers, chocolate-covered peanuts or raisins, dried fruit bits, or chopped, drained, maraschino cherries.

➤ Dust the tops of chocolate brownies with confectioners' sugar. Not only do they look more appetizing, but if there are any imperfections in the brownies, the confectioners' sugar will cover them up.

➤ Brownie sundaes are always a hit. Place a brownie square in the bottom of a bowl, top with ice cream and your favorite sundae toppings, and serve.

Remember, the idea is just to have fun with your cookies. Experiment with getting creative with your cookies before the holidays or special events, to give yourself a lot of time to become familiar with different techniques and doughs. You can try any or all of these suggestions, but sometimes the best accompaniment to any kind of cookie is a big glass of milk.

The Least You Need to Know

➤ Cookies come in many flavors and varieties; pick the ones you like.

➤ If your cookies spread too much during baking, try chilling the dough.

➤ Always check on your cookies after the minimum baking time given in the recipe.

➤ Store your cookies in an airtight container after they have cooled completely. If you don't plan on eating them within a few days, cookies freeze very well.

➤ Presentation makes a difference; feel free to dress up your cookies if you are taking them out.

All About Yeast Breads

Many people get nervous about baking bread from scratch. They think they have to have some secret talent to make it rise or come out tasting good. And since bread is so readily available and such a staple for many people, it's much easier to pick up a loaf at the local grocery store or bakery. While I'm not suggesting that you never pick up another store-bought loaf, I must say from all of the baking I have done over the years, there is nothing better than baking your own bread.

There is something so deeply satisfying, yet simple, about making your own bread. From the relaxing repetition of kneading the dough, to the slow, quiet rise, to the shaping of the loaves, to the heavenly smell of it baking in the oven, there is nothing quite like it. Bread is not overstated, nor is it decadent; it is simple and basic and has played a major role in history. With the invention of the bread machine, homemade loaves can be made in no time. But, to truly experience the wonderful experience of breadmaking, I believe everyone should bake at least one loaf of bread in their lives. I am sure it will not be your last.

General Information About Yeast Breads (Don't Be Afraid to Try Them)

Whole books have been dedicated to the art of breadmaking, and there are hundreds of different doughs which you can learn to bake. Instead of overwhelming you with too much information, I will stick to the basics to lay a good solid foundation on which you can build your bread-baking knowledge. Once you feel comfortable with the mixing and kneading and rising of basic bread doughs, you can move on to fancier types of loaves and rolls. First, it's important to understand how all the ingredients work together to have a better understanding about the making of bread.

Yeast

Yeast is the ingredient that makes bread rise. It is a live plant, which, when dissolved in warm water (not warmer than 110°F) and given something to eat, becomes active. Yeast needs food to stay alive. The sweetener added to the dough (usually sugar or honey) is the initial food for the yeast, then more sugar is found in the starch from the flour which sustains the yeast until it finally dies when it is baked in the oven.

There are several different types of yeast available. I like to use active dry yeast. It has a longer shelf life than fresh compressed cake yeast, is easy to store, and available in foil packs or jars coded with an expiration date. You can also use rapid-rise active dry yeast. If you do, just skip the proofing stage; rapid-rise yeast activates quickly and doesn't need to be proofed (for more on proofing, keep reading). One package of active dry yeast contains $1/4$ ounce or 1 scant tablespoon (scant means "barely"), so if your yeast isn't in the premeasured packages, measure out 1 level tablespoon, then gently shake back just a little. You should always store your yeast in the refrigerator. For more about yeast, see Chapter 5.

Bakers Beware!

If you are shopping for yeast, you might come across brewer's yeast, which is available in most health-food stores. THIS IS NOT A YEAST FOR BREAD-MAKING and should not be substituted for active dry yeast.

You can also substitute 1 square of fresh compressed cake yeast (available in 0.6-ounce squares) for 1 package of active dry yeast. Be sure to check the expiration date printed on the wrapper, since fresh yeast has a considerably shorter shelf life than dry active yeast.

Bread-machine yeast is designed to dissolve thoroughly when used in conjunction with a bread machine. If you are baking your bread without the use of a bread machine, don't use bread-machine yeast.

Yeast likes to be snug and warm, but not hot. The most common mistake made by first-time bread makers is to kill the yeast by overheating it. One of the first steps in breadmaking is to dissolve the yeast in warm water. Sometimes a temperature is given (not over 110°F). How will you be able to tell if the water temperature is correct? The most accurate way is to use a candy or meat thermometer. If you don't have one, you can measure the temperature almost as accurately just by feel. Your body temperature is about 98.6°F, so if you run the hot water until it is just slightly warm to the touch, but not uncomfortably hot, then that should be just about right.

What Is Proofing and Why Do It?

Proofing yeast—dissolving it in warm water, sometimes with a little sugar or flour, and waiting for it to react—was once an essential step in baking bread. The foam and the distinct odor the yeast produced was showing "proof" the yeast was still alive. Since yeast now comes well packaged with an expiration date, much of the guesswork is eliminated, but beginner bread bakers might want the sure thing. Feel free to proof your yeast if you want to make sure it is alive. The only yeast I do not recommend proofing is rapid-rise or quick-rise yeast, since it is not designed to be proofed. Just make sure any rapid-rise yeast has not reached its expiration date.

> **Bakers Beware!**
> Do not proof rapid-rise or quick-rise yeast. Because these yeasts are designed to make dough rise faster, they can use up a lot of their energy during the proofing stage, and not have enough oomph for the rising stage of the dough.

To proof yeast, combine one package (1 scant tablespoon) of yeast with $1/4$ cup warm water (not over 110°F) and $1/2$ teaspoon of sugar or flour. Stir well to dissolve the yeast and sugar, then let it rest for about five minutes, or until it becomes bubbly and foamy. This bubbling foam is your proof that the yeast is alive. Proceed with the rest of your recipe.

Let's say you have decided not to proof your yeast, only to discover, after many attempts at coaxing your bread to rise, that it just lies in the bottom of the bowl, unchanged. Don't despair! You can save your bread. This time, get out another packet of yeast, proof it as described in the paragraph above, and knead it into your dead dough. You will probably have to add a couple of tablespoons of flour to get dough to the the right consistency again. Knead the dough for a couple of minutes and then set it in a cozy warm place to rise again. This time it should work.

Flour

Flour is the main ingredient in bread. When you go to the store to buy ingredients, you might be astonished to find the number of different flours that are available. Flour contains proteins which, when liquids are added and the dough is kneaded, form gluten. This gluten gives the dough its elasticity, allowing the dough to stretch as it traps the gases released by the yeast, causing the bread to rise. The different varieties of flour have different amounts of gluten-making proteins, so it's good to know a little about your choices for breadmaking:

➤ *Bread flour.* Bread flour is protein-rich white flour, made from hard wheat that is high in gluten. This is a good choice for breadmaking because the gluten-rich dough has good elasticity and gives good volume when your bread rises. Bread flour also absorbs more liquid than all-purpose flour, so you might need less flour if your recipe calls for all-purpose flour and you are using bread flour. You might want to experiment with making the same recipe with all-purpose flour and bread flour and comparing the results; you may find the bread-flour loaf is a bit tastier, lighter, and better risen than your all-purpose loaf. Plus, the extra protein of the bread flour makes it a healthier choice.

Information Station

If you have eaten breads both above and below the Mason-Dixon line, you might have noticed that the texture of biscuits, for example, from Pennsylvania is different from that of the ones from North Carolina. That's because in baking there are two types of wheat: hard and soft. Hard wheat contains more gluten-forming proteins, making it good for yeast breads, and is mostly grown in the United States in Montana, the upper Midwest, and the Southwest. Soft wheat, or southern winter wheat, has less gluten but more starch, making it a better choice for biscuits, quick breads, and special fine-textured cakes because it gives them a more tender texture. This flour is grown is milder climates in the middle and eastern United States. Soft wheat is usually more finely ground and also absorbs less liquid than harder wheats.

➤ *Unbleached white flour.* Unbleached flour is a mixture of hard and soft wheats that has not been chemically whitened. It has a slightly higher protein content and more nutrients than all-purpose flour, making it a good choice for baking bread.

➤ *All-purpose enriched white flour.* This type of flour is by far the most common flour available, although it is not always the best choice. It is a mix of hard and soft wheats and has been chemically bleached. This process aids in the loss of some of its nutrients, which is why it is then enriched with additional vitamins. Because it is "all-purpose," it's a good flour to have around if you want to make a cake, some bread, or some cookies, although the results might not be as good as if you chose a flour specially intended for each purpose (cake flour for cakes and bread flour for bread).

➤ *Self-rising flour.* This flour is all-purpose flour with salt and baking soda mixed in it. I don't recommend it for yeast breads.

➤ *Whole-wheat flour.* Commercial whole-wheat flour is milled to include the flour, bran, and germ of the wheat. If a recipe calls for white flour, and you want to use whole-wheat, try substituting whole-wheat flour for half of the white flour and see what your results are. I have had much success in the past substituting half whole-wheat for white flour for traditional loaves of bread. Whole-wheat flour will produce a much denser loaf of bread and it also absorbs more liquid than white flour, so if you are substituting whole-wheat flour for white flour, add the minimum amount of flour called for in the recipe, then continue to slowly add more to make sure you don't toughen the dough.

A final word about flours: Although you may buy the same brand for 25 years, flour will vary in its absorbency properties and in the amount of moisture it contains. That is why many bread recipes will give a general amount of flour (4 to 6 cups) and it's up to you to determine how much flour to use that day. Always pay more attention to how your dough looks than the cup amount of flour you are adding to your dough. You should not pack flour into your measuring cup; instead just spoon it into the cup to measure it. And always add the flour slowly, don't dump all of it in at once. Good dough should be smooth and elastic and not stick to the sides of the bowl. It will give when it is kneaded and not be tough, and it shouldn't stick to your hands or the countertop.

Sweeteners

The usual sweeteners you will find in breadmaking are sugar and honey. While these typically do not make the bread sweet like a cake, the sweetener does add some flavor to the bread and it also feeds the yeast. When the yeast eats the sugar, it begins a fermentation process, which produces the gases that cause the bread to rise. The sweetener also browns during baking, helping produce a bread with a nice texture and golden-brown crust.

Salt

Salt is quite important in baking bread. It adds flavor and also controls the yeast growth, preventing the bread from over-rising. Salt was always the final ingredient added to the brioche dough I made when I worked in the bakery, and I have to admit I forgot to add it on more than one occasion. While it was not apparent when I put the dough into the bowl to rise overnight, the next morning I would arrive to find dough pouring out over the sides of the bowl and a rather flavorless, weakly structured dough. So, learn from my mistakes and don't forget to add the salt. But, that said, don't overdo it or else it will inhibit the proper growth of the yeast. Just use the amount called for in the recipe.

Fat

The addition of fat in bread recipes adds to the tenderness and texture of the bread and carries the flavor. Fats also act as a natural preservative, helping your loaf retain its moisture and stay mold-free longer than breads made without fat. When butter is used it adds a bit of color. Shortening or lard can be substituted for butter, measure for measure, and oil can also be used.

Eggs

Eggs are not essential to breadmaking, but sometimes they are called for in a recipe. The addition of eggs produces a richer dough and contributes a lovely pale-yellow color to the dough. You can also brush the tops of unbaked breads with beaten egg for a shiny finish.

Liquids

The typical liquids used in breadmaking are water, milk, and buttermilk. The liquids moisten the flour, which activates the gluten, and can also feed the yeast. Water gives bread a browner and crisp crust. Milk used for the liquid usually gives a velvety, creamier texture to the bread. Buttermilk adds a nice tangy flavor to bread. If you do use milk or buttermilk, warm it slightly (just so it is warm to the touch) to take the chill of the refrigerator off of it before dissolving the yeast in it. Yeast will also dissolve a bit more slowly in milk than in water.

Mixing and Kneading Breads

When you get ready to make bread, it's important to have all of your ingredients assembled in your work space. Typically, a recipe will ask you to dissolve the yeast in a liquid, and then you will add several other ingredients (butter, salt, sugar). Then it's time to add the flour. There are two ways to mix doughs together: with a mixer equipped with a dough hook, and by hand.

Dough hook for a stand mixer.

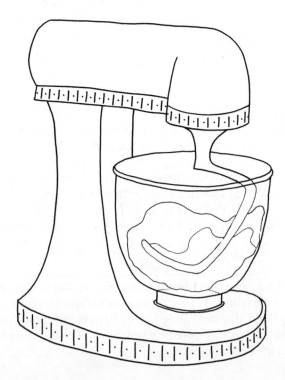

If you have a sturdy mixer with a good motor, then this is certainly the easy way to do it. Mixing bread dough by hand is a little more work, but it has its own rewards. Regardless of the mixing method you choose, it's very important to add the flour slowly. The first 2 to 3 cups will be absorbed quickly into the dough, making a wet, loose batter. You should then start adding the flour $1/2$ cup at a time, and continue mixing until the dough starts to come away from the sides of the bowl.

Bakers Beware!
Do not use a hand-held mixer to mix yeast bread doughs. The dough will become too heavy for the motor and you might burn out the engine. Unless you have a heavy-duty stand mixer with a dough hook attachment, I recommend mixing the dough by hand.

If you are using a mixer with a dough hook attachment, knead the bread for about 5 minutes on medium speed. Remove the dough from the bowl, and finish kneading by hand on a lightly floured surface. If you are mixing by hand, once the dough comes away from the sides of the bowl, turn the dough out onto a lightly floured surface. A large wooden cutting board, a clean counter-top, or a large slab of marble all make good kneading surfaces. Before you begin kneading, make sure your work surface is completely dry and you don't have obstacles in your way. Put away all of your ingredients except the flour, clear off a space and clean it if necessary, make sure it is dry, and then lightly dust it with flour. Rub your hands with a little flour, too. Never dump a lot of flour (more than 2 tablespoons) on dough you are kneading. Always lightly dust the dough with flour and when the flour is incorporated into the dough and it needs more, dust it again.

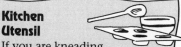

Kitchen Utensil
If you are kneading bread on a wooden board and find it is slipping or moving on the counter, wet a dishrag and place it between the board and the countertop. That should help steady the board.

Kneading dough develops the gluten and incorporates very tiny air pockets into the dough, which all help with the rising of the bread and its texture and look. As you knead the dough, you may notice it still feels a bit sticky or tacky. Just lightly dust the surface of the dough with additional flour and continue kneading and dusting until your dough is finished.

Okay, so you're ready to knead. Rest assured there's no mystery to it. You've turned the dough out onto a lightly floured surface and dusted the top of the dough with flour (don't use more than a tablespoon or two of flour for each dusting). Now press the heels of your hands into the top of the dough. You need to use some arm strength, so lean into the dough and push it hard into the kneading surface. Sometimes I link my fingers together, one hand on top of the other, as if I am giving CPR to the dough. It increases my kneading strength.

Fold the dough in half toward you, and press down again with the heels of your hands. Give the dough a quarter-turn, fold it again, and continue the pushing and kneading with the heels of your hands, always turning the dough and folding it so all the dough gets worked.

Kitchen Utensil
If you get tired while kneading and need to rest, that's okay. Just cover the dough with a clean dish towel and rest for five minutes. The dough will be glad to rest, too.

Continue to lightly dust the dough if it sticks to the board or your hands. Keep this up for about 10 minutes (3 to 5 minutes if you have used a mixer). If you are kneading by hand, you will not overwork the dough. This is a very important step in good breadmaking, so don't cut corners here. You will know you're done when your dough is smooth, elastic, and a bit satiny. If you press into the dough and it springs back, you have done the job.

Press the heels of your hands into the dough.

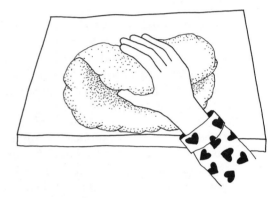

Fold the dough in half toward you and press down again with the heels of your hands.

Kneading is actually fun. You can smack, punch, toss, hammer, slam, or do whatever you choose to abuse your dough and it will reward you with good shape and texture. Bread dough is a good thing to take your aggressions out on, and if you make it often enough, you may find your arms are a bit more toned and you gain strength (hey, maybe there's an idea for a new type of gym class). For the more peaceful-minded baker, you may find that the pleasant rhythmic motion gives you time to let your mind wander, look out the window, or just sing to yourself. If you get tired before you finish, cover the dough with a clean towel and take a break. Once you have finished kneading, it's time to set the bread aside to rise.

Encouraging Bread to Rise

I find that the best bowl for rising is a heavy, large ceramic bowl. Ceramic bowls seem to be better insulators than metal or glass bowls. The temperature of metal or glass bowls might fluctuate with the exterior temperature, but they can also be used. Yeast likes it to be cozy and warm, so rinse the bowl out with warm water and dry it thoroughly. Then generously grease the inside of the bowl with softened butter or margarine or even shortening (don't use oil unless the recipe specifically calls for it). Form the dough into a ball and place it in the bowl. Roll the dough once around the bowl, to grease the dough itself. Dampen a clean dishtowel with warm water and drape it over the top of the bowl. If you don't have any clean dishtowels available, which I often find to be the case, just dampen five or six paper towels (don't separate them into individual sheets) and double it over the top of the bowl. You can also very loosely cover (don't seal) the top of the bowl with plastic wrap. The purpose of the cover is to keep the dough draft-free and to prevent anything from entering the dough as it rises, but the dough also needs to breath so you don't want to seal it off from air.

Many cooks agree that the best place to let dough rise is in a gas oven, turned off. The heat the pilot light gives off creates the perfect cozy spot for bread to rise and the oven itself should be draft-free. If you have an electric oven, you can place your bread to rise there. It isn't as warm as a gas oven, but it is draft-free. If you have two racks in your oven, place a pan of hot water on the bottom rack and the bowl on the upper rack. This creates a slightly warmer environment. The microwave oven, if it is large enough, is also a good draft-free choice. Make sure the bowl you choose fits in there, however. You can also place a cup of hot water in the corner of the microwave oven, if it fits, to add a bit of warmth, but it is not necessary. Of course, the kitchen countertop is fine, too. The dough needs to double in size, which usually takes 1 to 1½ hours. Always check it after the minimum time. If you are using rapid-rise yeast, check it after 30 to 40 minutes.

You will know your bread has finished rising when you can poke your finger into it about ½ inch and the indentation stays. If the dough springs back, continue letting it rise. Don't allow the dough to more than double in size. If a second rising is called for in a recipe, punch down the dough, give it a few quick kneads in the bowl, then re-cover the bowl and allow the dough to rise again. If you are going to shape the dough into loaves, punch down the dough and turn it out onto a lightly floured board. Knead the dough again for 2 to 3 minutes, then divide the dough (you can pull it apart or cut it with a knife), if necessary, into the portions you need. Let the dough rest for about 5 minutes before shaping the loaves.

Shaping and Baking the Loaves

Shaping loaves is not difficult. First, you should divide the dough according to how many loaves the recipe will make. Make sure you have as many loaf pans as loaves of bread the recipe will make. There are several different ways to shape your loaves. For the simplest method, simply pat each loaf into an oval about the size of the pan. You can gently stretch the dough down as you hold it to create a smooth top and place the dough in the prepared baking pan. Another method is to pat or roll the dough out into a rectangle slightly shorter than the loaf pan. Fold the dough in thirds, like a letter, or roll it up like a jelly roll. Tuck the ends under and place it seam side down into the prepared loaf pan. This method will give you a nice smooth finish. Cover the dough with a clean dishtowel and allow the bread to rise until it just comes up to the side of the pan, about 30 minutes.

Shaping a loaf of bread: Fold the dough in thirds and place it in the pan.

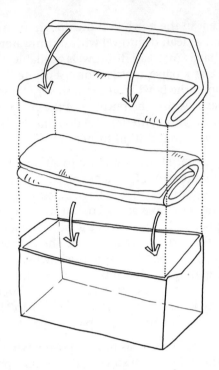

You can also braid bread dough. If you are making two loaves, divide the dough in half and then divide each half into three equal portions. Roll each portion out to look like a long snake, a few inches longer than the loaf pan, and braid the three portions together. Tuck under the ends and place it into the prepared bread pan to rise.

Braiding bread dough.

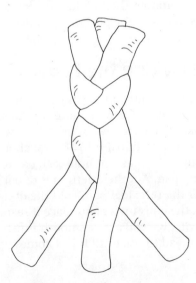

Chapter 14 ➤ *All About Yeast Breads*

In the first 15 minutes or so of baking, your bread will have an amazing growth spurt where the yeast gets really active and pushes up the bread before the crust begins to set. Always account for this sudden spurt of growth by not allowing your bread to rise over the top of the pans.

Always bake your bread in a preheated oven. Usually the baking time given for a recipe is accurate, but if you are unsure, give a thump on the bread (watch out, it will be hot!). If it sounds hollow, then it's done. If you are still unsure, you can go ahead and insert a long wooden skewer into the middle of the loaf. If it comes out clean, your bread is done. Don't judge doneness by the color of the loaf. If you find your bread is browning too quickly, cover it with aluminum foil for the last 15 or 20 minutes of baking.

Kitchen Utensil

If you want a soft crust, brush the top of your finished loaves with melted butter. For a shiny crust, brush the unbaked loaves with a beaten egg before the bread goes into the oven. For a crispy crust, place a pan of hot water on the bottom of your oven or on an oven rack set to its lowest setting in the oven. This is especially good for French bread.

Turn the bread out of the pans onto cooling racks when you remove them from the oven. They should slip out easily.

Let the bread cool at least 30 minutes before you slice it, otherwise you run the risk of ruining the bread you have worked so hard to make. Always use a serrated knife; a straight edge will press and squash the loaf. If you are having problems making even slices, turn the bread on its side and cut using very light pressure. Pressing too hard will also crush the loaf.

Storing Bread

Do not wrap your bread until it has completely cooled; otherwise, the warm bread will cause condenstion to form and it could mold quickly. Then store your breads in sealable plastic bags or wrapped tightly in aluminum foil. Since homemade bread does not contain any preservatives, it can get hard and go bad within a couple of days if not stored properly. Bread made with milk or fat has a tendency to stay fresher longer. Store your bread in the refrigerator if you don't think you will eat it within a couple of days.

Bread also freezes well, as a whole loaf or even cut in half. This is great inspiration to double up when baking bread to have a loaf to eat and a loaf for later. To crisp up a frozen loaf, defrost it, then place it in a 350°F oven for several minutes before serving.

Don't forget that stale bread also has some great uses: bread pudding, stuffing for turkey, homemade croutons, bread crumbs, and the absolute best—French toast.

The Yeast You Knead to Know

➤ Yeast needs a warm, cozy environment to live. Too hot a temperature kills yeast; too cold makes it sluggish.

➤ Kneading dough is very important for the final texture and look. Make sure you don't skimp on time.

➤ During the first 15 minutes of baking, the bread will have a growth spurt, so put your bread into the oven just when it reaches the edges of the loaf pans.

➤ Be sure you have enough pans to bake the number of loaves of bread your recipe will yield.

➤ Store your bread after it has completely cooled; you can also freeze bread with good results.

Chapter 15

All About Quick Breads, Muffins, and Biscuits

In This Chapter

➤ What puts the "quick" in quick breads?

➤ How to get great-looking and great-tasting muffins

➤ Tips for making mini-muffins and quick-bread loaves

➤ Tips for making fluffy, delicious biscuits

While everyone loves tender coffee cakes, muffins, and hot biscuits, oftentimes we find ourselves buying them from the bakery, deli, or in the refrigerated sections of the grocery store for convenience. Perhaps this is because you think you don't have the time or talent to whip up a batch of homemade muffins. Quick breads and muffins are the perfect introduction as you prepare to discover the joys of home-baked goods. The batters are not difficult to put together, most can be done in less than 15 minutes, and you can find a recipe that's right for any occasion.

Quick breads, such as banana bread or zucchini bread, are popular favorites for many people. In this chapter I'll talk about how to whip up batters for these breads. You'll learn how easy it is to jazz up quick breads with ingredients such as nuts, raisins, dried cranberries, chocolate chips, and dried fruits. There's also advice on making a wide variety of muffins, plus helpful hints for making tender, flaky biscuits.

Quick Tips About Quick Breads

Quick breads are quite popular because they are a snap to put together and can satisfy either a sweet or a savory desire. Since they are leavened with baking soda or baking powder, they don't require the rising time that yeast breads do, making them fast and easy to make. Just make sure your leaveners are fresh, so they will be sure to have optimal rising power.

The thing I like best about quick breads is that they are relatively indestructible when it comes to add-ins. If you want to experiment with adding about $1/2$ cup of nuts, dried fruit, chocolate chips, or coconut, go right ahead. What differentiates quick breads, muffins, and biscuits is the proportion of liquid to fat, flour, and eggs; quick breads having the most moisture and biscuits having the least.

Quick breads are generally baked in metal loaf pans. Shiny pans are best, but if you have dark, nonstick pans or glass pans, those are fine, too. Just lower the oven temperature by 25°F if you find the breads are browning too quickly.

Overmixing the batter can toughen the bread, so mix until the ingredients are just combined unless specified by the instructions. You may even want to consider mixing the breads by hand to avoid toughening the dough. Grease only the bottoms of the loaf pans for nut or fruit quick breads; the ungreased sides give the batter something to "cling" to as it rises and gives you a nicely shaped loaf with a gently rounded top.

Kitchen Utensil
If you find your quick breads are sticking in the pan a little, just run a butter knife around all four edges and try to release it from the pan again.

If your bread develops a large crack lengthwise down the center of the bread, don't worry that you have done anything wrong. The crusts of quick breads are usually thinner than yeast breads and have a tendency to crack. I think it gives the bread a great homemade look.

I find that many quick breads taste even better the second day, although they don't always stick around until then. You can wrap the cooled loaves in plastic wrap and store them in the refrigerator for up to one week. Well wrapped in aluminum foil and frozen, they can last several months.

Making the Perfect Muffin

Making a tender, moist muffin is really quite simple, but not knowing the proper technique can cause unpleasant results. The secret to bumpy rounded muffin tops and moist insides is to avoid overmixing the dough. You should only use a bowl and a spoon for mixing. Don't use a hand-held or stand mixer. When you combine the flour mixture with the liquids, just give it a few (no more than five) good turns with a sturdy wooden spoon. Yes, there will be, and should be, a tiny bit of unmixed flour in your batter. Believe it or not, the batter will "finish mixing" in the oven and the unmixed flour will not be present in the muffin. If you blend your batter until it is smooth and uniform, you will have made a cake-like batter, which will result in peaked or smooth tops. You want to have slightly rounded, bumpy-topped muffins baked to a golden brown.

Preparing the Pans

The easiest way to prepare muffin tins is to use paper liners. Just pop the liners in and then fill three-quarters full of batter. You don't need liners in order to make muffins, though. Just grease only the bottoms of the muffin cups. The sides of the cup should be left ungreased, unless the recipe calls for the entire cup to be greased. Not greasing the sides actually gives you a better-shaped muffin.

As soon as the muffins are done baking, let them sit for just one minute to set, then remove them from the muffin pan. They should tumble out when the pan is inverted; if some are reluctant to come out, just run a butter knife or a thin metal spatula around the muffin tin to loosen the muffin. If you leave muffins to cool in the muffin tins, they will become a bit soggy from the trapped steam.

Bakers Beware!
When you are filling muffin cups, be sure you only fill the cup three-quarters full of batter. Overfilling muffin tins will result in the batter spilling over onto the top of the muffin tin and your muffins will be oddly shaped. You may even have batter drip on the floor of the oven, which is always a mess. Be sure to wipe off any batter that has spilled onto the top of the muffin tin before baking.

Muffins can be stored in an airtight container, refrigerated, for three to five days. You can also freeze muffins for several months. Store the muffins in a large sealable plastic bag or an airtight plastic container. Just bring them to room temperature before serving. You can also split them and warm them in the oven.

Going Mini

The standard muffin cup is $2^1/_2 \times 1^1/_4$ inches; however, almost every muffin and quick-bread recipe can be baked in mini-loaf or mini-muffin pans. To determine the amount of baking time needed for these sizes, measure the volume of your baking pan. To do this, fill the pan to capacity with water (for muffin tins, just fill one cup), then pour the water into a glass measuring cup and read, and that is your capacity. When you bake, just fill your baking pans about three-quarters of the way full with batter, to allow room for the rising of the muffins or breads. If you fill the pan too much, it will spill over the edges of the baking pan onto the bottom of your oven. Bake your mini creations at 350°F and always check them after the minimum of time given. Remember, if you have greased extra muffin cups and don't have enough batter, fill them with a few tablespoons of water before baking to prevent the grease from burning onto the pan.

If Your Pan Holds...	Use This Much Batter	Baking Time
1/4 cup	3 tablespoons	10 to 15 minutes
1/3 cup	1/4 cup	15 to 20 minutes
1/2 cup	1/3 cup	15 to 20 minutes
3/4 cup	1/2 cup	20 to 25 minutes
1 cup	3/4 cup	30 to 35 minutes
2 1/2 cups	1 2/3 cup	40 to 45 minutes

Biscuit Basics

Fresh, hot, fluffy biscuits are a dinnertime dream for me. Just recently I came home from a particularly exhausting catering job. I dropped all of my bags by the door and sought out the closest comfortable chair. Before too long, a wonderful plate of hot homemade biscuits, smothered in a lush gravy, were presented to me. I tell you, those biscuits were quite resuscitating. And let me also share with you, the biscuits were made by my beau who does not fancy himself much of a baker, so if he can make fluffy, delicious biscuits, so can you.

While biscuits have great appeal all over these United States, below the Mason-Dixon line biscuits are a way of life. If you taste a "northern" biscuit and "southern" biscuit side by side, you'll notice quite a difference. That's because southern flour, made from soft winter wheat, is generally used for their biscuit making, producing a biscuit that is much more tender and lighter than those made with all-purpose flour. If you want to taste the difference, look for White Lily brand flour (or call 423-546-5511 for ordering information). Cake flour can also be used in place of all-purpose flour, measure for measure, for a lighter biscuit.

Information Station

Biscuits come from the French word, meaning twice cooked (*bis cuit*), and are a far cry from the light fluffy treats we are familiar with today. They began as dry, hard crackers or "hard tack" that sailors took with them since they would last during the long sea voyages. Later, shortening was added, but they were still hard because they were beaten for a long time. Finally, with the invention of baking powder, biscuits began their rise, and soon tender and fluffy became the motto for the biscuit.

Mixing Your Biscuit

Biscuits are a lot like pie pastry in the sense that too much handling will toughen the dough and the biscuit will not be as delicate. You don't want to overmix your biscuit dough, so it's important to work efficiently when making biscuits. The first step is to cut the fat into the flour so that it resembles coarse crumbs. This can be done one of two ways: either with a pastry cutter, or by using a fork or two knives. Then the liquid is added to the flour mixture and the ingredients are mixed together with a fork until they have just come together and the dough leaves the sides of the bowl. That is all the mixing of the dough you'll need. Don't use a hand-held or stand mixer to make biscuits; they don't need to be beaten.

Cutting and Baking

Turn the biscuit dough out onto a floured surface and either gently roll out the dough with a rolling pin or pat it out with your hands into a circle about $1/2$-inch thick. You can use either a 2-inch round cookie cutter or just flour the rim of a drinking glass to cut out your biscuits. Gather up the scraps, gently pat out the dough again, and cut out a few more biscuits. You don't want to cut out any more biscuits than that since overhandling the dough will make tougher biscuits. If you want biscuits with soft sides, place them in the pan so their sides are touching; if you want them to have crusty sides, place them about an inch apart on the baking sheet.

Storing Biscuits

Biscuits are really best when eaten hot, fresh out of the oven. You can make them a day ahead, but I would not suggest making them much more in advance than that. Store them in an airtight container when they have cooled completely.

The Least You Need to Know

➤ Quick breads are fast and easy to put together.

➤ Don't overmix your batters for any quick breads or biscuits. It will toughen the doughs.

➤ To avoid soggy crusts, don't allow breads and muffins to cool in the pans.

Part 5
Um...I Have A Question

This section is chock full of suggestions and ideas to answer the questions that will come up once you're baking. You'll learn what causes some of the most common baking problems and how to solve them. Then there are ideas for what to serve at different events, plus suggestions of sprucing up cakes and cookies. There are tips for special presentations and how to do some easy cake decorating when you want to make your cakes extra special. There's even a chapter that tackles the topic of fat and baked goods. You'll find information on storing your baked goods properly to ensure that they will remain fresh as long as possible. Finally, you'll find a chapter that tells you how to get that chocolate stain out of the tablecloth, and even how to bake a cake at 3,500 feet!

Chapter 16

What to Do If...

In This Chapter
➤ Simple solutions for near-disasters in the kitchen
➤ Help with a dry cake, a reluctant cake, cookies that bake unevenly, and much more

Okay, now you're baking. You've chosen a recipe and followed the instructions, yet something doesn't seem quite right. Small frustrations while baking can quickly turn the whole baking experience sour, and they can be time consuming and costly. It's good to equip yourself with the know-how to troubleshoot and problem-solve so you can rescue your recipe if you think it's in danger. In this chapter, you'll learn that while not all baking disasters can be averted, there are some things you can do to keep them from ruining your baking experience.

Help! My Cake Is Too Dry

One way to tell if your cake has finished cooking is to just look at it: It will pull away from the sides of the pan when it is done. This space is usually just a fraction of an inch, but sometimes when a cake is overcooked, it will have pulled away a considerable amount, maybe a quarter of an inch or so. There's a little trick we used in the bakery when cakes were overdone: We would brush them with simple syrup, which would remoisten the cake.

To make simple syrup, combine 1 cup water and 1 cup sugar in a small saucepan. Place over medium heat and cook, stirring, until the sugar dissolves and the mixture comes to a boil, about three minutes. Remove from the heat. This makes enough for a 9-inch layer cake. Simple syrup can be stored, covered, in the refrigerator for several weeks.

To use simple syrup, first cool the syrup to room temperature. While the syrup is cooling, even out the cake layers by carefully slicing the rounded dome off, if you like. With a pastry brush, paint the syrup all over the top and bottom of the cake to moisten it, allowing the syrup to soak in. The amount you will need depends on how dry your cake is. Then frost as usual.

You can add flavorings to this syrup, if you like, to give your dry cake a bit of a flavor boost. Add 2 or 3 tablespoons of liquor (such as rum, brandy, or bourbon) just before using. If you are using an extract, such as lemon or vanilla, add just 2 teaspoons.

If your cake still seems hopelessly dry because it baked too long, don't throw it away. Cut the cake into small squares and split the squares open. Melt about $1/2$ to 1 cup of jam and pour a few tablespoons on top of each serving to moisten, then top with whipped cream or ice cream. Call it something fancy like Secret Strawberry Surprise and no one will be the wiser. You may want to note on the recipe that the baking time seemed long and to shorten it the next time.

Help! My Cake Is Stuck in the Pan

The purpose of greasing and flouring baking pans is to keep your cakes and muffins from sticking in them once they've finished baking. For the most part, cakes, if cooked all the way through, usually leave the pan without a fight. Teflon coatings also make life a bit easier for the cook by providing a nonstick surface. This surface will lose its properties after a while, however, so if you're ever in doubt, it's always better to grease or line the bottom of the pan with waxed or parchment paper to be sure.

Bakers Beware!
When you take a cake out of the oven, set it on a wire cooling rack for a few minutes. If you try to remove the cake from the pan too quickly, the bottom of the cake will have a tendency to stick to the bottom of the pan and split the layer in half.

There are times, despite your best efforts, when the cake just refuses to leave the pan. There are a couple of tricks you can do to make cakes turn out easier. Try running a butter knife or a long, thin blade around the inside edge of the cake pan or muffin tin. This will loosen any cake that might be sticking to the sides. Place the cooling rack on top of the cake and flip the whole thing over. The cake should easily come out of the pan to finish cooling.

To remove an angel food cake from the pan after you have cooled it inverted, run a long, thin blade between the cake and the side of the pan to free it. Also, run the knife gently between the cake and the inside tube. Place a plate on top of the cake and turn it upside down, onto the plate. Gently wiggle or shake the pan to loosen the cake.

If your cake bottom is being very stubborn and simply refuses to leave the pan in one piece, with half of the cake deposited on your cooling rack and the other half stuck in the pan, don't despair. Grab a knife and scrape up the stuck bottom layer, then gently piece together the cake. Add a thickish layer of frosting and no one will be the wiser!

Muffins and cupcakes have a habit of sticking in the pan if they are too hot when flipped out. Let the muffins cool at least 5 minutes before trying to remove them, and always run a knife around them before inverting the pan.

Run a long, thin knife between the muffin and the side of the pan to loosen it.

Bundt cakes can be a bit trickier, especially if the pans are not well greased (all those nooks and crannies of the pan can make it a bit difficult). Here's a neat trick I learned for removing a bundt cake from the pan: Fold a kitchen towel or bathroom towel and wet it with steaming hot water. Leave it folded and place it in the sink. Remove the bundt cake from the oven and place it on the hot, wet towel for about 30 seconds. Then immediately turn out the bundt cake from the pan; it will come out cleanly and in one piece.

Help! My Cake Is Lopsided

If the lopsidedness is caused by a sloping oven, this is a problem indeed (see Chapter 6 for more on ovens). A lopsided oven is a rather difficult problem to overcome. If your oven is free-standing, you can try to insert little squares of heavy-duty cardboard underneath the oven to try and give it an even platform. You can tell if your oven is uneven by placing a glass baking dish halfway filled with water on your oven rack and looking to see if the waterline is straight. If your oven is severely lopsided, you can also place the cake pans on a baking sheet and prop something under the pan (make sure it's ovenproof; you could try a small stack of nickels) to offset the tilt. You will have to experiment with this to get it right.

Usually a sloping oven is not the problem, however. If your cake comes out of the oven with an irregular domed top, it may be because the batter was overbeaten. This is not a big problem, but if you are making a layer cake, it could cause your layers to shift and slide. To even out the layers, level your cake top by cutting it with a serrated knife. Choose the flattest surface of the layer cake and hold the knife parallel to the cake top. Slowly and gently cut straight across, making sure you are making an even cut across the top of the cake and not cutting down into the layer. Remove the cake dome and you should have a flat, even cake top.

Evening out the cake.

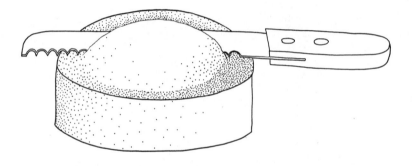

Information Station

When I worked at the bakery, we had to level cakes all the time, mostly carrot and chocolate cakes. Instead of throwing out the domed tops, we saved what was left once we'd finished snacking. Later, we turned them into crumbs by putting them in the food processor. We added these moist, flavorful crumbs to our cheesecake crumb bottoms or sticky roll fillings. Also, by leveling out the layers of the cake, we were able to sample what the cake tasted like without having to cut out a slice.

Help! My Cookies Look Like Pancakes

Every baker has suffered the problem of cookies that come out too flat. It's important to bake a test cookie to see how the rest of your batch will turn out. If there's a problem, it's better to discover it by baking just one cookie than by baking a whole batch.

If your cookies are spreading all over the baking tray while they bake in the oven, there are several tricks you can try to get them back in shape. First, make sure you're letting the baking sheet cool down between batches of cookies. The baking sheet should be cool enough for you to comfortably touch it before you put any dough on it. If you're sure that's not the problem, try adding a tablespoon or two of flour to the cookie dough and baking another test cookie. You can add up to 6 tablespoons of extra flour, mix it well, and bake another test cookie. If they are still spreading out too much, cover the dough and place it in the refrigerator for at least 30 minutes and up to two hours. Then bake another test cookie and see what that does. Keep the dough chilled while your cookies bake. You can also lower the oven temperature by 25°F and see if that helps.

If you try all of these adjustments and still nothing happens, I suggest just throwing out the recipe (or at least noting the page in the cookbook) and trying another.

Help! My Cookies Are Burned on the Bottom and Raw on Top

There is nothing more frustrating than removing your cookies from the oven to find they have scorched bottoms and doughy, raw tops. The first thing to do is check to see if your oven rack is in the right position. The rack should be in the center of the oven, not near the bottom or the top of the oven. If the rack is positioned too close to the bottom of the oven, where it is hotter, the bottoms of the cookies will burn before the rest of the cookie has baked.

If this is not the case, then your baking pans might be the culprits. Darker baking sheets (which sometimes include nonstick pans) tend to absorb heat more than the metal shiny ones, which will result in cookie bottoms baking faster than cookie tops. Lower your oven temperature by 25°F and keep your eye out for a sale on shiny metal baking sheets. They are not a bad investment and can save you from frustration in the kitchen.

Kitchen Utensil

If your cookies have burned a bit on the bottom, scrape off the burnt part and put the cookies in the freezer. Then, when you need a cookie-crumb crust, take the frozen cookies, process them into crumbs in the food processor, and voilà—cookie-crumb crust. You can use just about any flavor: chocolate chip, gingerbread, peanut butter, oatmeal, or sugar. It's a great trick!

If you do have the shiny metal sheets, then maybe they are too thin, allowing too much heat to penetrate. The easy way to fix this is to place one cookie sheet on top of another to create your own "insulated" cookie sheet. This should prevent the bottom of your cookies from burning.

Help! My Cookies Are Baking Unevenly

You may peer into the oven to discover that the cookies on the outside of the baking sheet have finished baking, while the cookies toward the center of the sheet have not. Or you may discover that half the sheet of cookies is browning, while the other half is not. Unless you have a high-tech convection oven (which blows around the air so every spot of the oven is the same exact temperature), your oven has hot spots and cool spots. For the most part, this will not interfere terribly with your baking. But, from time to time, you'll be reminded of the imperfections of your oven.

To combat hot spots and to produce nice, evenly baked cookies, the first thing to do is to make sure all of your cookies are the same size. If you make some big and some smaller, the small cookies will burn while the larger cookies will be gooey and raw.

Only bake one sheet of cookies at a time in the oven. Halfway through the baking time (most likely at the five-minute mark) give the cookie sheet an 180° turn in the oven, so the cookies in the back will be up front and those on the right will be on the left. That way, if there are hot spots, each side of the cookie tray will be evenly heated. This goes for sheet pans (brownies and single-layer cakes) too. And finally, don't overfill the cookie sheet. Leave about 1 inch between each cookie and about 1^1/$_2$ inches around the edge of the pan.

Help! My Pie Crust Is Burning

Sometimes a recipe calls for a pie filling to go into a partially baked pie crust, or sometimes a filling takes longer to bake than the pie pastry does, and you find the crust of the pie is browning too quickly.

If you find this is happening, there's no need for alarm. If you wrap up the edges of the pie in aluminum foil, or, if it's a double-crust pie, cover the whole top with aluminum foil, this will slow down the browning of the pastry so the filling can finish baking without burning the pastry itself. You can do this after the pie has baked for a bit and you notice the crust getting brown, or you can apply the foil prior to baking and then remove the foil about 10 to 15 minutes before the pie is done, so the crust will brown nicely in the last minutes of baking.

Cover the edge of the pie with aluminum foil and gently mold the foil to the edge of the pie crust.

Help! My Melted Chocolate Is Lumpy

You need to be careful when you are melting chocolate. Even the smallest drop of moisture (from a wet spoon or even the steam from the double boiler) can cause melted chocolate to become lumpy. Don't panic—instead, stir in 1 tablespoon of shortening (not butter or margarine, because they contain water) for every 3 ounces of chocolate. Stir constantly until smooth.

When melting chocolate in a double boiler, be sure the water level in the bottom pan is about an inch away from the bottom of the top pan.

Bakers Beware!
Chocolate burns easily if you melt it over too high a heat. If you suspect your chocolate is burnt, taste it. If it tastes burnt, throw it away and start again. That burnt taste will be transferred to your baked goods.

Help! My Bread Won't Rise

There are several reasons why your bread may not be excited about rising. First, yeast likes to be warm and cozy. If you have left the bowl in a cool, drafty place, the yeast will be sluggish, causing it to take a very long time to rise. If your kitchen is very cool, preheat your oven to the lowest setting (usually 200°F) for a few minutes (no longer than five, just take the chill off of it; if you have a gas stove with a pilot light, that alone should be warm enough). Turn off the oven, and place the bowl of dough, covered with a damp kitchen towel, in the warm oven. Let it sit there to rise with the door shut. If you still don't see a change in the dough within an hour, the yeast is probably dead.

There are several reasons why your yeast might be dead:

➤ *Did you use water above 110°F?* Hot water kills yeast. You want to use water that is just slightly above body temperature.

➤ *Is the yeast past its expiration date?* If you still have the packet of yeast you used, check the expiration date. If it has expired, there's your answer.

➤ *Did you proof rapid-rise yeast first?* Rapid-rise yeast is a special strain of yeast that has been made to cut down the rising time of breads. If you have used this type of yeast and proofed it first, that initial proofing could have used up all of the yeast's energy, leaving it too exhausted to make your dough rise. Next time, skip the proofing step if you want to use rapid-rise yeast.

If you suspect your yeast is dead, don't throw away the dough. All has not been lost, not by a long shot. You can mix fresh yeast into your existing dough and let it rise again.

Combine 1 tablespoon of yeast with ¹/₄ cup warm water (not over 110°F) and ¹/₂ teaspoon of sugar. Stir well to dissolve the yeast and sugar, then let it rest for about five minutes, or until it becomes bubbly and foamy. This bubbling foam is your proof that the yeast is alive. Knead the yeast mixture into your dead dough. You will probably have to add some additional flour (a handful or so) to get your dough back to the right consistency. Knead the dough for a couple of minutes and then set it in a cozy warm place to rise again. This time it should work.

Help! The Dough Has Risen, But Nobody's Home

Okay, let's say that your dough has just risen to perfection. The phone rings. Your friend's car has broken down and she needs you to go pick her up. Is your bread ruined? No. If your friend is hours away, punch down the dough, cover with plastic wrap, and put it in the refrigerator. The dough can stay there overnight, and will be ready for you in the morning. If your friend is just a few minutes away and you'll be back within an hour, you can punch down the dough, re-cover it with the towel, and let it rise again at room temperature. No harm done. If you're not sure how long you will be, pop the dough into the refrigerator to slow down the rising, and then when you're home again, remove it from the fridge and let it finish rising.

Okay, same friend but your dough is at a different stage. Now the dough is in the loaf pans, has finished rising, and is just moments from going into the oven to bake when your friend calls with her car problem. You can brush the top of the loaves with butter and pop them into the refrigerator. This will slow down the rising. If the dough still rises too much, you can take it out of the loaf pans, knead the dough for a few minutes, and set it back into the loaf pans to rise again.

Help! My Muffins Are Like Hockey Pucks

The reason muffins toughen and become hard is because the batter has been overworked. There is really nothing much you can do at this point to solve the problem except learn from your mistakes.

Muffins really don't need much mixing—just a couple of turns with a wooden spoon, and they are mixed. If the damage has been done, I suggest you finish baking the muffins. You can eat them as is, or, depending on what flavor they are, you can do several things with them. If they are a sweeter variety of muffin, cut them up and make a bread pudding with them. The additional moisture from the eggs and baking them will much improve their texture. If they are a savory variety, such as corn or bran muffins, you can cut them into chunks and make homemade croutons out of them. Sauté them in a little butter, olive oil, and seasonings (oregano, basil, onion, garlic) until they are lightly toasted and brown. Homemade croutons are great in salads and soups.

The Least You Need to Know

➤ Don't panic if you think you are having a problem.

➤ You can always salvage a mistake in the kitchen by turning the "mistake" into something else.

➤ Remember, all cooks make mistakes. The key is to learn from them.

Chapter 17

Simple Ideas for All Occasions

In This Chapter

➤ Suggestions for social functions

➤ Thoughts on what to serve

➤ Hints on well-matched flavors

It seems the older we get, the more we have to do. As you get married, buy a house, and/ or have kids, you may notice you are going to more social functions than ever before. There are housewarmings, bake sales, dinner parties...the list goes on and on. These social functions often revolve around food, and you certainly don't want to arrive empty-handed. You may find yourself wondering what to bring. Well, developing a fondness and a skill for baking answers this question. Once people discover what a great baker you are, there is no doubt that your desserts and other baked goods will be in great demand. In this chapter, I'll give you some specific suggestions for special events, plus guidelines for deciding what to bake, no matter what the occasion.

Menus for Many Events

I can't think of anyone who doesn't appreciate a freshly baked gift from the kitchen. It's always nice to bring a treat when you go to someone's home. Here are some simple ideas for some common events you might be attending.

Housewarming

A homebaked item is always such a treat, especially if you have not had time to unpack your kitchen. Here are some ideas on pairing housewarming food items and presents.

➤ Give your new neighbor shiny new loaf pans. Bake a loaf of bread and wrap it with the pans. Write down the recipe for the bread you made on a nice notecard so your new neighbor can make it again.

➤ Make a sheet cake and decorate it as the front of your neighbor's house, or make a door or mailbox with the address on it. If you present it on a nice cake tray or serving platter, that can also be his gift.

➤ Bake a pie in a disposable aluminum pan. Place the baked pie in a pretty pie plate and present both to your new neighbor.

Summertime Picnic

When attending summertime picnics, you want your choice to be sturdy enough to make the trip in the car. You also want it to be able to keep without having to be chilled. Here are some ideas:

➤ Line a basket with colorful napkins or a clean bandanna and fill it with cookies or brownies.

➤ For something different, try making bar cookies. They are easy to serve because you can cut them up in smaller squares and you don't have to worry about refrigeration, like you do with some cakes and pies.

➤ A homemade loaf of bread is always a treat for picnickers to create their own sandwiches.

Potluck

The hardest thing about potluck dinners is trying to decide what you're going to make. Make it easy on yourself by choosing items that don't have to be sliced or portioned out.

➤ Rolls are always a nice accompaniment to a meal. Think about making an assortment of them: white, whole-wheat, and pumpernickel are always crowd pleasers. Don't forget breadsticks and savory muffins, too.

➤ Make an assortment of cookies. Decorate the tray with colored napkins or frilly paper doilies. Think about purchasing a disposable tray if you're worried about getting your platter back.

➤ Cupcakes or muffins make a great potluck dessert because they are already in individual serving sizes—no cutting or knives needed.

Care Package

From kids away at camp or college to your friends in faraway places, everyone loves a care package. And what's better than a care package filled with treats you have made?

➤ Bake up several different types of sturdy goods: buttermilk scones, chocolate-chip cookies, brownies, cornbread. Pack them in a decorative metal tin or pack them in sealable plastic bags and in a shoebox.

➤ Bar cookies make excellent travelers. Pack them in an airtight plastic container so they won't get broken during travel.

➤ Make cutout cookies in the shape of the alphabet (there are cookie cutters to help you), so you can spell things out. Wrap up each "word" in individual plastic baggies. Enclose "clues" for the recipient so they can unscramble the message.

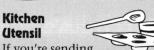

Kitchen Utensil

If you're sending out a care package and are worried about your cookies staying fresh, freeze them first before sending and try and insulate the container. While the cookies will defrost during shipping, they will be fresher when they arrive.

Deciding What to Serve

My philosophy for deciding what to serve is "Make what you like." After all, that means at least one person will like it! However, if you're like me and you like a lot of things, there are a few things to consider when you are narrowing down your choices. Think about the event. Will it be dessert for two, treats for a crowd, or something sweet for the younger set?

➤ Will you be serving just a few people? If so, look for a dessert with a lower yield, unless you want a lot of leftovers.

➤ Will your crowd include kids? They like sweet stuff, so cake and frosting will always be a sure hit. I recommend staying away from more esoteric things with ingredients like dried fruit and nuts.

➤ Will you want to serve a dessert wine after your meal? If so, steer away from chocolate or overly sweet desserts. They will detract from the wine.

➤ How will you serve your dessert? Would it be easier to slice from a whole cake or pie, or would it be easier to have individual servings such as cookies or cupcakes or pudding?

➤ Where will you be? Inside or outdoors? Do you need to refrigerate your dessert, or will it be okay at room temperature for a while?

➤ Does your dessert have to be ready in under an hour or do you have time to let it chill for a while?

Once you've narrowed down the characteristics your dessert has to have, it will be easier to choose what you want to make. Pay attention to the yield, prep, and cook time given for all the recipes to be sure it will be the right choice for you.

Flavorful Combinations

If you're looking for that little extra something, try the following flavoring combinations. You can flavor whipped cream or plain frosting with a few drops of extract or $1/2$ teaspoon of spice. You might be pleasantly surprised by the flavor boost it gives your desserts. If you're not feeling too adventurous, try flavoring the cream you serve with the coffee, or selecting a corresponding flavor of ice cream or sorbet to go with your dessert. Here are some delicious combinations that are sure-fire hits:

➤ *Chocolate/Orange.* Grate some orange zest into chocolate frosting.

➤ *Chocolate/Raspberry.* Serve fresh raspberries with a simple drizzle of melted chocolate.

➤ *Chocolate/Mint.* Mint ice cream is tasty when hot chocolate topping is added.

➤ *Chocolate/Apricot.* Spread apricot jam in between the layers of a chocolate layer cake instead of frosting.

➤ *Chocolate/Almond.* Make a cheesecake crust by grinding together chocolate graham crackers and almonds.

➤ *Chocolate/Cinnamon.* Hot cocoa with a sprinkle of cinnamon is very comforting.

➤ *Vanilla/Strawberry.* What's better in the summer than fresh strawberries with vanilla ice cream?

➤ *Vanilla/Lemon.* Sweeten a tangy lemon tart with some vanilla whipped cream.

➤ *Vanilla/Cherry.* What's better on top of cherry pie than pure vanilla ice cream?

➤ *Vanilla/Mango.* Fresh mango with whipped cream splashed with vanilla is a delicious treat.

➤ *Vanilla/Maple.* Looking to jazz up vanilla ice cream? Try a drizzle of pure maple syrup.

➤ *Vanilla/Hazelnut.* These two flavors make a wonderful coffee combination.

➤ *Pumpkin/Cinnamon.* Looking to jazz up some pumpkin nut bread? Try cinnamon.

➤ *Pumpkin/Maple.* A drizzle of maple syrup over pumpkin pie is a nice change from whipped cream.

➤ *Pumpkin/Rum.* Try adding a splash of rum to your pumpkin pie recipe.

➤ *Strawberry/Almond.* Strawberry shortcake for dessert? Flavor the shortcake or whipped cream with almond extract instead of vanilla.

➤ *Strawberry/Lemon.* Want to offer a variety of sorbets? Try this combination.

➤ *Blueberry/Lemon.* If you are making blueberry muffins, substitute lemon extract for vanilla.

➤ *Cherry/Almond.* Try flavoring whipped cream with a few drops of almond extract when you're topping a cherry pie.

The Least You Need to Know

➤ Homemade baked items are always a hit at social events.

➤ Think about the characteristics you want for your baked item before deciding on a recipe.

➤ There are many different flavor combinations to try if you are looking for something a little different.

Chapter 18

Easy Tips for Turning the Ordinary... Extraordinary

In This Chapter

➤ Tips for slicing a cake with ease

➤ Ideas for making simple decorations

➤ Instructions for making a good cup of coffee or tea

➤ Ideas for sprucing up the flavor of creams

When you spend your time baking, you want to be able to show off your finished product and enjoy all the oohs and ahhs when you put it on display. In this chapter, I'll give you some suggestions and ideas of how to make everything you bake just a little bit more special.

How to Cut Cakes

Believe it or not, there is a correct way to cut a cake. Well, it may not be "correct," but it does ensure you get slices of equal size. Most people cut out one slice of cake and then work their way around "eyeballing" each piece and ending up with irregularly sized slices. The problem shows itself when you are trying to feed ten people and you get to slice number eight and realize how tiny slices nine and ten will have to be. There is a simple technique for slicing cakes and pies that makes it easy to know how many slices of cake you will get even before you make the first cut. Plus, you have gone to all this trouble to make a cake, why just hack away at it? Neat slices of cake add to the appearance and appeal of eating it, too.

Pies and layer cakes can be cut the same way. You want to use a long, thin, sharp knife to cut. You also may want to have a cake server (a fancy, triangular spatula) to help you transfer the slices of cake or pie to the plates.

Cut cakes and pies into wedges. For a cake, begin by slicing it all the way in half. Then, depending on the richness of the cake or the number of people you have to serve, cut each half into four to six wedges. If you want to measure out the wedges before you cut into the cake, you can eyeball the wedge sizes you want to make, make a nick in the icing by gently letting the knife blade sink into the icing, and mark the cake all the way around. If you are satisfied with the sizes of the wedges, then proceed with cutting all the way through the cake. If you need more wedges, "erase" the cut mark by smearing the icing and re-mark the cake until you have the amount or size of slices you want. The same goes for pies. You can make a nick in the crust or a small cut in the top, or if the pie does not have a top crust, you can mark the filling.

Cut the cake into wedges.

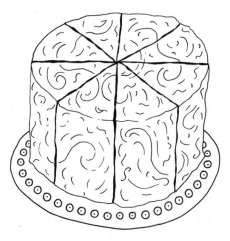

Cheesecakes can sometimes get messy when you cut them. The moist cake tends to stick to the knife, making the thickness of the knife grow with each slice. There are a few ways to conquer this problem. The first two suggestions are good if you are planning to cut the cake before you present it. Wet the knife with hot water and shake off any excess water (but don't dry it) and cut the cake. The heat and moisture from the knife allows you to get clean slices each time. You will have to re-warm and re-wet the knife every second slice or so. Another trick is to slice the cheesecake with clean dental floss. Get a piece of floss a few inches longer than the cake. Wrap the floss around your fingers and press down and through the cake. Then release one side of the floss and pull it through the cake. Repeat this until all of the cake is sliced. This provides nice, neat, clean slices.

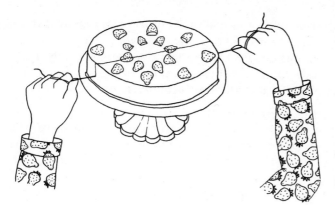

Cutting cheesecake using dental floss.

If you cut the cake at the table, you can always use two knives, one to slice and the other to scrape off the slicing knife in between slices.

Sheet cakes, bar cookies, and brownies all share the same cutting technique. It's easy, but you need to use a thin, sharp knife. You just have to cut the cake into equal-size squares. You can use the same technique you used on layer cakes to mark the icing before you actually slice to make sure you will be getting a high enough yield out of your cake or bars.

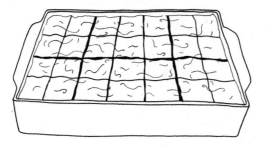

Cut the cake into equal-size squares.

Loaves should be sliced with a serrated knife. The thickness of each slice depends on the richness of the cake.

Presentation Is Everything

Food should look nice as well as taste good, so how you present your dessert really does make a difference. While it does not have to be picture-perfect, there are some simple things you can do to jazz up the presentation of your desserts.

More often than not, a decorated store-bought cake tends to be ornamental and have that "fussed over" appearance. While that is all well and fine for some people's taste, I prefer the simple and basic.

Kitchen Utensil
Remember, no one was born with the natural ability to decorate cakes and other baked goods, so go easy on yourself if it isn't just right the first few times. Techniques take time to perfect.

Try piping a simple shell border or stars around the edge of the cake instead of going crazy with design. I recommend simple designs for beginner designers. Recently, I baked a cake for a baby shower. On top of the cake I drew a very simple baby bottle with colored icing.

Not being a terribly artistic person myself, I think that less is definitely more. When I try to get too fancy, I usually have to explain my abstract art to those looking at the cake: "Okay, this is the baby stroller, and this is Anne…" The following are some suggestions for decorating cakes without having to apply to art school first.

Birthday:

Balloons (if the name is short, you could put the letters of the name in the balloons)

The age of the person

A present with a bow

A simple decorating idea for a birthday cake.

Anniversary:

A big heart

Two interlocking rings

The number of the years celebrated

Good Luck/Bon Voyage:

> Horseshoe
>
> Champagne glasses toasting with colored confetti (sprinkles or colored icings)
>
> Four-leaf clover
>
> Hot-air balloon

New Baby:

> Baby bottle
>
> Blocks with letters
>
> Rattle

If you have a lot of people to serve, sheet cakes are a good solution. They are the easiest to frost, and their large, flat top gives you lots of decorating room.

If you don't have a platter or plate large enough to accommodate a sheet cake, you can make your own. Find a sturdy corrugated cardboard box and cut out the cardboard large enough to accommodate your cake (use the cake pan to see how large your cake will be and leave at least a 2-inch border around the edge). Wrap aluminum foil around the cardboard and use that as your serving platter.

Quick, Spiffy Garnishes

There are times when frosting a cake is just not enough and you want to dress it up a little more. Garnishing a cake lets you make it personal. The following sections give you some ideas to make simple, fun garnishes.

Garnishes for Cakes

Cake garnishes don't have to be limited to sugary flowers or fancy decorations. Here are a few suggestions for some simple garnishes that use ingredients you probably already have on hand:

> ➤ Press sliced almonds, chopped nuts, shaved chocolate, or crushed candy (peppermint is a good idea) onto the frosted cake sides. To do this, frost the sides of the cake (don't frost the top), then hold the cake with one hand and press the garnish onto the side with the palm of your hand. Or sprinkle the garnish on a piece of waxed paper and roll the cake sides into the garnish. Set it back on the serving plate and finish frosting the top.

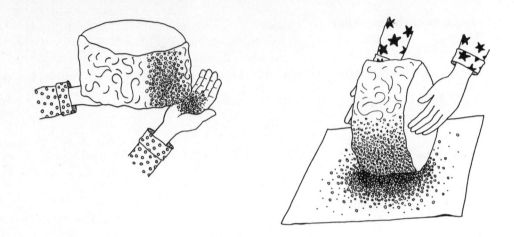

Two ways to garnish the sides of a cake: Press the garnish in with the palm of your hand or roll the cake in the garnish to coat.

➤ Lightly dust the top of an iced cake with ground spices, either cinnamon, nutmeg, or allspice (good for carrot cake, spice cake, or chocolate cake). Take a pinch of spice and sprinkle it on top. Don't shake the spice on directly from the can; you might add too much.

➤ Melt some chocolate and dip a fork in it, then drizzle the chocolate over top of the frosted cake.

➤ Make balloons with whole cookies (vanilla wafer or chocolate cream filled) and use licorice for strings.

➤ Colored and chocolate sprinkles or beads will add a little color to your cakes.

➤ Give your cakes a polka-dotted top by sprinkling candy-covered chocolates on top of the frosting.

➤ Forget the frosting and just dust the top of the cake with confectioners' sugar. You can cut out a message in a piece of paper, lay it on top of the cake, and then dust the top of the cake. When you remove the paper, your message will be written in sugar. You can also make a pretty pattern using the same method but using a paper doily instead.

You might also check out your local kitchen-supply store. There you'll find many garnishes such as candy flowers, candy letters, and even edible glitter.

Fruity Toppings

Fresh fruits always make a simple, elegant garnish. Cut up the fruit at the last minute to make sure it stays fresh. You can also garnish with whole pieces of fruit dipped in chocolate (strawberries are just about everyone's favorite) or you can use raspberries, blackberries, and even sliced peaches. Prevent discoloration by tossing the peaches in lemon juice before you use them for garnish. You can either garnish each slice of cake with fruit or you can top whole cakes or tarts with fruit.

Decorations for Plates

If you are serving a simple dessert that you don't want to bombard with creams or toppings, but you want to enhance its appearance, you can decorate the plates you serve it on. Try a few of these tricks:

➤ Grease the edge of the serving plate with shortening (just a thin coating). Sprinkle the edge with spices (cinnamon has a nice color) or cocoa, then tap off the excess. Place your dessert in the center of the plate and let your guests ogle.

➤ Get some squeeze bottles at a dime store and fill them with fruit sauce or chocolate sauce. Squeeze out a decoration (squiggles, lines, circles) onto each plate before serving.

Kitchen Utensil
Make your own fruit purées by peeling and slicing fresh fruits (such as mango, peaches, nectarines, or raspberries) and puréeing them in a food processor or blender. Press the fruit through a fine mesh strainer if it has a lot of seeds (as raspberries do), and transfer it to a squeeze bottle.

A simple piece of colorful fresh fruit also makes a nice garnish for plates.

How to Make Great Coffee and Tea

There is nothing like a good cup of coffee or tea to add to the satisfaction of a homemade dessert or breakfast goodie. A lot has happened to coffee in the past few years. No longer is your choice limited to regular or decaf. The world of coffees has expanded into lattes, espressos, plus all sorts of flavors for regular coffee from vanilla nut to pumpkin pie. With all of these choices, it's easy to find what you like.

During my breaks in college, I used to take over my sister's shifts at a coffee shop. It was when the coffee craze was just simmering on the East Coast, well before Starbucks and other coffee shops began popping up in every town. I worked for a lovely West Coast coffee fanatic, Jeff. While he could never fully convert me to taking my coffee black, he filled my head with all sorts of coffee trivia and impressed on me the virtues of a good cup of Joe, especially as an accompaniment to fresh baked goods.

A good cup of coffee has certain traits. It should be smooth, never bitter; with a full flavor and rich aroma. If you feel your pot of coffee misses the mark, take a quick read through the following sections to figure out what is going on.

The Beans

No matter what variety of bean you choose, they should be fresh. It is the oils in the beans that offer the great flavor of coffee. These oils will evaporate when exposed to air for too long, so it's important if you buy preground coffee to store it in an airtight container and keep in the refrigerator or freezer. If you buy whole beans and grind your coffee each time you make it, you will find the flavor to be quite good. You can find inexpensive coffee-bean grinders if you want to start grinding your own. Even whole beans can lose their essential oils, so be sure to store your beans in the freezer. Grinding frozen beans will not affect their flavor or performance.

The Measurement

A good rule of thumb when measuring coffee is to use 2 level tablespoons for every 8-ounce cup of water. Most coffepots are marked for 6-ounce cups, so don't use them to measure your water. Instead, use a glass measuring cup. If your coffeemaker makes ten 6-ounce cups, then it will make seven-and-a-half 8-ounce cups, so measure accordingly. Of course, you can adjust it to your taste.

If you think it is absolutely foolish to get out the measuring cups when making coffee, you can use the coffeepot to measure the water and use one heaping tablespoon for every "cup" of coffee that you use the pot to measure. Just remember to make a few extra cups of coffee if you serve your coffee in mugs because the mugs will hold more.

The Process

You have many choices when it comes to coffeemakers. The most common method is the electric drip coffeepot. There is not much to know about the electric pot. You measure out the grounds, measure out the water (remember, most pots are marked in 6-ounce increments), flip a switch, and in a few minutes you have a pot of coffee ready. A word of warning: Heat makes coffee taste bitter, so if you are the type to put a pot of coffee on in the morning and enjoy several cups throughout the morning, you run a high risk of burning your coffee or making it bitter by leaving it on the hot plate. Instead, get a thermal coffeepot (they are not expensive). Once your morning pot is brewed, pour it into the thermos and it will keep your coffee hot all morning long without burning it.

Kitchen Utensil
Coffee and tea stains are a real drag for ceramic cups and metal pots. Baking soda works magic as a stain remover. Just sprinkle some into the bottom of your cup or pot and add enough water to dissolve it (about $1/4$ cup). Scrub the stain and rinse. Baking soda always rinses clean.

Other popular methods of brewing coffee are the drip method and the plunger pot. I am not a coffee purist, but I grew up on drip coffee and really like its clean taste. For the drip method, you usually pour hot (just below boiling) water over coffee grounds which are set in a cone and paper filter and it drips directly into a coffeepot or cup. Since the pot does not rest on a heat element, you should plan on serving the coffee once it has finished brewing. A plunger pot (also called a French press) uses a similar method. Measure out the coffee into the pot, pour the hot, not boiling, water directly into the grounds, and let it steep for 5 minutes. Then push down the plunger (which is really a fine mesh strainer that is attached to the lid), and the grounds remain at the bottom of the pot. If you do use a plunger pot, be sure you use coffee that's more coarsely ground. If your coffee is ground too fine, it will sneak though the plunger and into your cup of coffee.

A plunger coffeepot.

Information Station

If you have tried everything and your coffee still tastes funny, it may not be you, it might be your coffeemaker. It's probably time for a cleaning. If you use your coffeemaker every day, I recommend cleaning it once a month (or follow your manufacturer's instructions). To clean your coffeemaker: Fill the upper compartment where you put the water with a 50/50 vinegar-water solution (If you have a 10-cup coffeemaker, that would be 5 cups of vinegar and 5 cups of water). Run it though your coffeemaker. Then fill up the compartment again with plain water and run it through. That should fix it.

No matter which method you choose, if you think your coffee is too weak, do not pour it through the grounds again. You will end up with really bad-tasting coffee. If your coffee is too weak, you just have to throw it away and start all over again.

Ground Rules for Good Coffee

If you have embarked on the good cuppa Joe quest, here are some tips to keep in mind:

➤ Always use fresh cold water. Filtered water is also a good choice if you have heavy or chlorinated water.

➤ Always use the right grind for the way you prepare your coffee: drip for the drip method, coarse for the plunger pot, and fine ground if you have an espresso machine.

➤ Glass or porcelain coffeepots are best for holding coffee. Metal might give a funny taste to your coffee, although stainless steel is not a bad choice.

➤ Always clean your equipment well. Wash baskets and pots after every use with mild detergent and/or baking soda. You can soak baskets in a baking soda solution to get them clean.

Jazzing Up Coffees

Because of the wide variety of flavored coffee beans, instant coffee, and specialty coffee mixes available, it's easy to offer more than just plain coffee to your guests. However, if all you have on hand is regular coffee and you yearn for something different, try sprinkling a teaspoon of ground cinnamon into your grounds for a nice flavor change. If flavored coffees are a bit overwhelming for your taste buds, mix half flavored coffee with half regular coffee to tone down the flavor. A friend of mine, Matt, makes a wonderful flavored coffee blend using 2 parts hazelnut, 1 part Irish cream, and 1 part vanilla almond. It's truly a wonderful blend.

Information Station

If you want to make your coffee more "adult," here are some suggestions for some delicious add-ins for each cup. For an extra-special finish, dollop some whipped cream on top.

➤ 2 tablespoons chocolate-flavored syrup

➤ 2 tablespoons orange liqueur

➤ 2 tablespoons any coffee-flavored liqueur and 2 tablespoons chocolate syrup

➤ 1 tablespoon Irish whiskey

➤ 2 tablespoons amaretto

➤ 1 tablespoon crème de menthe

➤ 1 tablespoon Frangelico or any other hazelnut-flavored liqueur

Tea Talk

The American Tea Council says that Americans drink 7.5 gallons of tea per capita yearly. Well, I know I am doing my share, since I probably drink that much a month. There is nothing better after a hard day than to snuggle down on the couch with a pot of tea close by. When I lived in England, I easily grew accustomed to their ritual of morning and afternoon tea. It seemed there was never anything so pressing that it could not wait until my cup of tea was finished.

The most popular supermarket variety teas you'll usually see are black teas. They are usually Pekoe or Orange Pekoe cut teas. They come in premeasured bags and are usually not too bad. However, if you become more interested in tea, you should be a bit adventurous and try some newer varieties, such as Ceylon, Darjeeling, Assam, Keemun, Lapsang Souchong, and Oolong. Blended teas, such as Earl Grey, English Breakfast, Irish Breakfast, and Jasmine and Russian teas are also a pleasant change. Be sure to store all tea and tea bags in airtight containers. Try to buy a supply you know you will use up within six to eight months.

Information Station

Tea can refer to the hot beverage you drink, the leaves you use to make it, and the plant from which it comes. *Black tea* and *green tea* are two types of tea available. Black tea is fermented tea leaves, while green tea comes from unfermented leaves. While all teas come from the same species of plant, the various climates and soils in which it grows gives us the varied flavors of tea. *Blended teas* are teas that have spices, oils, and other herbs mixed in with the tea leaves to give them distinctive flavors.

There is a huge variety of herbal and spiced teas on the market today, which make a fine cup of tea on their own, or you can mix them with black teas for fruity overtones in the taste. My two favorite mixtures are mint tea with regular Orange Pekoe or herbal lemon tea with Earl Grey.

The Measurement

You should use 1 teaspoon of tea per cup (8 oz.) of water. Some people like to add an additional teaspoon for the pot but I think that often makes the tea too strong. Of course, feel free to adjust the measurement to your taste. If you have premeasured tea bags, add one bag of tea per 2 cups of water; for herbal teas, add one bag of tea per cup of water. I'm not a fan of overly strong tea, so I will not add more than three bags of a black tea per pot of tea.

Information Station

If you use loose tea leaves and don't want them floating in your tea, you can strain them out using a tea strainer, which is a tiny mesh strainer that sits on top of your teacup. Otherwise, you can purchase a tea ball (sometimes shaped like a house or, oddly enough, a ball) to hold your tea. Or look for teapots with built-in infusers. They look like cylinders with little slits in the bottom. Measure your loose tea into the infuser, drop it into the pot (it's made to fit into the top), cover, and let the tea quietly steep. You can leave the infuser in or take it out before you serve.

The Process

There is not much of a secret to making good tea. Start with fresh cold water. If you have a tea kettle, pour out any water that was sitting in it and start fresh. Bring the water to a boil. Fill the teapot or cups with hot water and let them sit while you're waiting for the water to boil, about 3 minutes. Dump out the water and measure out the loose tea, or have the tea bags ready, and place them in the warmed pot or cups. Pour the boiling water into the pot or cups, cover, and let the tea steep, undisturbed, for about 5 minutes for the pot and 3 minutes for the cup. Remove the tea bags (do not dunk them or squeeze them) and serve. If you find the tea is too strong, it's okay to dilute the pot with additional hot water until it is to your liking.

A tea ball.

Tea and coffee can be served with a choice of sweeteners and creams: honey, sugar, half-and-half, light cream, or milk. Lemon is also good with many teas. If you want to add milk or sweetener to your hot beverages, be sure to add it first to the empty cup. The heat from the tea or coffee will warm the milk. If you pour in the milk after you have served the tea, the milk will cool the tea.

If you want to make iced tea or iced coffee, double the amount of grinds or tea you will brew to counteract the dilution of the addition of ice cubes. Sweeten your coffee or tea with sugar or honey before it cools completely to make sure it thoroughly dissolves.

Whipping and Flavoring Creams

A dollop of whipped cream on top of cakes and pies is always a welcome treat. While there are a whole variety of premade whipped toppings available, it's easy to make your own. Begin with one pint of heavy (whipping) cream (light cream or half-and-half will not whip up) and place it in a chilled bowl. With an electric or hand mixer or a wire whisk (you can chill these too), beat the cream until it begins to thicken and stiffen. Add 2 tablespoons of granulated sugar or 4 tablespoons of confectioners' sugar, plus 1 teaspoon of vanilla. Beat a little bit more until soft peaks form. Taste. Adjust the sweetness, if desired. One cup of heavy cream will yield 2 cups of whipped cream.

Try substituting different flavored extracts for the vanilla. Some of my favorites are almond, lemon, and maple. Almond cream is great in coffees, on cherry pies, and in fruit cobblers. Lemon cream is great paired with lemon tarts or anything minty, and maple cream is delightful on pancakes, pies, and baked apples.

Bakers Beware!
Never add both lemon and cream to your tea—you'll curdle the milk! You can; however, add milk to your herbal lemon tea.

Bakers Beware!
Be careful! You don't want to beat the cream much beyond soft peaks, or you'll end up with butter instead of whipped cream. You can try to salvage over-beaten cream by folding in fresh, unbeaten cream. Do not whip it in. The cream will be not as stiff, but usable.

The Least You Need to Know

➤ Cutting cakes and pies properly will ensure the right yield.

➤ Decorating desserts can be fun, but remember, less is sometimes more.

➤ Fresh cold water, proper measurements, and the right temperature are the keys to successful coffee and tea.

➤ For something different, try flavoring the creams you serve with coffee and dessert.

Chapter 19

The Skinny on Low-Fat Recipes

In This Chapter

➤ What is fat and why do we need it?

➤ How to choose the fats you eat wisely

➤ Tips on lowering the fat content in your favorite recipes

"Low-fat" and "fat-free" seem to be the hot catch phrases when it comes to talk about baking and food in general these days. One of the perks of baking things ourselves is that we have control over what we put into our baked goods, thereby controlling what we put into our bodies. While we should all be conscious of what we eat and how much we eat, all the media attention on fats has made people overly sensitive to the idea of eating something that contains fat. Let's take a closer look at fat, its role in baking, and how to reduce it if you're watching what you eat.

Recap on the Role of Fat

You actually need fat in your diet. Not only is fat a fuel source for many of your tissues, it's also a concentrated source of energy. It transports essential vitamins and helps the body use carbohydrates and protein. A totally fat-free diet would be very unhealthy for you.

Fats also help make foods taste good. They hold flavor and also act as a flavor carrier. That is why when recipes cut down on fats, you will notice there is often an increase in the amount of seasoning to compensate for this. Fats contribute to the "mouthfeel," lingering on your tongue and coating your tastebuds. And after a meal, they make you feel full and satisfied because fats digest slowly. So, if they do all this good stuff, why do fats have such a bad reputation?

All calories are not created equal. Fat calories do not work the same as calories you get from proteins or carbohydrates. Your body converts fat calories into body fat more easily than it does other calories. Since your body uses fat calories more efficiently, it needs fewer of them. What you don't need is stored, causing you to gain weight. Keep in mind, the excess of any kind of calorie will be stored as fat, although fat is metabolized and stored most easily. Since it takes fewer calories to get the same job done with fat as it would take with carbohydrates or proteins, we actually need fewer calories from fat to get things done. Or, at least, it would be smarter to get fewer calories from fat and make our bodies work a little harder at burning calories that we obtain from nonfat sources (carbohydrates, protein, etc.) rather than storing them up.

Kitchen Utensil
Don't be seduced by all the fat-free items lurking on your grocer's shelves. While they may be fat-free, they are not calorie-free, although we often trick ourselves into thinking we can overindulge since we are skimping on the fat. Try purchasing the "real thing"—you might find it more satisfying—and just watch your serving sizes more carefully.

But fat is a necessary part of baking. It not only adds flavor to our baked goods, it also creates a flakiness and tenderness we have grown to like. Fats, when used with discretion and skill, will enhance any baked product for all the reasons we have mentioned before: texture, taste, and satisfying feeling. Fats also contribute moisture to baked goods. If you have ever had a fat-free muffin, you may have noticed that the texture is more sponge-like and the flavor is lighter and not altogether pleasant.

So, now that we seem to be caught up in a huge frenzy, afraid to let anything with fat touch our lips, the first advice I give is to relax about it. Remember, total deprivation is overkill, and one rich dessert will not sacrifice your figure forever. All things in moderation. If you are looking to cut down on fats for health reasons, there are a few things you should keep in mind when selecting what to bake.

Information Station

The future of fat is upon us. The FDA has already approved Simplesse and is looking to approve Olestra. Olestra is made of sucrose and vegetable oil, which are bonded together. The result is a molecule that is too big to be digested; therefore, Olestra does not add any calories. Simplesse is a popular fat substitute made of egg whites or milk protein. It has a texture similar to fat and is usually used in desserts such as ice cream and frozen yogurt.

Choosing Your Fat Wisely

If you have decided to bake something and you're trying to be fat-conscious, you can cut down on the fats in a recipe. The easiest thing to do is look for recipes that use a minimum of fat. Angel food cake and meringue cookies are good choices. There are many lower-fat recipes in this book. Know which foods are rich in fat and try to find adequate substitutions for them, without sacrificing flavor. Above all, don't feel guilty if you really want to make a rich cake. Just serve smaller slices and top the cake with slices of fresh fruit instead of ice cream or whipped cream. It's fine to have a rich dessert every so often. There is no reason to feel guilty about it.

Remember, sweets can be part of a healthy diet and it is okay to have a few cookies or slice of cake every so often. Most of the problem is not with the fat in our foods, but with the portions we allow ourselves to eat. If we spend each night sitting on the couch with cookies or cake and wash it down with big glasses of milk (which I certainly have been known to do on more than one occasion), then it starts to show on our bodies if we are not burning those calories during the day. If you're like me, and most of your day is spent at a desk, you need to be careful about your overall calorie consumption. Cookies and cakes often get blamed for our expanding waistlines, but they can be incorporated into anyone's diet as long as we stay active and burn the daily calories we consume.

If you have a small family and one cake is too much to eat, you can always cut the recipe in half and just make a one-layer cake. Cake and cookies also freeze well, so you can save some for later, too. Another thing I like to do if I am baking a lot is to bring what I don't want to eat into the office. It gets snatched up so quickly there and everyone appreciates it, and I'm grateful that folks have helped me finish up the goodies.

Bakers Beware!
Do not substitute reduced-fat or low-fat butter, margarine, or spreads with less than 65 percent fat for butter in recipes. They will not perform the way regular margarine or butter will and the effects will be undesirable. The low-fat and nonfat spreads have a lot more water and won't bind the way regular butters will.

You can also do calorie trade-offs. For example, if you are anticipating eating a rich dessert, you can forego the butter on your bread (which is 100 calories of pure fat per tablespoon), skip the rich salad dressing, or pass on the fries or chips, to make room for the dessert calories. Again, these are just lifestyle decisions for you to consider if you are trying to watch your diet.

How to Lower the Fat in Your Favorite Recipes

The fats used in baking are primarily butter, margarine, shortening, and oil. They are not the only sources of fat, however. Dairy products also have lots of fat in them, as do nuts. Choosing reduced-fat dairy products or reducing the amount of nuts you use in a recipe will help lower the amount of fat. Remember, a reduction of fat in a recipe automatically means a reduction in calories all the way around. Don't go crazy, though—you still want your dessert to taste good.

If you are trying to reduce the fat in your recipes, here are some tips that might help:

➤ To cut down on the eggs in a recipe, you can substitute egg whites, which have zero fat. To substitute for one whole egg, use two whites. For two whole eggs, use one whole egg plus one white or three egg whites. Keep in mind that too many egg whites will have a drying effect, so don't go crazy with substitution.

Information Station

You can freeze extra egg whites or yolks you have left over. Add a pinch of sugar to the egg yolks to prevent them from becoming sticky. Freeze both the yolks and whites separately in ice cube trays so you know it is one yolk or white per cube. Always defrost frozen eggs in the refrigerator. If you want to freeze whole eggs, beat the egg lightly, sprinkle in a few grains of salt or sugar, and freeze in the tray. If you don't use ice cube trays, be sure you mark how many eggs you have frozen per container so you'll be able to defrost the right amount later.

➤ Low-fat or nonfat plain yogurt makes a great substitute for sour cream. You can also find reduced-fat and nonfat sour cream, but be careful, because they are not always the best choice for baking. Read the label to make sure it's made from cultured skim milk and not made from other artificial ingredients and water, which will not work.

➤ Frozen yogurts make a fine substitution for ice cream or whipped cream toppings.

➤ Choose skim milk in place of whole milk if it is called for in a recipe. You can also substitute buttermilk, which is low-fat and gives the flavor a nice tang.

➤ Nuts are a great source of fat. If you like the flavor of nuts in a recipe, cut down the amount to mere tablespoons. If you finely chop them, they will stretch farther in a recipe. Toasted nuts also have a richer flavor, so you will need fewer of them.

➤ Use a nonstick cooking spray when greasing pans. It has great releasing action, and you don't add calories to your baked goods.

Kitchen Utensil
Melt some premium frozen vanilla yogurt in a saucepan over very low heat. Drizzle the melted yogurt over desserts— it tastes just like cream!

➤ Thick fruit purées and applesauce can be successfully substituted for part of the fat in a recipe. You may want to start experimenting with your own favorite recipes, if you want to redo a recipe. You can experiment with a "how-low-can-you-go" by substituting the purée for the part of the butter. Remember, the texture will not be the same.

The Least You Need to Know

➤ You do need some sort of fat in your diet, so don't shun fats completely.

➤ Choose naturally fat-free desserts such as angel food cake or meringue cookies.

➤ Choose lower-fat ingredients, if desired, when baking.

Chapter 20

Storage for All Your Creations

In This Chapter

- ➤ Tips for storing all your baked goods
- ➤ How to freeze frosted and unfrosted cakes
- ➤ The best ideas for storing cookies
- ➤ Uses for aluminum foil, plastic wrap, and waxed paper
- ➤ Sealable plastic containers versus tins

Okay, so you have baked your cake, cookies, pies, and breads and now you are wondering what to do with them. You want them to stay fresh and good tasting, but maybe you're not sure how long something will keep or what the best method is for storage.

You can keep most cookies and bars covered and at room temperature for at least a day. The most important thing you should keep in mind is that you don't want your baked goods to sit in the open. They will dry out much faster. Slices of bread or cake can get dry and stale in just a few hours. If you want your baked goods to stick around for a few days, you might want to keep them refrigerated or even frozen. In this chapter I'll give you some advice on storage and the best ways to keep your treats fresh.

Storing at Room Temperature

Chances are if you don't live alone, you won't have to worry about your freshly baked goods hanging around too long. From the first sniff of anything baking, you'll soon have an audience in the kitchen, waiting for the treats to be cool enough to sink their teeth into. As long as you want the items to be consumed right away, most freshly baked items can be left on a plate for a while.

Most cookies, cakes, and pies (unless they're made with cream, custard, or meringue) can sit on the counter for the better part of the day (about 12 hours) before they need to be stored. If they need to be stored in the refrigerator, the recipe will say so. Otherwise, most cookies can be stored in an airtight plastic container on the kitchen counter for up to three days. Cookie jars are cute, but unfortunately most of them don't have an airtight seal. But if you have a high turnover for your cookies, meaning they will float out of the cookie jar within a few days, a cookie jar is fine to use.

As long as your cake does not contain custard, raw egg, fresh whipped cream, or meringue topping, all of which require refrigeration, it can be stored at room temperature for several days. To store your cakes, you can purchase a cake saver, which is a large plastic cake holder with an airtight lid that fits on top. I find them very useful because I can fit a cake on a serving plate on the base of the cake saver, snap on the lid, and even if the plate slides around, it does not damage the frosted sides of the cake at all.

A cake saver.

Kitchen Utensil
To prevent the cut surface of the cake from becoming stale while it is being stored, press a piece of waxed paper or aluminum foil against it.

You can also use a cake dome, usually a metal or plastic cover that you place over the cake itself. The dome does not provide an airtight seal, but if the cake will be around for just a few days, that shouldn't matter. If you don't have either of those items, a large mixing bowl can be inverted over the cake. Just make sure it's large enough that it won't smash down the top of the cake or touch the sides. A bowl is also slightly more difficult to lift because it doesn't have a handle, but it does provide an adequate cover.

Information Station

If you will be traveling with your cake and its appearance is important to you, carry some extra frosting and your frosting spatula (and pastry bag, if necessary) with you. That way, if your cake has suffered some nicks and bruises along the way, you can fix it up in a jiffy and people will be none the wiser.

Whole fresh-fruit pies can be kept on the kitchen counter, covered, for about a day. Store any leftovers, covered, in the refrigerator.

Bread can be stored at room temperature, sealed in a plastic bag, for several days. Home-made bread tends to lose its freshness faster at room temperature, so you might want to keep it in the refrigerator even if you plan on using it up within a day or so. Of course, before you put away your bread (or any baked good), make sure it has cooled completely. Otherwise, moisture will accumulate, making it spoil faster.

Keeping Things Cool

Cheesecakes must be stored in the refrigerator, as should any cakes, cookies, or pies with custard, raw egg, fresh whipped cream, or meringue topping. Any cake *can* be stored in the refrigerator, unless otherwise specified in the instructions, to extend its freshness. If you keep a cake in the refrigerator, be sure that it is well covered in either a cake saver or with a cake lid or bowl. You can also wrap the cake in aluminum foil or plastic wrap. If you place a cut cake uncovered and unwrapped in the refrigerator for more than a few hours, it will most likely pick up a refrigerator flavor, the icing will harden, and the cake will dry up and become stale.

You can store cookies in the refrigerator in a airtight plastic container for about two weeks. After the first week, they will not be as fresh as they once were, but you can always pop them in the oven for a few minutes or even zap them in the microwave for a few seconds if you want that fresh-from-the-oven feeling. If you can't be bothered, I find a not-so-fresh cookie makes a perfect dunker in milk. It sops up lots of milk, but doesn't fall apart. Mmmm, yum.

Pies can be stored in the refrigerator for several days as long as they are well wrapped. You can store pies in a

Bakers Beware!
If you are traveling with a cake or pie that needs to be refrigerated, keep it in the air-conditioned part of the car with you. Do not put it in the trunk. If you don't have air conditioning, and your cake fits in a cooler, keep it there. Otherwise, double-box the cake and surround it with ice packs (one box to hold the cake, and the other box to hold the ice packs around the boxed cake).

cake saver or just cover them with plastic wrap or aluminum foil. After a day or two, the crust may become a bit soggy, but you can rewarm the pie in the microwave or oven, if you like.

Since homemade breads lack the preservatives that store-bought breads have to increase their shelf life, your breads will not keep for nearly as long. To extend the life of your bread, store it in the refrigerator. I have kept bread, wrapped in a plastic bag and refrigerated, for up to a week without any molding problem. Fresh bread is always best eaten within a few days from when it is baked, but sometimes that's not possible.

If you think your bread is past its prime, don't throw it away. Bread recycles into so many great things. If it's still somewhat soft, make it into toast for a sandwich. You can also slice it up and use it for French toast. The drier bread sops up the egg without disintegrating and makes a tasty breakfast treat. You can also cut the bread into cubes, toss with melted butter and some spices, and bake for about 5 to 10 minutes, until the cubes are golden brown, to make croutons. If your bread is rock-hard, you can grate it using the large holes of a food grater and make bread crumbs. These crumbs can be stored in a sealable plastic bag for several weeks and can easily be frozen. However, if your bread is at all moldy, throw it away.

Bakers Beware!
Always label and date any item you put in the freezer. You might even want to keep a master list on the freezer door so you know what's inside. Frozen unbaked doughs have a relatively short freezer life, so always know what you have on hand so you can use it up in time.

The Deep Freeze

The freezer is a huge help to bakers because it allows you to prepare foods when you have the time, freeze them, and then defrost them when you need them.

Even though most items freeze well, keep in mind that if you have the time to bake your items fresh, that is always the best choice. There is an inescapable loss of moisture in frozen goods, and they have a tendency to dry out faster after they are brought back to room temperature for baking. Never freeze custards or cream pies.

Bread Doughs

Prepare the bread dough as usual. Allow the dough to rise once, punch it down, then shape it into loaves no more than 2 inches thick. Try to use the frozen bread dough within 10 days to make sure the yeast does not die. Defrost the loaves in a 250°F oven for about 45 minutes, then bake as instructed.

Rolls can be frozen in the same manner, but don't keep them in the freezer for more than a week. Freeze the individual rolls on a baking tray for 2 hours, then wrap them in an airtight container. When defrosting rolls, allow them to rise in a warm area, covered, until doubled in bulk (anywhere from $1^1/_2$ to 4 hours) and bake as instructed.

Cookies

Many cookie doughs can be frozen. You'll get the best results from those with a lot of fat in them. Uncooked cookie dough will last about two months frozen. You can shape the cookie dough into long logs, wrap them in plastic wrap, and freeze. Once frozen, double-wrap the log in aluminum foil or put it in an airtight container. Be sure to label the dough. You can even slice the cookies before you freeze them to make preparing them easier. If you want to experiment with different doughs, start with chocolate chip, oatmeal, or peanut butter cookies. Bake the cookies in a 350 to 375°F oven for 8 to 10 minutes. They will be tough to cut through if they are completely frozen, so let them defrost in the refrigerator for several hours before using. Do not set them out at room temperature or they may become too difficult to work with. Cut the dough chilled.

Baked cookies are easy to freeze. Just stack them in an airtight plastic container with waxed paper between each layer and pop them in the freezer. You can also store cookies in sealable plastic bags. Just about every cookie freezes well (the exception is meringue cookies), but you may find filled cookies and some bar cookies with dried fruit will be a bit softer once they are defrosted, although still just as good in flavor.

Cakes

I don't recommend freezing cake batters. The leavening used to make cakes rise may react differently after being defrosted, and the flavor of the cake will also change.

Baked cakes can be frozen for several months. Cool the cakes completely before wrapping them in plastic wrap, then in aluminum foil. You can also wrap the layers well, then seal them in a large, plastic bag. The purpose is to create an airtight package for your cake layers. Label each item (you can write directly on the plastic bag or foil, or you can label a piece of masking tape and stick it onto the wrapped cake).

Information Station

It is tradition to freeze the top layer of your wedding cake, and then defrost it and eat it on your first anniversary. There are many funny stories about this: One woman actually mixed up the packages and ended up freezing one of her wedding presents instead of the cake. Weeks later, as she was opening her wedding presents, she discovered a very stale cake, and in her freezer was a frozen crystal bowl!

You can also freeze frosted layer cakes. Place the frosted cake in the freezer, unwrapped. Once the cake has frozen through, wrap it in plastic, then in aluminum foil. If your

Kitchen Utensil
To freeze pies (baked or un-baked), frosted cakes, pastry, or rolls, place them on a baking sheet, uncovered, in the freezer until frozen (anywhere from 45 minutes to several hours). Then wrap tightly and store so that they will not get crushed. Never leave anything unwrapped in the freezer for more than 9 hours.

freezer is large enough, I recommend placing the cake in a cake saver or placing a bowl over the cake, or placing it in a cake box to prevent it from getting crushed or from other freezer items smashing up against it.

Cake layers, unfrosted, can be frozen for up to two months, unless it is a meringue cake or pie, which does not freeze at all. A frosted layer cake will keep frozen for up to four months. Spice cakes should not be stored for more than a month to ensure that the flavor stays true. If you are freezing a frosted cake, be sure the frosting is frozen solid before you wrap it up. Defrost the cake at room temperature, unwrapped but covered with a cake dome or cake-saver lid, until ready to serve.

Pies

Assemble the pie in a pie plate that you do not mind sacrificing to the freezer for a while. If this is a problem, you might want to purchase aluminum-foil pie plates for freezing. The best pies to freeze are fresh-fruit pies. You can freeze whole pies, baked or unbaked, and pop them in the oven to bake when you want them.

Kitchen Utensil
When freezing pie pastry, be sure to label it to indicate whether it is dough for an 8-inch or 9-inch pie.

To freeze an uncooked pie, prepare the pie as usual, except use $1^1/_2$ times the amount of cornstarch, tapioca, or flour. For example, if the recipe calls for 1 tablespoon, increase it to $1^1/_2$ tablespoons. Freeze the pie solid before wrapping it in plastic wrap and aluminum foil or putting it in an airtight container. Bake the pie, unthawed, for 15 minutes in a 425°F oven, then reduce the temperature to 375°F and continue baking for about 40 minutes more. If the pie has a top crust, be sure to poke air holes in the top crust before baking.

To freeze a baked pie, first bake it completely. Let it cool completely, then wrap it tightly in heavy-duty aluminum foil and place it in the freezer. If the pie is to be served cold, thaw it for several hours in the refrigerator or at room temperature. To serve the pie warm, place the frozen pie in a preheated 375°F oven for about 30 minutes.

If you're not ready to make the pie, or if you want to save time later, you can also freeze pie pastry. Pie pastry made with shortening or butter freezes very well. You can freeze pie pastry in many different ways. You can just wrap the dough in an airtight container. When you're ready to use it, just defrost the dough, roll it out, and use as instructed.

You can also roll out the dough and place it on a greased baking sheet to freeze. Once frozen, just wrap and label. Defrost and use as normal. Or you can press the pie crust into a pie plate and freeze it like that. You might want to use disposable foil pie plates unless you don't mind storing the pie plate in the freezer for a while. Freeze the crust in the pie plate until frozen solid, then wrap tightly and seal in an airtight container, double-bag it in large sealable plastic bags, or place the pie shells in a box to fit for extra protection from the other objects in the freezer. You can bake these shells without thawing them at 425°F for 10 to 15 minutes.

Avoiding Freezer Burn

Air left in containers dries out the food during storage, which can cause freezer burn. The additional moisture that is drawn from the food forms those ice crystals which you find on the lids of many home-frozen items. Freezer burn can also occur if foods are not wrapped tightly enough.

When wrapping food for freezing, choose only wrappers that are moisture-proof to keep your foods from drying out. This also keeps freezer odor from penetrating your foods. Heavy-duty aluminum foil is great for the freezer because it can be molded to the shape of the item being frozen. Large sealable freezer bags are also a good choice for freezing irregularly shaped items. You can press out all the additional air to get a good seal. Double-wrapping or bagging items is another good idea. Plastic wrap should be used first, then follow with heavy-duty aluminum foil for the best seal. Also, look for hard, plastic freezer containers in which to store your baked goods to protect them from any damage in the freezer. Wrap the items in plastic and foil, then place them in the containers for the best protection.

Wrap It Up!

No kitchen is complete without a supply of plastic wrap, aluminum foil, and waxed paper. Plastic wrap is good as an airtight seal for food. I like it because you can see through it and know what you have stored. Plastic wrap also won't react with any acidic or alkaline ingredients, which makes it good for storing all ingredients. It's microwave-safe, too. You can also create airtight seals over bowls and other containers. Find the brand of plastic wrap you like best. It should cling to itself and you should also be able to pull it tightly without it ripping.

Aluminum foil is also a great tool in the kitchen. Unlike plastic wrap, aluminum foil can be used in the oven for baking. It's also handy for wrapping up items because it molds to whatever shape you want, which is great for irregularly shaped items. Because it molds to itself, you can create an airtight seal with aluminum foil. And it is great for the freezer. Write directly on the foil so you know what you have wrapped up. Aluminum foil cannot be used in the microwave.

Waxed paper is also very useful in the kitchen. It can be used to line baking sheets and pans and to separate

Kitchen Utensil

If you are using a baking sheet to catch drips, place a piece of aluminum foil on top of the baking sheet. All the drips fall on the foil, not the baking sheet, meaning no burnt-on mess, and clean-up that's a snap.

layers for storage. It's safe for the microwave and can be used to wrap up items as long as an airtight seal is not required. Also, a sheet of waxed paper can act like a movable part of your kitchen counter or a bowl you don't need to wash. Spread out a sheet on your counter and sift ingredients onto it or use it to hold bread crumbs or any other coating.

Sealable Plastic Containers Versus Decorative Tins

I must admit, I am a big fan of plasticware. It's perfect for everything from packing lunches and holding leftovers to storing everything you can bake. Don't skimp on quality when you purchase plastic containers. Look for sturdy containers with good lids that offer airtight closure. Be sure that the lids fit well and you don't have to struggle each and every time you want to seal it. If you have a microwave, you might want to choose a brand of microwave-safe plasticware.

Sealable plastic containers make great storage items because the airtight seals keep your baked items fresher longer. Clear plastic allows you to see what you have stored (which is a great memory aid) and they are generally spacious and can fit many items.

Decorative tins are great for gift items and can serve as the holder and wrapping if you like to give baked goods as gifts. There are a few things you should keep in mind, though, when you choose decorative tins. Tins generally do not have an airtight seal, which means that baked items will not stay fresh as long as they would if they were stored in plastic containers. The second thing is that they do not have as much holding capacity as plastic containers. Tins are great if you want to give a sampling of cookies or brownies to a friend, but if you want to send a few dozen cookies as a care package, I would send them in a plastic container.

The Least You Need to Know

➤ Know how long you want to store your baked goods before you choose which way to store them.

➤ Freezing baked items is a great way to keep them on hand, but make sure your baked items are well wrapped and stored properly.

➤ Airtight plastic containers are great for storing just about anything. Think about investing in a few for storage.

Stuff Your Parents Never Told You

There are many things you may encounter in the kitchen that you don't expect—a big chocolate stain on your favorite white shirt, a nick on your knuckles, a burn on your hand. Or you may be wondering how to prepare a recipe to accommodate living at a different altitude. In this chapter we'll take a look at how to deal with these predicaments. You'll discover you have the tools to deal with just about anything thrown your way!

How to Conquer Stains

Despite your best attempts at being neat, you'll still manage to spill things or be left to deal with stains others have made on the tablecloth. The following sections list the most common types of stains and some suggestions on how to remove them. This advice is for natural cotton or linen fabrics. If you have wool, silk, or other synthetics, follow the manufacturer's instructions for laundering. Never rub a stain; rubbing will further penetrate the stain into the fabric. Instead, just blot the stain with something absorbent.

Wine and Fruit Juices

If you get to the spill in time, these types of stains are usually not that terrible. Have a bottle of plain seltzer water handy to douse the stain. I also pour regular table salt onto the fabric (except for silk). Soak the fabric for 30 minutes to several hours, if possible, and then launder as usual. If you spilled on a white tablecloth, try rubbing a little lemon juice and salt into the stain and setting it out in the sun for a while to see if you can bleach it out.

Coffee and Tea

The best way to remove a fresh coffee stain is to stretch out the fabric and pour boiling water directly over the stain. If you have a large rubber band and a smallish colander, stretch the stained fabric over the colander and secure it with a rubber band. Place the colander in the sink and carefully pour the water over the stain. Be very careful doing this; you don't want to burn yourself. This way, the hot water just washes down the drain. If the coffee or tea has stained your countertop or dishes, try removing it with a paste of baking soda and a few drops of water.

Chocolate

Soak the stain in cold water for about 20 minutes, then rub some liquid detergent into it and launder as usual. If that doesn't work, you can try my suggestion for coffee and tea stains or try a grease solvent (follow the manufacturers instructions carefully) and launder again.

Wax

I feel like an expert on wax removal, thanks to a thoughtless roommate I had a while back. I am not exactly sure how it happened, but I came home one weekend to discover wax was spilled all over my couch, newly finished wood floors, and on a suitcase that was sitting nearby. He promised to clean it up, but as the weeks went by, there was no change in the conditions. So I took it upon myself to conquer the wax.

Wax can be a little tricky; you need to let it harden before doing anything to it. Don't rub it or try and scrape it while it's still warm. If you spilled wax on a tablecloth or something like that, the best thing to do is to put the item in the freezer for a few hours. The hardened wax should pop right off. If you can't fit it in the freezer, you can apply ice cubes to the wax. The wax leaves behind a greasy feel, so apply a grease solvent before you launder the item.

Kitchen Utensil
You can find grease solvents and other stain-fighting products where you buy laundry detergent in the supermarket.

If the wax has fallen on something that won't fit into the freezer (like a couch), allow the wax to harden and remove as much of it as possible. Then place a thin, cotton rag or tissue paper on the stain and run a warm iron (set the iron on the lowest setting, you don't need a lot of heat) over the area for just a few seconds. Repeat as necessary, getting a new blotting rag each time. Once you have removed the stain, you might want to further clean the area with a grease solvent or fabric cleaner. This also works for crayons, but the dyes in the crayons that give them color will probably leave a permanent stain.

Greasy Stains

Grease stains are quite a challenge. If you notice the stain right away, blot some cornstarch onto the stain and let it sit for about 30 minutes, then launder it. The cornstarch should help absorb the grease. If not, you can rub laundry detergent directly into the stain to help break up the grease. Otherwise, I suggest purchasing a grease solvent to help you.

Ink Pens

I know this may sound a little crazy, but after years of doing homework on my bed (with a white comforter) and a mishap with a pen and a washing machine, I know this works: hairspray. Yes, hairspray. I find that inexpensive aerosol hairspray works the best. Just zap the pen stain with the hairspray and then launder it right away. Large, inky blots may need a second treatment. If it's a thin fabric, make sure the ink doesn't bleed through and stain the other side of the garment. Soon, you, too, will be singing the virtues of hairspray.

Food Safety Tips

The way you handle food has a lot to do with how safe it is to eat. The best rule to keep in mind is that freshest is best, so always rotate your ingredients when you buy fresh (first in, first out). Use up what you had before you start the new batch. I think it's important to be aware of what you have to do (or not do) in order to prevent the spread of bacteria around your kitchen, but I also advise that you use your common sense. A clean kitchen, clean utensils, and frequent washing of hands are the best precautions to take. And always cook your ingredients all the way through. When serving, keep hot foods hot and cold foods cold. The middle ground is where bacteria loves to grow and multiply (between 40°F and 140°F). Make sure that when you have finished serving egg and meat dishes you refrigerate them right away.

There's been a lot of attention in the media lately about salmonella. The shells of the egg will protect the inside of the egg, but once the shell is broken, that barrier no longer exists. That is why many people no longer suggest separating eggs by passing them from shell to shell. If the outside of the shell is contaminated, you

Kitchen Utensil

If you have any other questions about food safety, call the USDA's Meat and Poultry Hotline at 800-535-4555, or call the Center for Disease Control, Prevention and Foodborne Illness at 404-332-4597 (24-hour recorded information).

can pass that on to the inside of the egg. If you have any questions about the quality and freshness of your eggs, check the date of freshness printed on the carton. Look for an 800 number, also on the carton, and you can call the distributor to see if there has been an outbreak. For more about salmonella, see Chapter 5.

Many recipes call for ingredients to be at room temperature. Ingredients will reach room temperature within 20 minutes of being removed from the refrigerator. Never leave eggs at room temperature for more than one hour. Don't let cooked egg or chicken dishes sit out at room temperature for more than 30 minutes.

Avoid cross-contamination. If you use a plate to hold raw meat, get a clean plate to hold the cooked meat. This includes utensils. Cross-contamination can also happen with your hands. After handling raw meats, wash your hands thoroughly with soapy water before you handle other ingredients.

Cleaning up should be done with as much care as when you handle the ingredients. Wash all utensils and cutting boards that have come in contact with eggs or meats with hot, soapy water immediately after you finish using them. Never reuse utensils that have come in contact with raw meats without washing them first. Discard all wrappings associated with the raw ingredient.

Kitchen Utensil
To sanitize your cutting board or countertops, use 2 teaspoons of bleach, 1 tablespoon distilled vinegar, and 1 gallon of water. Use this mixture to rinse the board, sink, and utensils and wipe down the countertops.

Make sure your milk is fresh. One sniff should tell you if it has soured or not. Check the expiration date on the carton of milk before you buy it. Most supermarkets will stock the fresher items in the back of the cooler case, so shop wisely and compare dates. Butter can also go rancid if stored too long. If in question, smell a little bit of it. If it doesn't smell right, discard it and get fresh butter. Butter, milk, and eggs should be stored away from strong smelling odors such as fish, cheese, and cabbage. Never leave milk at room temperature for more than 30 minutes. Remember: When in doubt, throw it out!

Overall, if you make sure your ingredients are fresh (this means everything from your eggs down to fruits and nuts), handle raw meats carefully, keep your kitchen tidy, and refrigerate your items once they are used, you should not have a problem.

First Aid in the Kitchen

Your kitchen can be a dangerous place. You are surrounded by fire, sharp objects, and hot things. A lot can happen, and you want to be prepared. There is a lot you can do to prevent accidents from happening. Following are some basic kitchen safety tips:

➤ Make sure you have a working fire extinguisher in the kitchen at all times, and know how to use it.

➤ Lid handles and metal utensils left in a pot while cooking will get hot. Be careful!

➤ Do not wear open-toe shoes when baking in case something hot spills or you drop a knife.

➤ Do not wear loose, baggy clothes when you cook. These can hang over a flame or get caught in equipment.

➤ Be sure your sleeves are rolled up, and if you have long hair, pull it back or wear a cap.

➤ Keep your knives sharp. Dull knives can slip and end up cutting you because you have to use more pressure to cut. Store all knives carefully.

➤ Keep your hands and utensils away from the moving parts of kitchen equipment. Never use equipment that has missing parts or is broken.

➤ Do not try to scrape down the sides of a bowl until the mixer has stopped completely.

➤ Never put your hand or utensil inside a working blender or mixer.

➤ Keep kitchen towels and paper towels away from the stovetop and don't hang kitchen towels off the oven door. If there is a fire in the oven or broiler, they can catch fire easily.

➤ Check to make sure there is nothing in the oven before you preheat it. Adjust the racks, if necessary, when the oven is cool.

➤ After opening a can, dispose of the sharp-edged top carefully. Either drop it into the bottom of the empty can or wrap it in paper before you throw it out. An unwrapped lid can be very dangerous even in the trash if you push down to make more room for additional garbage. The same is true for broken glass.

➤ Wipe up spills as soon as they happen, especially on the floor; otherwise you might slip and fall.

➤ Don't use thin, decorative oven mitts or potholders to handle hot pots and pans. They are cheaply made and not well insulated. Look for thick, well-insulated, or heavy-duty potholders (mitts made for outdoor barbecuing are usually good quality). And if your potholder wears thin, throw it away and purchase a new one. Use potholders or oven mitts that are clean and dry. If your potholder becomes wet, it will transfer the heat from the pan right to your hand.

Burns

The best way to prevent burns from the oven is to purchase heavy-duty oven mitts, which cover your entire hand plus part of your forearms. You can even buy oven mitts that go up to your elbows (not a bad idea).

Remember, steam burns too, so be careful and shield your face and hands from steam when removing a lid from boiling water or from something covered in the oven.

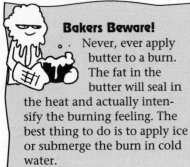

Bakers Beware!
Never, ever apply butter to a burn. The fat in the butter will seal in the heat and actually intensify the burning feeling. The best thing to do is to apply ice or submerge the burn in cold water.

If you do burn yourself by touching something hot, immediately apply ice or submerge your hand in ice water. If something spills on you, remove the clothing immediately. Do not apply a burn cream until after the burning sensation is gone. A first-degree burn will turn red. A second-degree burn will have a blister. For anything more severe, you need to call your doctor. Also, if the burning sensation does not subside within an hour or so, consult your doctor.

When you have pots and pans on the stovetop, be sure you turn the handles away from the edge of the stove. A small child could pull on the handle, or the handle could catch on you or something you're wearing.

Proper positioning of a pot on the stovetop.

Cuts

Working with knives and other sharp objects also requires care. If you do cut yourself, immediately wash the area with antiseptic and apply direct pressure to the area with a clean gauze pad or towel. Then apply an antiseptic cream and bandage. If the cut is deep and there is heavy bleeding, apply direct pressure and seek medical attention.

Holding your fingers properly will help prevent serious cuts. Always tuck your fingers under, not hold them straight out, as you hold an ingredient for cutting. That way, if the knife slips, you will nick your knuckle and not slice the very sensitive tips of your fingers. Also, wash knives immediately after use. Never place them in a sink of soapy water. If you forget the knives are there and reach into the water, you may end up with a cut.

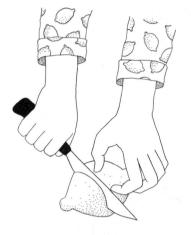

The proper finger positioning for cutting.

Information Station

Pick up a box of thin, disposable gloves at the drugstore and keep them in the kitchen. They are extremely useful, especially if you get a minor cut. Just slip on a pair and you will keep your cut sterile while you continue to work. They are also very good if you are handling hot chilies. The oil from the chilies can get under your nails, and if you rub your eyes or touch your nose after you handle them they can cause severe irritation. By wearing gloves, you prevent the oils from ever touching your skin. Gloves are also handy when handling raw meats.

Fire

No matter how infrequently you cook, you should always have a fire extinguisher in the kitchen. Read the manufacturer's instructions and keep it in working order. Make sure you understand how to use it.

Never douse a grease fire with water (oil and water do not mix). If it's a small flare-up, try to cover the flames with a lid (no more oxygen, no more fire). Otherwise, baking soda or salt will extinguish flames.

Don't wear baggy clothes and do tie back long hair when you work in the kitchen, so if there is a fire, there will be less chance of it transferring to you or your clothes. Always have the number to the fire department by the phone and stay close to the kitchen when you have items in the oven. Don't leave the stove unattended if you have things cooking on the stovetop.

High-Altitude Adjustments

People who live at elevations above 3,500 feet face some interesting cooking challenges. The higher altitude causes different reactions in baking, thanks to the change in air pressure and humidity. You may notice that once-dependable recipes suddenly become a bit out of whack.

When air pressure is reduced as it is at higher elevations, water boils at a lower temperature and liquids evaporate much faster. Gases also expand more rapidly, so you may find your cake rises so much that it actually collapses upon itself. This means your tried-and-true recipes may start behaving poorly when the altitude increases.

Recipes have to be adjusted to compensate for this. Unfortunately, there is no definite outline or rule of thumb to apply to the high altitude, so you are left to trial and error for the most part. If you are new to high-altitude cooking, you can contact your local U.S. Department of Agriculture Extension Service, listed in the phone book under county government, for help with any questions. Also, check out your local library or bookstore for books on high-altitude cooking. Or contact Colorado State University in Fort Collins, Colorado. Many products also have 800 numbers you can call for help.

Here are some things to keep in mind when you are baking at higher altitudes:

➤ If you are boiling foods, they will take longer to cook because the temperature at which water boils is between 203–207°F, not the usual sea level 212°F.

➤ Cream your butter and sugar for a shorter amount of time and beat the eggs less, so there is less air incorporated into your finished product and it will not rise as much.

➤ Most baked goods made with baking powder or baking soda will be better off if the following adjustments are made: Increase the liquid by 1 to 4 tablespoons, decrease the leavening by one-quarter, decrease the sugar by 1 to 3 tablespoons per cup, and/or use a larger pan size (for example, if an 8-inch-square pan is called for, increase the pan size to a 9-inch-square pan). For butter-rich cakes, decrease the butter by 1 to 4 tablespoons.

➤ You may even want to increase the oven temperature by 25°F and shorten the baking time to compensate for the loss of moisture.

➤ If egg whites are your primary leavener, beat them only to soft peaks so there is less air incorporated into them.

➤ Quick breads, cookies, biscuits, and muffins require the fewest adjustments. Experiment with increasing the liquid by $1/4$ to $1/2$ cup and decreasing the leaveners and sugar by one-quarter, if necessary.

➤ For cookies, increase the oven temperature by about 25°F and decrease the baking time by a few minutes to compensate, thereby giving the cookies less of a chance to dry out.

➤ Yeast breads will rise more rapidly at higher altitudes, so adjust the rising time to be shorter and be watchful of your breads since they may over-rise. Also, the flour may dry out faster, so use the minimum amount called for in the recipe, or decrease the amount of flour by $1/4$ to $1/2$ cup or increase the liquid by $1/4$ to $1/2$ cup.

➤ Cooked frostings will become concentrated more quickly because of the faster evaporation of the water. Watch very closely and reduce the recipe temperature by 2°F for every 1,000 feet above 3,500 feet.

The Least You Need to Know

➤ Tend to stains as soon as you discover them. Your chances for removing them will be much greater.

➤ Food safety is important in every kitchen. Be aware of the specific things you need to know when handling certain ingredients.

➤ Prevention is the best cure for accidents. Be smart and safe in the kitchen.

➤ When making adjustments for high-altitude baking, because most are trial and error, start with the smallest changes and go from there. The higher up you are, the more you will have to adjust.

Part 6
The Recipes

Now that you know a lot about baking, it's time to try out your knowledge. The best part is that you get to eat the results! Each recipe has prep and bake times allotted to it. A level is also assigned to each recipe: Easy, Intermediate, or Challenging, so as you get more and more practice, you can increase the level of the recipes you can do. Easy recipes require nothing more than measuring ingredients and mixing them up. Intermediate recipes might have a trickier step or additional technique. Challenging recipes have specific techniques which, if done incorrectly, might affect the baked product. But, not to worry, as you practice, you will become more and more familiar with ingredients and baking.

Chapter 22

Let's All Eat Cake

A good cake is moist and flavorful and has a nice texture. Cakes are wonderful because they are so versatile—perfect for big celebrations or small affairs. And cakes don't have to be in layers; there are bundt cakes, pound cakes, and cupcakes, too. In this chapter you'll find some of the most classic cake recipes, such as a basic yellow cake, carrot cake, and chocolate cake. But there are some exciting new flavors you might be interested in trying out, such as Siembora's Apple Cake or Banana Sour Cream Bundt Cake. Whichever cake you choose, you *can* have your cake and eat it, too!

Basic Yellow Cake

Prep: 10 minutes

Bake: 25 minutes

Yield: One 9-inch, 2-layer cake

Level: Easy

My grandmother says this cake is easier to make than a mix. I think so, too, and it's just as quick to make. Try topping this cake with Chocolate Frosting, Mocha Frosting, or Basic Vanilla Buttercream Frosting (all recipes are found at the end of this chapter).

2 cups all-purpose flour

$1^1/_3$ cups sugar

$^1/_2$ cup shortening

1 teaspoon salt

1 cup milk

1 tablespoon baking powder

2 large eggs

1 teaspoon vanilla extract

Preheat the oven to 375°F. Grease two 9-inch cake pans.

Combine all the ingredients together in a large mixing bowl and beat until smooth, 3 to 4 minutes (the batter will be thin). Stop the mixer several times to scrape down the sides of the bowl.

Pour the batter into the prepared pans and bake for 25 to 30 minutes, or until a toothpick inserted into the center comes out clean. Remove the cakes from the pan and cool on a wire rack.

Martha's Chocolate Cake

Prep: 15 minutes

Bake: 25 minutes

Yield: One 9-inch layer cake, or one 8-inch layer cake and 6 cupcakes

Level: Easy

Martha, who is one of my best friends, told me that she used to sit in her math class when she was in grade school and dream of having a slice of this cake when she got home from school. This cake is so moist and delicious it will keep you dreaming, too. Frost it with Martha's Favorite Frosting (see recipe later in this section) for the real McCoy.

2 cups all-purpose flour

1 teaspoon salt

1 teaspoon baking powder

2 teaspoons baking soda

3/4 cup unsweetened cocoa powder

2 cups sugar

1 cup vegetable oil

1 cup hot coffee

1 cup milk

2 large eggs

1 teaspoon vanilla extract

Preheat the oven to 325°F. Grease and flour either two 9-inch cake pans, or two 8-inch cake pans and 6 muffin cups.

Sift together the flour, salt, baking powder, baking soda, cocoa, and sugar into a large mixing bowl. Add the oil, coffee, milk, eggs, and vanilla. Beat at medium speed for 2 minutes (the batter will be thin).

Pour the batter evenly into the two 9-inch cake pans, or fill 6 muffin cups halfway with batter and divide the remaining batter between the two 8-inch pans. Bake 25 to 30 minutes, until a wooden toothpick inserted into the center of the cake comes out clean (check on the cupcakes after 15 minutes). Let the cakes cool 15 minutes before removing them from the pans. Let them cool completely on wire racks before frosting.

Carrot Cake

Prep: 25 minutes

Bake: 30 minutes

Yield: 12 to 14 servings

Level: Easy

This is quite a cake, a three-layer beauty. If you don't have three pans, just bake two of the layers, then wash and reuse one of the cake pans. Think about making this cake a day in advance. It tastes even better the second day. Frost it with Cream Cheese Frosting (see recipe later in this section).

1¹/₂ cups vegetable oil	1 tablespoon ground cinnamon
2 cups sugar	2 teaspoons baking soda
4 large eggs, beaten	1 teaspoon salt
1 teaspoon vanilla extract	3 cups grated carrots
2 cups all-purpose flour	1 cup walnuts, coarsely chopped (optional)

Preheat the oven to 325°F. Grease and flour three 8- or 9-inch cake pans.

In a large mixing bowl, beat together the oil and sugar. Add the eggs and vanilla and mix to combine. Sift together the flour, cinnamon, baking soda, and salt and add to the oil/sugar mixture. Stir in the carrots, and walnuts, if using. Pour the batter evenly into the pans. Bake for 30 minutes, or until a wooden toothpick inserted into the center comes out clean. Remove the cakes from the pans and let the cakes cool completely on wire racks before frosting.

Applesauce Cake

Prep: 20 minutes

Bake: 1 hour 15 minutes

Yield: One loaf

Level: Easy

2 cups all-purpose flour	¹/₂ teaspoon ground nutmeg
1 cup sugar	¹/₂ teaspoon ground allspice
1 teaspoon baking powder	¹/₂ cup vegetable oil
1 teaspoon baking soda	¹/₂ cup applesauce
1 teaspoon salt	2 large eggs
1 teaspoon ground cinnamon	1 cup chopped walnuts or pecans
¹/₂ teaspoon ground cloves	

Preheat the oven to 350°F. Grease a 9 × 5 loaf pan.

Sift together the flour, sugar, baking powder, baking soda, salt, and all of the spices into a large mixing bowl. Add the oil and applesauce and mix for 2 minutes at medium speed. Beat in the eggs; mix for 2 minutes longer. Fold in the nuts and pour the batter into the loaf pan. Bake for 1 hour and 15 minutes, or until a toothpick inserted into the center comes out clean. Cool the loaf in the pan for 10 minutes. Remove from the pan and finish cooling on a metal rack.

Siembora's Apple Cake

Prep: 20 minutes

Bake: 45 minutes

Yield: One bundt cake; 16 servings

Level: Easy

This cake has been a staple in my family's house for as long as I can remember. This cake keeps incredibly well and I think it keeps getting better the longer it sits. The traditional way to make this cake is to pour half of the batter into the bundt pan, then layer in the apples, then top it with the rest of the batter. Then you have a lovely ring of apples when you cut into the cake. I, personally, find it too fussy, so I just mix the apples into the batter and pour it all into the pan. Suit yourself with either method.

For the apples:

1/4 cup sugar

1 teaspoon ground cinnamon

4 large tart apples (Granny Smith or winesap), peeled, cored, and thinly sliced

For the cake:

2 cups sugar

1 cup vegetable oil

4 large eggs

2 1/2 teaspoons vanilla extract

3 cups all-purpose flour

1 tablespoon baking powder

Pinch of salt

1/4 cup orange juice

Preheat the oven to 375°F. Grease a 12-cup bundt pan.

Prepare the apples: In a small mixing bowl, combine the sugar, cinnamon, and sliced apples. Set aside.

Prepare the cake: In a large mixing bowl, beat together the sugar, oil, eggs, and vanilla until light, about 2 minutes. Slowly add the flour, baking powder, and salt. Mix in the orange juice. Stir in the apples, just to combine. Pour the batter into the prepared bundt pan. Bake for 45 to 60 minutes, or until a wooden toothpick inserted into the center comes out clean. Let the cake cool for 15 minutes before removing it from the pan. Finish cooling the cake on a wire rack.

Angel Food Cake

Prep: 15 minutes   **Yield:** 10 to 12 servings
Bake: 40 minutes   **Level:** Intermediate

This recipe calls for cake flour. Be sure you don't purchase self-rising cake flour by mistake (it will be marked on the box). You can double-check if you're not sure by reading the ingredients. If there are any leavening agents present, the flour is self-rising.

1 cup cake flour

1½ cups confectioners' sugar

2 cups large egg whites (about 6 to 8 eggs)

¼ teaspoon salt

1 teaspoon vanilla extract

¼ teaspoon almond extract

1 cup granulated sugar

Preheat the oven to 350°F.

Sift the cake flour with the confectioners' sugar twice. Set aside.

With a wire whisk or the whisk attachment of an electric mixer, beat the egg whites, salt, vanilla, and almond extract together until they are foamy and just begin to form soft peaks. Gradually add the granulated sugar, about 2 to 3 teaspoons at a time, and continue beating until stiff peaks form. Do not overbeat.

Add the flour mixture to the egg whites in thirds and gently fold with a rubber spatula to combine (about four turns) after each addition. Carefully pour the mixture into an ungreased 10-inch tube pan. Bake the cake 40 to 45 minutes. It will be golden brown and spring back when you touch it. Remove the cake from the oven and turn it up-side down over a funnel or neck of a bottle, or rest it on the feet of the tube pan, if available. Let the cake cool inverted. Remove it from the pan and serve.

Jelly Roll

Prep: 30 minutes
Bake: 8 minutes

Yield: 10 to 12 servings
Level: Intermediate

Instead of using raspberry preserves for a jelly roll, feel free to substitute a buttercream filling, sweetened whipped cream, pudding, or any flavor of jam or preserves. If you use pudding or whipped cream, be sure to keep the jelly roll refrigerated.

$^3/_4$ cup all-purpose flour

1 teaspoon baking powder

$^1/_2$ teaspoon salt

4 large eggs

$^3/_4$ cup granulated sugar

1 teaspoon grated lemon peel

Raspberry preserves, at room temperature

Confectioners' sugar, for sprinkling

Preheat the oven to 375°F.

Line a 15 × 10 × 1-inch baking pan with waxed paper. Set aside. Sprinkle a clean kitchen towel with confectioners' sugar and set aside.

In a small bowl, sift together the flour, baking powder, and salt. Set aside.

In a medium-size bowl, beat the eggs until they thicken slightly and turn a light yellow, about 2 minutes on medium speed. Beat in the granulated sugar, about 2 tablespoons at a time, and continue beating on medium speed for about 5 minutes. Add the lemon peel. Gently fold in the flour mixture and spread the mixture into the prepared pan.

Bake 8 to 10 minutes, until the cake springs back gently when touched and a wooden toothpick inserted into the center comes out clean. Invert the cake onto the prepared kitchen towel and allow to cool for just 2 minutes. Remove the pan and carefully peel off the waxed paper. Beginning at the narrow end, roll the cake in the towel and place on a wire rack, seam side down, to cool, about 20 minutes.

Unroll the cake and spoon the preserves onto the cake. Spread to cover, leaving a $^1/_4$-inch border around the cake's edges. The preserves should be spread about $^1/_4$-inch thick. Roll up the jelly roll again and place it seam side down onto the cake plate and let rest for about 30 minutes. Sprinkle with additional confectioners' sugar before serving.

Banana Sour Cream Bundt Cake

Prep: 20 minutes   **Yield:** About 12 servings
Bake: 45 minutes   **Level:** Easy

This is a lovely, dense cake that travels quite well. If you want, throw in a cup of chocolate chips. You can dress up the cake with a dusting of confectioners' sugar.

$^1/_2$ cup (1 stick) butter, softened

$1^1/_4$ cups sugar

2 large eggs

1 cup mashed ripe bananas (about 3 bananas)

$^1/_2$ teaspoon vanilla extract

$^1/_2$ cup sour cream

2 cups all-purpose flour

1 teaspoon baking powder

1 teaspoon baking soda

$^1/_4$ teaspoon salt

$^1/_2$ cup chopped walnuts

$^1/_2$ teaspoon ground cinnamon

Preheat the oven to 375°F. Grease well a 10-cup capacity ring mold or bundt pan.

In a large bowl, beat the butter until light, about 1 minute on medium speed. On low speed, slowly beat in 1 cup of the sugar. Beat in the eggs, one at a time. Add the mashed bananas, vanilla, and sour cream.

Sift together the flour, baking powder, baking soda, and salt. Fold the flour into the creamed mixture, just to blend (do not overbeat).

In another bowl, combine chopped walnuts, the remaining $^1/_4$ cup sugar, and cinnamon. Sprinkle half of this mixture over bottom of well-greased ring mold or bundt pan. Spoon in half of the batter.

Sprinkle in remaining walnut mixture and cover with rest of banana and sour cream batter.

Bake for 45 minutes or until cake is brown and starts to pull away from sides of mold, or until a wooden toothpick inserted into the center comes out clean. Let the cake cool in the pan for 10 minutes before turning it out to a wire rack to cool.

Classic Pound Cake

Prep: 20 minutes　　　　　　　　**Yield:** One loaf; 12 to 16 servings
Bake: 60 minutes　　　　　　　　**Level:** Easy

This rich, dense cake is perfect on its own, but you can serve it with a scoop of ice cream, fresh fruit, a drizzle of chocolate sauce, or a sprinkling of confectioners' sugar.

1³/₄ cups all-purpose flour　　　　　³/₄ cup sugar
³/₄ teaspoon baking powder　　　　　3 tablespoons milk
¹/₄ teaspoon salt　　　　　　　　　　3 large eggs
³/₄ cup (1¹/₂ sticks) butter, at room temperature　　1¹/₂ teaspoons vanilla extract

Preheat the oven to 350°F. Grease and flour a 9 × 5 loaf pan.

Sift together the flour, baking powder, and salt in a medium-size bowl. Set aside.

In another bowl, cream together the butter and sugar with an electric mixer on medium speed until well incorporated, about 1 minute. Add the milk and the eggs, one at a time, then add the vanilla and continue beating to mix well. Slowly add the flour, about ¹/₂ cup at a time, mixing on low speed, just until blended.

Scrape the batter into the prepared loaf pan. Bake 55 to 60 minutes, or until a wooden toothpick inserted into the center comes out clean. Let the cake rest 10 minutes before inverting it onto the cooling rack.

Ginger Cake

Prep: 15 minutes　　　　　　　　**Yield:** One 8-inch cake
Bake: 30 minutes　　　　　　　　**Level:** Easy

This cake forms a crispy outer layer, but the inside is a moist, delicious cake. Finding the ginger may be your only challenge. Preserved ginger comes in jars and can easily be found in Asian markets or in gourmet markets.

1 large egg, beaten　　　　　　　　1 cup sugar
1 cup (2 sticks) butter　　　　　　　¹/₃ cup preserved ginger, drained and sliced
2 cups all-purpose flour

Preheat the oven to 350°F.

Reserve 1 tablespoon of the beaten egg in a small bowl. In a medium bowl, mix together the butter, flour, sugar, and the remaining beaten egg with an electric mixer for 1 minute on medium speed. Press the dough into an 8-inch-square baking pan (it will be about 1 inch thick). Press the middle of the cake down.

Brush the reserved egg on top of the batter and decorate with the sliced ginger. Bake for 30 minutes, or until a wooden toothpick inserted into the center comes out clean. Cool on a wire rack.

Chocolate Cupcakes

Prep: 15 minutes   **Yield:** 12 cupcakes
Bake: 20 minutes   **Level:** Easy

If you like, you can use $^1/_4$ cup shortening and $^1/_4$ cup butter ($^1/_2$ stick) in place of the $^1/_2$ cup shortening called for in the recipe. Just make sure they are both at room temperature. Frost these cupcakes with Basic Vanilla Buttercream Frosting or Chocolate Frosting (both recipes are found later in this chapter), or just sprinkle them with confectioners' sugar.

$^1/_2$ cup shortening, at room temperature	$^1/_2$ teaspoon salt
1 cup sugar	1 teaspoon baking soda
1 large egg	$^1/_2$ cup buttermilk
$1^1/_2$ cups all-purpose flour	$^1/_2$ cup hot water
$^1/_2$ cup cocoa	1 teaspoon vanilla extract

Preheat the oven to 375°F. Grease 12 muffin cups or line them with paper liners.

In a medium-size mixing bowl, cream together the shortening and sugar until light and creamy with an electric mixer, about 1 minute. Beat in the egg.

In a small bowl, combine the flour, cocoa, and salt. Stir the baking soda into the buttermilk and stir to dissolve. Add the flour mixture alternately with the buttermilk to the shortening mixture, beginning and ending with flour (flour, buttermilk, flour, buttermilk, flour) and mix just until combined. Add the hot water and vanilla and mix well. Pour the batter into the muffin tins and bake for 20 minutes, or until a toothpick inserted into the center comes out clean. Wait 5 minutes before removing the cupcakes from the pan. Cool the cupcakes on a wire rack completely before frosting.

Molly's Date-Chocolate Cupcakes

Prep: 25 minutes

Bake: 25 minutes

Yield: 18–20 cupcakes

Level: Easy

Dates and chocolate are the perfect mixture. My great-aunt Molly liked to add two chocolate kisses to her cupcakes, but my grandmother advises that only one be used. You can use your judgment.

1 cup chopped dates	2 cups all-purpose flour
1 cup hot water	1 teaspoon unsweetened cocoa
1 teaspoon baking soda	1 teaspoon salt
1 cup sugar	1 teaspoon vanilla extract
$1/2$ cup shortening	$1/2$ cup chopped walnuts
1 large egg, beaten	18 to 20 chocolate kisses, or more if desired

Preheat the oven to 350°F. Grease 18 to 20 muffin cups or line them with paper liners.

Place the dates in a small bowl and add the hot water and baking soda. Set them aside to cool.

While the dates are cooling, in a mixing bowl cream together the sugar and shortening on medium speed, about 1 minute. Add the beaten egg and all of the dates with the soaking liquid; mix to combine. Sift together the flour, cocoa, and salt and add to the date mixture. Stir in the vanilla and nuts.

Fill each muffin cup $2/3$ full of batter. Anchor a chocolate kiss in each cupcake and press it down so the batter covers it. Bake 25 minutes. Remove the cupcakes from the pan and cool on a wire rack.

Kitchen Utensil

If you have already greased 20 muffin cups and discover you only have enough batter for 18, pour a little bit of water into the empty greased cups to prevent them from burning during baking.

Classic Cheesecake

Prep: 25 minutes

Bake: 1 hour, 15 minutes

Chill: 4 hours

Yield: One 9-inch cheesecake; serves 12 to 16

Level: Easy

2 cups graham cracker crumbs (about 1 package)

4 tablespoons ($1/2$ stick) butter, melted

5 large eggs

$1/4$ cup heavy (whipping) cream or half-and-half

2 pounds (four 8-ounce packages) cream cheese, at room temperature

$1^1/2$ cups granulated sugar

Grated rind of 1 lemon

2 teaspoons vanilla extract

Heat the oven to 300°F.

In the bottom of a 9-inch springform pan, combine the graham cracker crumbs and the melted butter. Press into the bottom of the pan and place the pan in the refrigerator until you are ready to add the filling.

In a large mixing bowl or a blender, combine the remaining ingredients and mix on medium-low speed until well blended, about 3 minutes. Stop the mixer at least three times to scrape down the bottom and the sides of the bowl with a stiff rubber spatula.

Pour the batter into the chilled crust and set on a baking sheet. Bake the cheesecake until the center is set (it might still wiggle a little but it should not be soupy in the middle), about 1 hour and 15 minutes. Turn off the oven and open the oven door and let the cheesecake cool in the oven for 20 minutes, then finish cooling on a wire rack. Cover and refrigerate the cheesecake for 4 hours or overnight to set. Serve chilled.

Pumpkin Cheesecake

Prep: 20 minutes   **Yield:** 10 servings
Bake: 50 minutes   **Level:** Intermediate
Chill: 6 hours

My former boss Anne asked me if there would be a pumpkin cheesecake recipe in this book, so here it is. You can use a blender to make this recipe; just be sure to tap the container a few times on the countertop to release any air bubbles before you pour the mixture into the springform pan. This cheesecake is wonderfully rich and very pumpkiny.

For the crust:

2 cups graham cracker crumbs, about 1 package (cinnamon graham crackers are good)

5 tablespoons butter, melted

For the filling:

1 cup sour cream

2 8-ounce packages cream cheese, at room temperature

1 cup sugar

2 cups (one 16-ounce can) canned or fresh pumpkin (not the seasoned pie filling)

$1/2$ teaspoon ground nutmeg

$1/4$ teaspoon ground allspice

1 tablespoon vanilla extract

2 tablespoons bourbon or maple syrup

4 large eggs

Preheat the oven to 300°F.

Make the crust: Mix the cracker crumbs and the butter together until the crumbs are moistened and press them into the bottom of a 9-inch springform pan. Your crust should be about $1/4$-inch thick and a quarter of the way up the side of the pan.

Prepare the cheesecake: In a blender or large mixing bowl, combine all the cheesecake ingredients and mix until well blended, about 2 minutes. Stop the blender or mixer several times to scrape down the sides (cream cheese has a tendency to stick to the sides of the container). Pour the filling into the prepared pan.

Bake 50 to 60 minutes or until it is set (it may still wiggle a little but the center should not be soupy). Turn the oven off and crack the door a little and let the cheesecake cool inside the oven, 30 minutes. Remove the cheesecake from the oven and finish cooling on a wire rack. When the cheesecake has cooled, cover the top with plastic and chill for at least 6 hours or overnight.

Information Station

If you are feeling daring, try using fresh pumpkin. It takes a little while longer to prepare, but I think it's well worth it. Look for the small pumpkins (sugar pumpkins) around October or November in the grocery store or at the farmers market. You will need one that weighs about 4 pounds. Cut the pumpkin in half and remove the seeds. Bake the pumpkin, cut side down, in a baking dish with $1/2$ cup of water for about 1 hour, or until tender. Set aside until it's cool enough to handle (about 20 minutes). Peel the skin off of the pumpkin and purée the flesh in a food processor or blender. I like to add a little bit of liquid (a few tablespoons of water at a time) to help make a smoother purée. You will need 2 cups puréed fresh pumpkin to make this recipe.

Frostings

Many people think cake is just an excuse to eat frosting. So, for them, here is a collection of rich, satisfying frostings.

Cream Cheese Frosting

Prep: 5 minutes   **Level:** Easy

Yield: 3 cups (enough for an 8- or
9-inch layer cake)

If you use this frosting, be sure you refrigerate the cake. Let the cake come to room tempera-ture before serving. Also, make sure both the cream cheese and butter are at room temperature so when you blend them together, they will be smooth and not have little bits of cold butter or cream cheese peppered throughout. Begin with 2 cups of confectioners' sugar and adjust it to your liking. You can add up to 4 cups of confectioners' sugar if you have a big sweet tooth.

12 ounces cream cheese, at room temperature   2 tablespoons milk

$^1/_4$ cup ($^1/_2$ stick) butter, at room temperature   1 teaspoon vanilla extract

$2^1/_2$ cups confectioners' sugar

Beat the cream cheese and butter together on medium speed until well blended. Add the sugar gradually, $^1/_2$ cup at a time, and beat until blended. Stop the mixer several times during this process to scrape down the sides of the bowl. Mix in the milk and vanilla. Cover and refrigerate if you are not using immediately. Bring to room temperature before frosting a cake to make it more spreadable.

Kitchen Utensil

Boost the flavor of cream cheese frosting with the addition of 1 teaspoon grated lemon or orange rind.

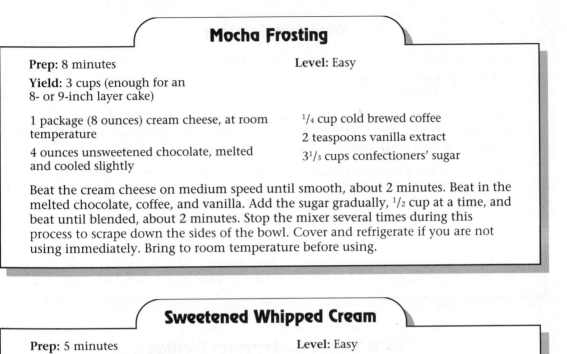

Mocha Frosting

Prep: 8 minutes

Level: Easy

Yield: 3 cups (enough for an 8- or 9-inch layer cake)

1 package (8 ounces) cream cheese, at room temperature

4 ounces unsweetened chocolate, melted and cooled slightly

$^1/_4$ cup cold brewed coffee

2 teaspoons vanilla extract

$3^1/_3$ cups confectioners' sugar

Beat the cream cheese on medium speed until smooth, about 2 minutes. Beat in the melted chocolate, coffee, and vanilla. Add the sugar gradually, $^1/_2$ cup at a time, and beat until blended, about 2 minutes. Stop the mixer several times during this process to scrape down the sides of the bowl. Cover and refrigerate if you are not using immediately. Bring to room temperature before using.

Sweetened Whipped Cream

Prep: 5 minutes

Level: Easy

Yield: 3 cups (enough for an 8- or 9-inch layer cake)

Nothing beats a piece of pie or cake or, for that matter, most anything that has a dollop of sweetened whipped cream on top.

$1^1/_2$ cups heavy (whipping) cream

$^1/_2$ cup confectioners' sugar, or more to taste

1 teaspoon vanilla extract

Beat the cream in a chilled mixing bowl until it begins to thicken, about 2 minutes. Add the sugar and vanilla and continue beating until soft peaks form. Do not overbeat or you will end up with butter.

Kitchen Utensil

If you want to use Sweetened Whipped Cream to frost a cake, increase the amount of heavy cream to 2 cups. Dissolve 1 envelope unflavored gelatin in 2 tablespoons cool water in a small saucepan. Place the saucepan over very low heat and melt (the mixture should be just warm). Allow the mixture to cool to lukewarm. Add it to the heavy cream after you beat in the sugar and vanilla and while the cream still forms soft peaks.

Chocolate Frosting

Prep: 10 minutes   **Level:** Easy

Yield: 3 cups (enough for an
8- or 9-inch layer cake)

1 pound semisweet chocolate or one 16-ounce bag semisweet mini chocolate chips

$^3/_4$ cup heavy (whipping) cream

$^1/_4$ cup ($^1/_2$ stick) butter

1 tablespoon vanilla extract

Cut the chocolate into small bits and place in a mixing bowl (you can skip this step if you are using the mini chips).

Combine the cream and butter in a small saucepan and bring to a full boil over medium heat. Remove from the heat as soon as it boils and pour it over the chocolate, mixing constantly on low speed until the chocolate melts and is thoroughly combined. Add the vanilla and continue mixing until smooth. Allow the frosting to thicken (about 1 hour in the refrigerator) before frosting the cake. If you find the frosting has gotten too hard, just leave it out at room temperature until it softens.

Basic Vanilla Buttercream Frosting

Prep: 10 minutes   **Level:** Easy

Yield: 3 cups (enough for an 8- or
9-inch layer cake)

$^3/_4$ cup ($1^1/_2$ sticks) butter, softened

3 to 4 cups confectioners' sugar

$1^1/_2$ teaspoons vanilla extract

Cream the butter on medium speed in a mixing bowl. Slowly beat in the sugar until smooth and creamy and sweet enough for your liking, about 2 minutes. Add the vanilla. Refrigerate the frosting if you are not using it immediately. Soften the frosting to room temperature before using.

Kitchen Utensil

Beat in 2 ounces of melted unsweetened chocolate if you want a chocolate buttercream frosting.

Martha's Favorite Frosting

Prep: 40 minutes   **Level:** Intermediate
Yield: About 2 cups

This frosting is very sweet. It requires a bit of time to make but if you do it while the cake cools, by the time you are finished, the cake will be ready to be frosted.

1 cup milk	$^1/_2$ cup shortening
5 tablespoons all-purpose flour	1 cup sugar
$^1/_2$ cup butter, softened	1 teaspoon vanilla extract

Combine the milk and flour in a 1-quart saucepan and cook, whisking often, until thick and smooth, about 4 minutes. Cover and refrigerate until cool, about 20 minutes.

In a mixing bowl, beat together the butter, shortening, sugar, and vanilla until smooth and creamy, about 2 minutes. Add the chilled mixture and beat for about 10 minutes, or until creamy.

Chapter 23

Pies of Our Eyes

Here is quite a collection of pies, from classic apple and blueberry to luscious banana cream and peaches-and-cream. If you have any questions along the way, be sure to refer to Chapter 12.

Pumpkin Pie

Prep: 10 minutes

Bake: 35 minutes

Yield: One 9-inch pie

Level: Easy

Pastry for a 9-inch pie (recipe follows later in this chapter)

³/₄ cup firmly packed light brown sugar

¹/₂ teaspoon salt

1 teaspoon ground cinnamon

¹/₂ teaspoon ground ginger

1 15-ounce can canned pumpkin (not pie filling)

¹/₄ teaspoon ground cloves

1 teaspoon vanilla extract

2 large eggs

1 12-ounce can evaporated milk

Preheat the oven to 375°F.

Prepare the pastry for a 9-inch pie plate and line the pie plate, leaving a 1-inch overhang. Crimp the edges of the pie crust.

Combine all the remaining ingredients in a large mixing bowl and blend until smooth. Pour the mixture into the unbaked pie shell and bake until set and a toothpick inserted into the center comes out clean, 35 to 45 minutes. Cool the pie on a wire rack before serving or refrigerate until ready to serve.

You'll-Be-Glad-You-Tried-It Apple Pie

Prep: 30 minutes   **Yield:** One 9-inch pie

Bake: 40 minutes   **Level:** Intermediate

The best apple pies are those with just a hint of spice. Check out your local farmers market or vegetable stand to get a good variety of apples, which will perk up the flavor of any pie. Keep your eyes peeled for varieties like Cortland, Macoun, Ida Red, Stayman, Mutzu, and Gravensteins. Golden Delicious and Granny Smiths are fine, too. Don't use Red Delicious apples, though. They are only good for eating.

Pastry for a 2-crust pie (recipe follows later in this chapter)

8 cups peeled, sliced apples (about 3½ pounds)

Juice of 1 lemon (about 1 tablespoon)

¼ cup firmly packed light brown sugar

⅓ cup granulated sugar

3 tablespoons all-purpose flour

1 teaspoon ground cinnamon

½ teaspoon ground nutmeg

1 teaspoon vanilla extract

2 tablespoons cold butter, cut into little pieces

Preheat the oven to 425°F. Prepare the pastry for a 9-inch pie plate and line the pie plate with half of the dough, leaving a ½-inch overhang.

In a large bowl, toss the apples with the lemon juice. Add both sugars, the flour, cinnamon, nutmeg, and vanilla and toss to coat all the apples. Place the apples in the pie plate and scatter the butter pieces over the top of the apples.

Roll out the top pastry and carefully lay it over the apples. Pat the pastry over the apples. Fold the edges of the bottom pastry over the top pastry and crimp the edges of the pastry. Cut 6 to 8 slits in the top crust for vents.

Place a piece of aluminum foil on a baking sheet (to catch any drips). Place the pie on the baking sheet and bake 40 to 50 minutes, until the crust is golden brown and juice bubbles through the slits in the top crust. Cool the pie on a wire rack before serving.

Blueberry Pie

Prep: 30 minutes

Bake: 30 minutes

Yield: One 9-inch pie

Level: Intermediate

Blueberries are in season during the month of July and into August. Get some fresh blueberries when they're in season and put them in your freezer, so you can make fresh blueberry pie in the fall.

Pastry for a 2-crust pie (recipe found later in this chapter)

$1/2$ cup sugar

$1/4$ cup all-purpose flour

$1/2$ teaspoon ground cinnamon

$1/4$ teaspoon ground nutmeg

6 cups fresh or frozen blueberries (do not thaw the frozen berries)

1 tablespoon lemon juice

1 tablespoon cold butter, cut into 4 pieces

Preheat the oven to 425°F. Prepare the pastry for a 9-inch pie plate and line the pie plate with half of the dough, leaving a $1/2$-inch overhang.

In a large bowl, toss together the sugar, flour, cinnamon, and nutmeg. Add the blueberries and lemon juice and mix to coat. Place the blueberries in the pie plate and scatter the butter pieces over the berries.

Roll out the top pastry and carefully lay it over the blueberries. Pat the pastry over the blueberries. Fold the edges of the bottom pastry over the top pastry and crimp the edges of the pastry. Cut 6 to 8 slits in the top crust for vents.

Place a piece of aluminum foil on a baking sheet. Place the pie on the baking sheet and bake 30 to 40 minutes, until the crust is golden brown and juice bubbles through the slits in the top crust. Remove the pie from the baking sheet to wire racks to cool.

Cherry Crumb Pie

Prep: 25 minutes   **Yield:** One 9-inch pie

Bake: 40 minutes   **Level:** Intermediate

If you don't want the crumb topping, you can make a double crust instead.

Pastry for a 9-inch pie (recipe follows later in this chapter)

$^1/_4$ cup sugar

4 tablespoons instant tapioca

6 cups pitted fresh or canned, drained sour cherries

$^1/_2$ teaspoon almond extract

2 tablespoons cold butter, cut into small pieces

For the topping:

1 cup all-purpose flour

$^3/_4$ cup sugar

$^1/_2$ cup (1 stick) unsalted cold butter, cut into small pieces

$^1/_2$ cup ground almonds

Preheat the oven to 400 °F.

Prepare the pastry for a 9-inch pie plate and line the pie plate with half of the dough, leaving a 1-inch overhang. Crimp the edges of the pie crust.

Combine the sugar, tapioca, cherries, and almond extract. Toss to combine and place the cherries in the pie plate. Scatter the butter pieces over the cherries.

Combine all the topping ingredients and blend so the mixture resembles coarse crumbs (you can do this in a food processor, if desired). Scatter the topping over the cherries.

Place a piece of aluminum foil on a baking sheet. Place the pie on the baking sheet and bake 40 to 50 minutes, until the crust is golden brown and juice bubbles through the topping. Cool on a wire rack before serving.

Kitchen Utensil

Sour cherries have a very short season, and more than likely you'll find a good supply of frozen tart cherries. You can substitute frozen unsweetened tart cherries, thawed and drained, for the fresh cherries in this pie. You can also use canned, drained cherries. Do not use canned pie filling.

Carol's Peaches-and-Cream Pie

Prep: 20 minutes

Bake: 40 minutes

Yield: One 9-inch pie

Level: Intermediate

Sound delicious? It sure is. To make assembling this pie easy, select freestone peaches, not clingstone, so the pits will come out easily.

Pastry for a 9-inch pie (recipe follows later in this chapter)

$^3/_4$ cup sugar

3 tablespoons all-purpose flour

5 ripe peaches, peeled and halved (pits removed)

$^3/_4$ cup heavy (whipping) cream

1 teaspoon ground cinnamon

Preheat the oven to 450°F.

Prepare the pastry for a 9-inch pie plate and line the pie plate, leaving a 1-inch overhang. Crimp the edges of the pie crust.

Combine the sugar and flour. Place half of the flour-sugar mixture in the bottom of the pie plate. Place the peach halves, cut side down, in the pie plate. Sprinkle the peaches with the remaining flour-sugar mixture. Slowly pour in the cream. Dust the top of the pie with cinnamon.

Bake the pie for 10 minutes, then lower the temperature to 350°F and bake for another 30 minutes.

Cool on a wire rack. Chill the pie when it has completely cooled. Keep refrigerated.

Kitchen Utensil

If your crust has browned but the pie has not finished baking, cover the browned crust with aluminum foil to finish baking.

Pecan Pie

Prep: 20 minutes   **Yield:** One 9-inch pie, about 8 to 10 servings

Bake: 45 minutes   **Level:** Intermediate

Pecan pie is a great Southern tradition; the pecan is actually one of the few ingredients indigenous to America (blueberries, Concord grapes, and cranberries are a few others). Make this pie to serve at your next barbecue or cookout. Be sure you purchase fresh pecans for this pie.

Pastry for a 9-inch pie (recipe follows later in this chapter)

3 large eggs, separated

$\frac{1}{2}$ cup firmly packed light brown sugar

1 teaspoon vanilla extract

1 cup light corn syrup

1 cup pecan pieces

2 tablespoons butter, softened

2 teaspoons cornstarch or flour

Preheat the oven to 350°F.

Prepare the pastry for a 9-inch pie plate and line the pie plate, leaving a 1-inch overhang. Crimp the edges of the pie crust.

In a medium-size mixing bowl, beat together the egg yolks, brown sugar, and vanilla. Add the corn syrup, pecan pieces, butter, and cornstarch.

In a separate bowl with clean, dry beaters, beat the egg whites to stiff peaks. Fold the stiffly beaten egg whites into the egg yolk mixture. Pour the mixture into the unbaked pie shell and place the pie on a baking sheet. Bake 45 minutes. Cool the pie on a wire rack before serving.

Chocolate Cream Pie

Prep: 25 minutes   **Yield:** One 9-inch pie

Bake: 15 minutes (for the pie shell)   **Level:** Challenging

Chill: 1 hour 30 minutes

The only baking this pie requires is the time it takes to prebake the crust, making this a great pie to make in the summertime when you don't want to heat up the kitchen. This pie needs to be refrigerated, so it's not a good choice for picnics.

Pastry for a 9-inch pie (recipe follows later in this chapter)	2 1-oz squares unsweetened chocolate, chopped into small pieces
$1/4$ cup cornstarch	3 large egg yolks
1 cup sugar	2 tablespoons butter
$1/4$ teaspoon salt	$1/2$ teaspoons vanilla extract
2 cups milk, at room temperature	Sweetened whipped cream (see recipe in Chapter 22)

In the top part of a double boiler, mix the cornstarch, sugar, and salt. Gradually whisk in the milk. Cook the mixture over simmering water until it thickens, stirring constantly with a whisk, about 10 minutes. Add the chopped chocolate to the thickened mixture and continue stirring until melted through, about 3 minutes.

Place the egg yolks in a small bowl and beat them slightly. Slowly add about a ladleful (about $1/4$ cup) of the hot mixture to the egg yolks. Stir the egg yolk mixture back into the hot mixture in the double boiler. Cook 5 minutes. Cool. Add the butter and vanilla and stir until the butter is melted and smooth, about 3 minutes. Pour into the cooled baked pie shell and chill until set, about $1^1/2$ hours. Top with the sweetened whipped cream.

Banana Cream Pie

Prep: 20 minutes

Bake: 20 minutes (for the pie crust)

Chill: 1¹/₂ hours

Yield: One 9-inch pie

Level: Challenging

This pie is such a treat, especially because bananas are always in season. You make the vanilla pudding for this pie, which makes it special. If you're looking for a shortcut, you can substitute instant vanilla pudding, add some sliced bananas to it, chill it in a prebaked pie crust, and top it with whipped cream.

Pastry for a 9-inch pie (recipe follows later in this chapter)

¹/₄ cup cornstarch

²/₃ cup sugar

¹/₄ teaspoon salt

2 cups milk, warmed

3 large egg yolks

2 tablespoons butter

¹/₂ teaspoons vanilla extract

3 ripe bananas, sliced

Sweetened whipped cream (see recipe in Chapter 22)

In the top part of a double boiler, mix the cornstarch, sugar, and salt. Gradually whisk in the milk. Cook the mixture over simmering water until it thickens, stirring constantly with a whisk, about 10 minutes.

In a small bowl, lightly beat the egg yolks. Slowly add a ladleful (about ¹/₄ cup) of the hot mixture to the egg yolks and mix well. Stir the egg yolks back into the milk mixture in the double boiler. Cook 5 minutes. Cool slightly, then stir in the butter and vanilla until the butter melts; then add the banana slices. Pour into the cooled baked pie shell and chill until set, about 1¹/₂ hours. Top with the sweetened whipped cream.

Tart Lemon Tart

Prep: 15 minutes   **Yield:** One 9-inch tart

Bake: 20 minutes   **Level:** Easy

You must use freshly squeezed lemon juice for this tart in order for it to be as lip-puckering good as it is. If you like lemon, you will love this tart. Remember to zest the lemon before you squeeze it for the juice.

$1^1/_4$ cups graham cracker or butter cookie crumbs

2 tablespoons butter, melted

$^1/_2$ cup (1 stick) butter

$^3/_4$ cup freshly squeezed lemon juice (about 4 lemons)

1 cup sugar

4 large eggs

1 teaspoon vanilla extract

Zest of 1 lemon

Preheat the oven to 350°F.

Combine the graham cracker crumbs and 2 tablespoons melted butter in a small bowl and mix to moisten the crumbs. Transfer the crumbs to the bottom of an 8-inch springform pan. Press evenly to cover.

In a 1-quart saucepan, combine the $^1/_2$ cup butter, lemon juice, and sugar. Cook over medium-low heat, stirring constantly, until the butter melts and mixes in with the sugar, 3 to 4 minutes. Stir in the eggs, one at a time, the vanilla, and the lemon zest. Continue stirring until the mixture just begins to thicken, 2 to 3 minutes (don't let it thicken too much; it should coat the back of a spoon). Remove the mixture from the heat and gently pour it into the prepared pan. Place the springform pan on a baking sheet. Bake 15 to 20 minutes, until just set (it will not be golden brown). Cool the tart, then refrigerate it for a few hours until ready to serve.

Wonderful Pear Tart

Prep: 10 minutes   **Yield:** One 8-inch tart

Bake: 60 minutes   **Level:** Easy

If you try just one recipe in this book, this is the one. This is my absolute favorite tart. It's incredibly easy to put together. When you press the batter into the pan it may not seem like a lot, but as it bakes it rises nicely. You don't have to have pears on hand—tart baking apples, peeled peaches, and fresh apricots (just cut them in half and pit, but don't peel the apricots) also work well. Each time I make this tart, I get rave reviews. I'll bet you will, too.

$^3/_4$ cup sugar

$^1/_2$ cup (1 stick) unsalted butter, softened

1 cup all-purpose flour

1 teaspoon baking powder

2 large eggs

2 to 3 pears, peeled, cored, and cut into $^1/_4$-inch slices

1 teaspoon ground cinnamon, or to taste

1 tablespoon sugar, or to taste

Juice of one half of a lemon

Preheat the oven to 350°F.

In a medium-size mixing bowl, cream together the sugar and butter until smooth, about 1 minute. Add the flour, baking powder, and eggs and mix well. Spoon the batter (it will be thick) into an 8-inch springform pan and spread it around evenly to cover the bottom. Arrange the slices of pear on top of the batter in a decorative fashion. Drizzle the lemon juice on top, sprinkle with the cinnamon and sugar, and bake for 1 hour. Cool the tart, then remove the springform before serving.

Grandma's Pie Crust

Prep: 20 minutes **Yield:** One or two 9-inch pie crusts

Bake: 15 minutes, if desired **Level:** Intermediate

Chill: 1 hour

Don't be intimidated by making a pie crust. Remember, just handle the dough as little as possible, let it chill for an hour, don't over-flour the board, and you'll be in good shape. This pie crust is made with shortening, so it is very flaky.

For a 1-crust pie:

1 cup all-purpose flour

$1/4$ teaspoon salt

$1/3$ cup shortening

2–4 tablespoons ice water

For a 2-crust pie:

2 cups all-purpose flour

1 teaspoon salt

$2/3$ cup shortening

3–5 tablespoons ice water

Mix together the flour and salt in a mixing bowl. Cut the shortening into the flour mixture with a pastry blender, two knives, or a fork. It should resemble small crumbs. (You can also use a food processor—just pulse together the flour and shortening a few times until it resembles crumbs or coarse meal, then transfer it to a mixing bowl to add the water.) Add the water, a tablespoon at a time, and lightly mix together with a fork until the dough forms a ball. Handle the dough as little and as lightly as possible.

Divide the dough in half. Form each half into a flattened disk and wrap tightly with plastic wrap. Chill the dough 1 hour.

To roll out a pie crust:

Begin rolling the dough with a rolling pin (dusted with flour) on a lightly floured surface from the center of the chilled dough outward (don't roll back in or push the rolling pin back and forth), lifting and turning the pastry occasionally to make sure the dough is not sticking. Also, don't press down hard when rolling out the dough— the weight of the rolling pin is all the pressure you need. Roll the dough out to $1/8$-inch thick or less; it should be at least 2 inches larger than the pie dimensions (if you have a 9-inch pie plate, the dough should be 11 inches across). If the dough rips while you're rolling it, repair it by pressing the two torn sides together. If the dough begins to stick, rub more flour into the work surface or rolling pin.

For a 1-crust pie: Fold the pie crust in half and slide it into the pie dish. Press the crust firmly into the bottom of the pie plate. Trim the crust for a 1-inch overhang. Fold and roll the extra pastry underneath, so the edge is even with the pie plate. (See Chapter 12 for more about trimming pastry edges.) Fill and bake as directed.

For a 2-crust pie: For a baked pie crust, heat the oven to 450°F and prick the bottom of the pie with a fork or place a sheet of waxed paper on the bottom of the crust and weigh the pastry down with pie weights or dried beans. Bake the crust for 12 minutes. Remove the waxed paper and pie weights and bake for 3 minutes more. Cool on a wire rack and fill.

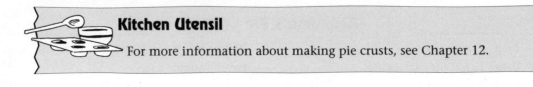

Kitchen Utensil

For more information about making pie crusts, see Chapter 12.

Kitchen Utensil

For a bit of a flavor boost, add 1 teaspoon of the spice called for in the pie to your pastry crust. If you're making an apple pie, for example, add a teaspoon of cinnamon or nutmeg to the crust.

Old-Fashioned Pie Dough

Prep: 15 minutes

Chill: 2 hours

Yield: Enough for one 8- or 9-inch, double-crust pie

Level: Intermediate

This crust uses a combination of butter and shortening for a buttery flavor and flaky crust.

2$^1/_2$ cups all-purpose flour

$^1/_2$ tablespoon sugar

1 teaspoon salt (optional)

$^1/_2$ cup (1 stick) cold unsalted butter, cut into 1-inch pieces

$^1/_2$ cup shortening, chilled and cut into 1-inch pieces

1 large egg, beaten

$^1/_4$ cup ice water

In a large bowl, using a pastry blender, combine the flour, sugar, and salt (if using). Using your fingertips or pastry blender, cut the butter and shortening into the flour mixture until it resembles coarse meal. (There will be a few larger or smaller pieces.) Combine the beaten egg and cold water in a small bowl. While stirring lightly with a fork, pour egg and water into flour mixture in a fast and steady stream. Continue stirring, occasionally cleaning off the dough that collects on the fork, until flour is almost completely mixed in, but dough does not form a ball.

Empty the dough onto a flat work surface. Lightly work in the flour completely by using the heel of your hand to press and push the dough just until it holds together, 2 or 3 times. (This is not kneading.) Shape the dough into a 6-inch disk. There should be many tiny flecks of butter visible. Wrap the dough tightly in plastic wrap or wax paper, and refrigerate it for at least 2 hours or overnight. When ready to use, divide the disk in half and roll each half into evenly rounded 13-inch circles.

Stir-and-Roll Pie Pastry

Prep: 20 minutes   **Yield:** Dough for one 8- or 9-inch pie crust

Bake: 8 minutes, if necessary   **Level:** Easy

This is another variation of a pie crust. The texture will be slightly more dense and less flaky than a traditional pie crust because you are using oil instead of butter or shortening. One advantage to this crust is that you don't have to let the dough chill before rolling it out and using it. Like all pie crusts, do not overhandle the dough.

1^1/$_2$ cups all-purpose flour ^{1}/$_3$ cup vegetable oil

^{1}/$_2$ teaspoon salt   3 tablespoons cold milk or water

Mix together the flour and salt in a medium-size bowl. Pour the oil and milk into a mixing bowl and whisk until it is frothy. Pour all of the liquid at once into the flour. Stir lightly with a fork until mixed and dough is formed. Gently press the dough together to make a ball. Roll the dough out between waxed paper. Place the dough in an 8- or 9-inch pie pan and press in the pan. Flute the edges and prick thoroughly with fork.

For a prebaked crust: Preheat the oven to 425°F. Bake the crust 8 to 10 minutes.

Kitchen Utensil

If you're cooking for someone who might be allergic to dairy products, this is a great pie crust to make, since you can substitute water for the milk and mix as directed.

Chapter 24

Cookie Monster Mania

Freshly baked cookies are always a hit, no matter what time of year. You don't even need a reason to make cookies because they are just nice to have around. You'll find a wide variety of cookies here, from the all-time favorite Oatmeal Raisin, Chocolate Chip, and Peanut Butter to the new flavors of Chocolate Toffee Bars and Apricot-Date Half-Moons.

Chocolate Drop Cookies

Prep: 15 minutes

Bake: 8 minutes per sheet

Yield: About 4 dozen cookies

Level: Easy

These little gems are little chocolate drops of cookies. To make these double chocolatey, stir in 1 cup of chocolate chips, or you can turn them into reverse chocolate chip cookies by using vanilla chips.

$1^1/_2$ cups semisweet chocolate chips

$^3/_4$ cup ($1^1/_2$ sticks) butter

$^1/_2$ cup confectioners' sugar

1 egg yolk

$1^1/_4$ cups all-purpose flour

Preheat the oven to 350°F.

Melt the chocolate chips in a double boiler placed over simmering water. Set aside.

In a large mixing bowl, beat together the butter, sugar, and egg yolk on medium speed until creamy, about 1 minute. Stir in the flour and melted chocolate. Drop the dough by the teaspoonful onto an ungreased baking sheet about 1 inch apart. Bake for 8 to 10 minutes. Let the cookies cool on the baking sheet a few minutes before transferring them to a rack to cool.

Classic Oatmeal Raisin Cookies

Prep: 15 minutes, plus 15 minutes soaking time, if desired

Yield: About 4 dozen cookies

Bake: 10 minutes per sheet

Level: Easy

These cookies are my dad's favorite. To keep the raisins plump, I like to soak them in hot water before adding them to the batter. You can start the soaking 30 minutes before you start the recipe for plump, moist raisins, if desired.

1 cup raisins

$^1\!/_2$ cup (1 stick) butter

$^1\!/_2$ cup shortening

$^3\!/_4$ cup firmly packed brown sugar

$^3\!/_4$ cup granulated sugar

2 large eggs

2 teaspoons vanilla extract

$1^1\!/_2$ cups all-purpose flour

1 teaspoon baking soda

1 teaspoon ground cinnamon

$^1\!/_2$ teaspoon salt

$^1\!/_4$ teaspoon ground cloves

3 cups rolled oats (quick-cooking or old-fashioned, but not instant)

Preheat the oven to 350°F.

Place the raisins in a small saucepan. Add enough water to cover. Bring the water to a boil over high heat. As soon as the water comes to a boil, remove from the heat and let sit 15 minutes or up to 30 minutes; drain.

In a mixing bowl, beat the butter, shortening, brown sugar, and granulated sugar together until creamy, about 1 minute. Add the eggs and vanilla and beat well, 1 minute more.

In a separate bowl, combine the flour, baking soda, cinnamon, salt, and cloves. Add the flour mixture to the butter mixture and mix to combine. Stir in the oats and the drained raisins.

Drop the cookies by rounded teaspoonfuls onto an ungreased cookie sheet with about $1^1\!/_2$ inches between each cookie. Bake 10 to 12 minutes. Remove the cookies to a wire rack to cool.

Kitchen Utensil

Jazz up ordinary oatmeal cookies by adding $^1\!/_2$ cup chocolate chips, or substitute chocolate-covered raisins in place of regular raisins. Walnuts are also a good addition; try adding a $^1\!/_2$ cup. Or you can update the classic by using dried cranberries or blueberries in place of the raisins.

Peanut Butter Cookies

Prep: 15 minutes
Bake: 12 minutes per sheet

Yield: About 4 dozen cookies
Level: Easy

Who can resist peanut butter cookies? They make such perfect dunkers in milk and seem to be a universal favorite with the younger set. If you want to go a little wild, throw in 1 cup of chocolate chips for that peanut-butter-cup flavor. For a really dense, chewy cookie, mix the batter by hand.

1 cup (2 sticks) butter, softened
1$^1/_2$ cups firmly packed light-brown sugar
$^1/_2$ cup granulated sugar
2 large eggs
1$^1/_2$ teaspoons vanilla extract

1$^1/_2$ cups peanut butter, smooth or chunky
3$^1/_4$ cups all-purpose flour
1$^1/_2$ teaspoons baking soda
$^1/_2$ teaspoon salt

Preheat the oven to 325°F.

Cream together the butter and both sugars until well blended, about 2 minutes. Add the eggs, vanilla, and peanut butter and mix well, about 2 minutes more. Add the flour, baking soda, and salt. Drop the dough by the teaspoonful onto an ungreased baking sheet about 2 inches apart. Flatten the top of the cookies with the tines of a fork, if desired. (To keep the fork from sticking to the dough, dip it in granulated sugar prior to flattening each cookie.) Bake 12 to 15 minutes. Let the cookies rest on the baking sheet a few minutes before removing to the wire rack to cool.

Crisp Sugar Cookies

Prep: 20 minutes
Bake: 10 minutes

Yield: About 4 dozen cookies
Level: Easy

Try to make the cookies all the same shape to make sure they bake evenly.

1 cup (2 sticks) butter
$^1/_2$ cup granulated sugar
$^1/_2$ cup confectioners' sugar
$^1/_2$ teaspoon baking soda
$^1/_2$ teaspoon cream of tartar

$^1/_2$ teaspoon salt
1$^1/_2$ teaspoons vanilla extract
1 large egg, beaten
2$^1/_2$ cups all-purpose flour
Granulated sugar, for dipping (start with $^1/_3$ cup)

Preheat the oven to 375°F.

Cream together the butter and both of the sugars until light and creamy, about 2 minutes. Add the baking soda, cream of tartar, salt, and vanilla and mix to blend. Add the beaten egg and the flour. Shape the dough into balls (about the size of a walnut) and place on a baking sheet about 3 inches apart. Dip the bottom of a glass into additional granulated sugar; press on each cookie until it's about $^1/_4$-inch thick. Bake 10 minutes until lightly brown. Remove the cookies to a wire rack to cool.

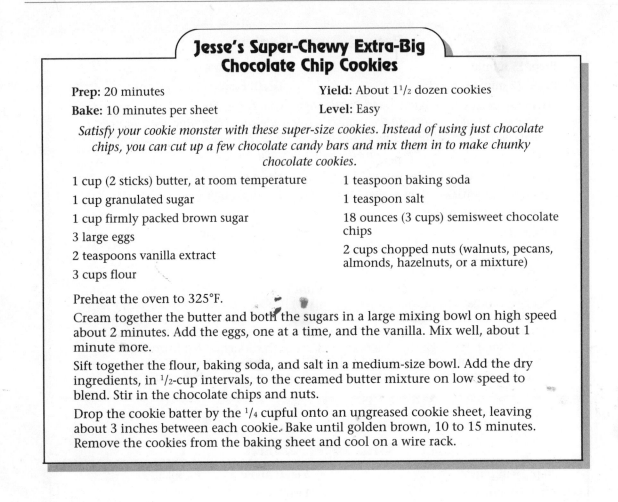

Jesse's Super-Chewy Extra-Big Chocolate Chip Cookies

Prep: 20 minutes

Bake: 10 minutes per sheet

Yield: About 1¹/₂ dozen cookies

Level: Easy

Satisfy your cookie monster with these super-size cookies. Instead of using just chocolate chips, you can cut up a few chocolate candy bars and mix them in to make chunky chocolate cookies.

1 cup (2 sticks) butter, at room temperature

1 cup granulated sugar

1 cup firmly packed brown sugar

3 large eggs

2 teaspoons vanilla extract

3 cups flour

1 teaspoon baking soda

1 teaspoon salt

18 ounces (3 cups) semisweet chocolate chips

2 cups chopped nuts (walnuts, pecans, almonds, hazelnuts, or a mixture)

Preheat the oven to 325°F.

Cream together the butter and both the sugars in a large mixing bowl on high speed about 2 minutes. Add the eggs, one at a time, and the vanilla. Mix well, about 1 minute more.

Sift together the flour, baking soda, and salt in a medium-size bowl. Add the dry ingredients, in ¹/₂-cup intervals, to the creamed butter mixture on low speed to blend. Stir in the chocolate chips and nuts.

Drop the cookie batter by the ¹/₄ cupful onto an ungreased cookie sheet, leaving about 3 inches between each cookie. Bake until golden brown, 10 to 15 minutes. Remove the cookies from the baking sheet and cool on a wire rack.

Grandma's Classic
Chocolate Chip Cookies

Prep: 15 minutes

Bake: 8 minutes per sheet

Yield: About 3 dozen cookies

Level: Easy

You can substitute mini chocolate chips, butterscotch chips, or even mint-flavored chips for the regular chocolate chips in this recipe. Just be sure to have a glass of milk handy when you eat them. If you prefer your cookies chewier and a bit flatter, use 1 stick of butter and omit the shortening.

$^1/_4$ cup ($^1/_2$ stick) butter, softened

$^1/_4$ cup shortening

$^1/_2$ cup brown sugar, firmly packed

$^1/_2$ cup granulated sugar

1 large egg

$^1/_2$ teaspoon vanilla extract

1 cup plus 2 tablespoons all-purpose flour

$^1/_2$ teaspoon salt

$^1/_2$ teaspoon baking soda

1 cup (6 ounces) semisweet chocolate chips

$^1/_2$ cup chopped walnuts (optional)

Preheat oven to 350°F.

In a large mixing bowl, cream together the butter, shortening, and both of the sugars until smooth, about 2 minutes. Add the egg and vanilla and beat 1 minute more. In a separate bowl, combine the flour, salt, and baking soda, then add to the creamed mixture and beat another minute. Stir in the chocolate chips and nuts, if using.

Drop the batter by the teaspoonful onto an ungreased cookie sheet approximately 2 inches apart. Bake about 8 to 10 minutes or until golden brown. Remove the cookies from the baking sheet and cool them on a wire rack.

Information Station

The invention of the chocolate chip cookie can be attributed to a very smart lady, Ruth Wakefield, owner of the Tollhouse Inn in Massachusetts. Story has it that in 1940, she was substituting a chopped-up chocolate bar for the nuts in the butter cookies she was making. She expected the bar to melt evenly throughout the cookie, but instead she was left with a lovely chocolate-studded cookie. A guest at the inn described the cookie to a friend at a Boston newspaper. Word got around, and soon the cookie became a local favorite. Then Nestle got involved, bought the recipe, and began marketing chocolate chips, offering Ruth's recipe on each package. And the rest, my friends, is history.

Gingersnaps

Prep: 15 minutes   **Yield:** About 5 dozen cookies

Chill: 1 hour   **Level:** Easy

Bake: 8 minutes per sheet

Not only do these cookies make a great snacking treat, but you can save a dozen or so in the freezer and use them the next time you want to make a crumb crust for a cheesecake. They'll last up to 6 months in the freezer.

1 cup sugar

$^3/_4$ cup (1$^1/_2$ sticks) butter, softened

$^1/_4$ cup molasses

1 egg

2$^1/_4$ cups all-purpose flour

1$^1/_2$ teaspoons baking soda

$^1/_4$ teaspoon salt

1 teaspoon ground cinnamon

$^1/_2$ teaspoon ground cloves

$^1/_2$ teaspoon ground ginger

$^1/_4$ teaspoon ground nutmeg

Granulated sugar, for rolling (about $^1/_2$ cup)

In a large bowl, cream together the sugar and butter on medium speed until smooth, about 1 minute. Add the molasses and egg and continue beating until light and fluffy. Stir in the flour, baking soda, salt, cinnamon, cloves, ginger, and nutmeg. Cover the bowl and chill for 1 hour.

Preheat the oven to 350°F.

Place about a half a cup of granulated sugar on a plate; add more sugar if needed. Shape the dough into 1-inch balls. Roll the balls in granulated sugar and place them on a baking sheet about 2 inches apart. Bake the cookies 8 to 10 minutes or until set. Remove the cookies from the baking sheet and cool on a wire rack.

Lemon Cookies

Prep: 15 minutes   **Yield:** 7 dozen cookies

Chill: 1 hour   **Level:** Easy

Bake: 9 minutes per sheet

Try these cookies if you are looking for something a little different. The lemon and almond flavors make a nice flavor combination.

1 cup (2 sticks) butter, softened	4 cups all-purpose flour
1/2 cup granulated sugar	1/2 teaspoon baking soda
1/2 cup firmly packed light brown sugar	1 tablespoon grated lemon peel
3 tablespoons fresh lemon juice	1/2 cup finely chopped almonds
1 large egg	

In a large mixing bowl, with an electric mixer on medium speed, cream together the butter and both of the sugars, about 2 minutes. Add the lemon juice and egg and beat well. Sift the flour and baking soda together and add to the butter mixture, mixing well. Add the lemon peel and nuts and mix until well blended. Shape into four logs, each 2 inches in diameter, and wrap tightly in plastic wrap. Chill until firm, about 1 hour or overnight.

Preheat the oven to 375°F. Cut the dough into 1/8-inch slices and place them about 1 inch apart on a cookie sheet. Bake for 9 minutes or until lightly browned. Cool the cookies on a wire rack.

Chocolate-Mint Surprises

Prep: 20 minutes

Chill: 2 hours

Bake: 10 minutes

Yield: About 3 dozen cookies

Level: Intermediate

My grandmother passed on this recipe, which used to be a staple at Christmastime before the company that made large mint-flavored chocolate drops went out of business. I found undecorated milk-chocolate praline drops and gave the cookies the hint of mint by adding mint extract to the batter. If you can't find undecorated praline chocolate drops, you can use 5 or 6 chocolate chips in place of each drop. The dough is very soft, so you might want to make up all the cookies and keep them in the refrigerator while each batch bakes.

1 cup (2 sticks) butter, at room temperature

1 cup granulated sugar

1/2 cup lightly packed light brown sugar

2 large eggs, lightly beaten

2 tablespoons water

1 teaspoon vanilla extract

1 teaspoon mint extract

3 cups all-purpose flour

1 teaspoon baking soda

1/2 teaspoon salt

About 36 large undecorated chocolate praline drops

Cream together the butter and both of the sugars until light and fluffy, about 2 minutes. Add the eggs, water, vanilla, and mint extract. Add the flour, baking soda, and salt and mix until blended. Cover the dough and refrigerate at least 2 hours or overnight.

Preheat the oven to 375°F. Grease a baking sheet with shortening.

Pinch off a generous teaspoon of dough and enclose a chocolate praline drop in the dough. Place the cookies on the prepared baking sheet, about 2 inches apart. Bake 10 to 12 minutes or until golden brown. Remove the cookies from the baking sheet to a wire rack to cool.

Agnes's Chocolate Toffee Bars

Prep: 20 minutes

Bake: 25 minutes

Yield: 16 2^1/$_2$-inch bars

Level: Intermediate

When I was a child, it was not Christmastime at my grandparent's house unless these bars filled up at least one of the large cookie jars. They are wonderful. You can also top these bars with shredded coconut, if you like.

1 cup (2 sticks) butter, at room temperature

1 cup brown sugar, firmly packed

2 cups all-purpose flour

^{1}/$_4$ teaspoon salt

1 teaspoon vanilla extract

1 large egg

1 12-ounce bag of semisweet chocolate chips (2 cups)

^{1}/$_2$ cup walnuts or pecans, finely chopped

Preheat the oven to 350°F.

Cream together the butter and sugar on medium-high speed until light and fluffy, about 3 minutes. Add the flour, salt, vanilla, and egg and mix together until thoroughly blended.

Press the batter into a 9 × 11-inch baking pan. Bake for 25 minutes.

While the bars are baking, place the chocolate chips in the top of a double boiler placed over simmering water for about 7 minutes, stirring occasionally, until melted and smooth.

When the bars are finished baking, spread the melted chocolate over the hot bars. Sprinkle with the chopped nuts. Let the bars cool slightly, but cut them while they are still warm.

Anisette Biscotti

Prep: 25 minutes   **Yield:** About 40 biscotti

Bake: 60 minutes   **Level:** Intermediate

These cookies are easy to make and so satisfying, with their distinctive flavor of black licorice. The logs get a bit wider and flatter as they bake, so compensate for this by making them a little more narrow before they go into the oven. Waxed paper might smoke or steam a little bit in the oven, but overall it will be fine.

3 large eggs

1 cup granulated sugar

$^1/_2$ cup (1 stick) unsalted butter, melted

2 teaspoons anise extract

3 cups all-purpose flour

$^1/_4$ teaspoon salt

1 tablespoon baking powder

Preheat the oven to 350°F. Line a baking sheet with waxed paper or parchment paper.

Beat the eggs on high speed about 2 minutes, until light and frothy. Keep the mixer on high speed and slowly add the sugar, $^1/_4$ cup at a time, and drizzle in the melted butter. Add the anise extract and mix well.

Reduce the speed to low and add the flour, salt, and baking powder and mix just until blended (the dough will be soft and a little glossy from the melted butter). Divide the dough in half and form each half into a log about 10 to 12 inches long, 2 to 3 inches high in the middle (they will flatten when they bake). If the dough seems sticky, lightly dust your hands with flour. Place the logs on the baking sheet. They should fit side by side. Bake 30 minutes, until firm but not hard.

Reduce the oven temperature to 300°F.

Let the logs cool 20 to 30 minutes before slicing them on the diagonal into half-inch slices. Return the slices to the baking sheet (you will need two sheets for all the slices) and return to the oven for 30 more minutes, or until they are dry and crispy.

Note: the biscotti will bake all the way through the first time, so you don't have to rebake it if you don't want to. It is a lovely, tender cookie baked just once.

Apricot-Date Half-Moons

Prep: 15 minutes to make; 20 minutes to fill **Yield:** About 2¹/₂ dozen cookies
Chill: 2 hours **Level:** Intermediate
Bake: 12 minutes

If you have never tried a filled cookie, this is a good place to start and quite delicious.

For the pastry:
¹/₃ cup confectioners' sugar
³/₄ cup (1¹/₂ sticks) unsalted butter, softened
³/₄ cup small-curd cottage cheese
1 teaspoon vanilla extract
1 teaspoon grated lemon peel
1³/₄ cups all-purpose flour
Pinch of salt

For the filling:
¹/₂ cup chopped dates
¹/₂ cup chopped dried apricots
¹/₄ cup sugar
2 tablespoons water
2 tablespoons brandy
1 teaspoon vanilla extract
1 large egg, beaten (optional)

In a large mixing bowl, cream together the sugar, butter, and cottage cheese (it will not get completely smooth like just butter and sugar would), about 2 minutes. Add the vanilla and lemon peel. Add the flour and salt and continue mixing until the dough just comes together. Gather the dough into a ball and chill for 2 hours.

Once the dough is almost finished chilling, combine all of the filling ingredients except the vanilla and egg in a small saucepan and cook, stirring frequently, over low heat until thickened, about 3 minutes. Transfer to the bowl of a food processor and pulse several times to blend (it will be thick and sticky). Stir in the vanilla.

Preheat the oven to 375°F. Cut the dough ball in half and roll out one half to about ¹/₈-inch thickness on a lightly floured surface. Using a drinking glass or a cookie cutter, cut out 2-inch round circles. Place about ¹/₂ teaspoon of the filling in the center of the dough, fold it in half, and pinch closed. Repeat with the remaining dough. Brush each half-circle with the beaten egg, if desired.

Bake 12 to 15 minutes, until lightly golden brown. Remove to a wire rack to cool.

Kitchen Utensil

For the filling, you can double the amount of apricots and omit the dates, if you like, or get wild and substitute some dried cranberries, blueberries, or even raisins.

Grandma's Buttery Knots

Prep: 15 minutes

Chill: 1 hour

Bake: 8 minutes each sheet

Yield: About 4 dozen cookies

Level: Intermediate

You can press little bits of red candied cherries for holly berries and add little jagged "leaves" cut out of green citron, if you feel like dressing these cookies up for the holidays. My grandmother just uses red and green sugars because "the kids didn't like citron." I think the sugars are a little easier to use, anyway. If you find the dough too sticky when you're rolling out the knots, very lightly dip your fingers in flour. Do not use too much. Moisten your fingers and dip them in the sugar, then press the sugar onto the knot and it will stick much easier.

$^3/_4$ cup (1$^1/_2$ sticks) butter, softened

$^3/_4$ cup shortening

1 cup sugar

2 teaspoons grated orange peel

2 large eggs

1 teaspoon vanilla extract

4 cups all-purpose flour

Red and green decorating sugar, if desired

Cream together the butter, shortening, and sugar in a medium-size mixing bowl on medium-high speed for about 2 minutes. Add the orange peel, eggs, and vanilla. Mix well for 1 minute. Stir in the flour.

Cover the dough and chill for at least 1 hour or overnight.

Preheat the oven to 400°F.

Break off about a teaspoon of dough and roll it out to the size of a pencil, about 6 inches long and $^1/_4$-inch thick. Form each piece into a circle, bringing one end over the other. Place on an ungreased baking sheet. Sprinkle a pinch of red or green sugar on the knot, if desired. Bake 8 to 10 minutes, until set, but not browned. Transfer to a wire rack to cool.

Granola Bars

Prep: 25 minutes   **Yield:** 24 granola bars
Bake: 15 minutes   **Level:** Intermediate

These come from my friend, Jesse, who likes her granola bars crunchy like the kind you buy in the grocery store. She warns, though, that the crispier they get, the easier they fall apart. But that's okay; these bars are great bite-size too.

$1^1/_2$ cups rolled oats (not instant)
1 cup all-purpose flour
$^1/_2$ cup flaked sweetened coconut
$^1/_2$ cup raisins
1 cup assorted chopped nuts (peanuts, pistachios, hazelnuts, walnuts, sunflower seeds)

$^1/_2$ teaspoon salt (omit if using salted nuts)
2 tablespoons ground cinnamon
$^1/_2$ cup (1 stick) butter or vegetable oil
$^1/_2$ cup light corn syrup
$^1/_4$ cup honey
1 tablespoon vanilla extract

Preheat the oven to 350°F.

In a large bowl, combine the oats, flour, coconut, raisins, nuts, salt (if using), and cinnamon. Set aside. In a small saucepan, combine the butter, corn syrup, honey, and vanilla and cook over low heat until the butter is melted. Pour the butter mixture over the oat mixture and stir until well combined.

Press the mixture into a 9 × 13 baking pan. If the mixture is sticking to your hands, wet them a little. Bake for 15 to 20 minutes, until lightly brown. Watch that they do not burn. Let the bars cool completely before slicing into $1^1/_2$ inch bars.

Lib's Pecan Delights

Prep: 15 minutes   **Yield:** About 18 cookies
Bake: 30 minutes   **Level:** Intermediate

My Aunt Lib claims everyone will want a copy of the recipe when you make these. It's very easy to put together. Remember to separate the egg carefully. Even a drop of egg yolk will prevent your whites from whipping up to their fullest volume. You can easily make this recipe using an electric mixer or a hand-held egg beater.

1 large egg white $1^1/_2$ cups pecans, coarsely chopped
$^3/_4$ cup light brown sugar, lightly packed

Preheat the oven to 250°F. Line a greased baking sheet with waxed paper. Grease the waxed paper.

Beat the egg white to soft peaks. Add the sugar, two tablespoons at a time, and continue beating to incorporate the sugar. Gently fold in the pecans.

Drop the batter by teaspoonfuls onto the cookie sheet about an inch apart. Bake for 30 minutes. Turn the oven off and let the cookies cool in the oven. Then remove and transfer the cookies onto a serving plate.

Poppyseed Thumbprints

Prep: 25 minutes
Bake: 20 minutes per sheet

Yield: About 30 cookies
Level: Easy

Here's a twist on the classic—poppyseeds add a great flavor to this cookie. I suggest using raspberry jam, but you can use whatever flavor you like.

1 cup confectioners' sugar
1 cup (2 sticks) butter, softened
1 large egg
1 teaspoon vanilla extract

2 cups all-purpose flour
3 tablespoons poppyseeds
$^1/_2$ teaspoon salt
$^1/_2$ to $^2/_3$ cup raspberry preserves

Preheat the oven to 300°F.

In a large mixing bowl, beat together the sugar and butter until light and fluffy, about 1 minute. Mix in the egg and vanilla, about 2 minutes more. Stir in the flour, poppyseeds, and salt. Drop the batter by the teaspoonful about 2 inches apart onto a baking sheet. Gently press your thumb in the center of the dough to form a depression (do not press all the way through to the baking sheet). Fill each cookie with about $^1/_2$ teaspoon of preserves. Bake the cookies about 20 minutes or until the edges of the cookies turn lightly brown. Remove the cookies from the baking sheet to wire racks to cool.

Russian Tea Balls

Prep: 20 minutes
Bake: 10 minutes

Yield: 4 dozen cookies
Level: Easy

These tea balls are also known as Mexican Wedding Cakes. Don't crank up the speed of the mixer too quickly or a big puff of confectioners' sugar will go flying.

1 cup (2 sticks) butter, softened
$^1/_2$ cup confectioners' sugar
1 teaspoon vanilla extract

$2^1/_4$ cups all-purpose flour
$^1/_2$ teaspoon salt
$^3/_4$ cup finely chopped walnuts
Additional confectioners' sugar, for rolling (about $1^1/_2$ cups)

Preheat the oven to 400°F.

In a large mixing bowl, beat together the butter, confectioners' sugar, and vanilla. Stir in the flour, salt, and chopped nuts, and mix thoroughly. Roll into 1-inch balls and place on an ungreased baking sheet. Bake about 10 minutes, until set but not brown. While the cookies are still warm, roll them in additional confectioners' sugar; cool on wire racks. Roll in powdered sugar again.

The Ultimate Brownie

Prep: 20 minutes

Bake: 30 minutes

Yield: 16 brownies

Level: Easy

These brownies are from my grandmother's file. She found this recipe in California more than 40 years ago. They are gooey and simply delicious. She likes to add raisins when she adds the nuts and that is just how I like them, too.

$^1/_2$ cup (1 stick) butter	$^1/_2$ cup all-purpose flour
2 ounces (2 squares) unsweetened chocolate	1 teaspoon baking powder
1 cup sugar	1 teaspoon vanilla extract
1 cup chopped pecans	2 large eggs
$^1/_2$ cup raisins (optional)	

Preheat the oven to 350°F. Grease an 8-inch square glass baking pan.

Melt the chocolate and the butter in a small saucepan, stirring constantly, over very low heat. Transfer the melted chocolate to a medium-size mixing bowl and add the sugar, pecans, raisins (if using), flour, baking powder, and vanilla. Stir well. Mix in the eggs, stirring to blend thoroughly.

Spread the batter evenly into the prepared pan. Bake about 30 minutes, until a wooden toothpick inserted into the center comes out clean. Set the pan on a wire rack and allow the brownies to cool in the pan before slicing them into 2-inch squares.

Kitchen Utensil

Finding that cookie dough sticks to your hands? Wet your hands with cold water before handling the dough and you will find they won't get as sticky.

Black and White Brownies

Prep: 20 minutes

Bake: 40 minutes

For the brownie:

$1^1/_2$ cups (9 ounces) semisweet chocolate chips

$^1/_2$ cup sugar

$^1/_4$ cup ($^1/_2$ stick) butter, softened

2 large eggs

1 teaspoon vanilla extract

$^1/_2$ teaspoon salt

$^2/_3$ cup all-purpose flour

Yield: 16 $2^1/_4$-inch brownies

Level: Intermediate

For the cream cheese topping:

1 8-ounce package cream cheese

$^1/_2$ cup sugar

2 tablespoons butter, softened

2 large eggs

2 tablespoons milk

1 tablespoon all-purpose flour

$^1/_2$ teaspoon vanilla extract

$^3/_4$ cup (4 ounces) semisweet chocolate chips

Preheat the oven to 350°F. Grease and flour a 9-inch square baking pan.

Prepare the brownie: Melt $1^1/_2$ cups chocolate chips in a double boiler placed over simmering water. Set aside.

In a large mixing bowl, beat together the sugar and butter until creamy, about 2 minutes. Add the eggs, vanilla, and salt; mix until smooth, about 1 minute. Mix in the flour and then the melted chocolate. Pour the batter evenly into the prepared baking pan.

Prepare the cream cheese topping: In a large bowl, mix together the cream cheese, sugar, and butter until creamy, about 1 minute. Add the eggs, milk, flour, and vanilla; mix to combine. Gently stir in the chocolate chips. Carefully pour the cream cheese topping over the brownie base. Bake for 40 to 45 minutes. Set the pan on a wire rack and cool the brownies completely in the pan before cutting.

Lemon Bars

Prep: 20 minutes   **Yield:** About 24 two-inch squares

Bake: 40 minutes   **Level:** Easy

Remember to grate the peel from the lemons before you cut them in half to juice them.

$2^1/_4$ cups all-purpose flour   2 cups granulated sugar

1 cup (2 sticks) butter, softened   1 teaspoon baking powder

$^1/_2$ cup confectioners' sugar   Grated rind and juice from 3 large lemons

4 eggs, lightly beaten

Preheat the oven to 350°F.

Mix together 2 cups of the flour, the butter, and the confectioners' sugar. Pat the mixture into the bottom of a 13 × 9-inch baking pan. Bake the crust 20 minutes.

While the crust is baking, beat together the eggs, the remaining $^1/_4$ cup flour, granulated sugar, baking powder, and lemon peel and juice. Remove the crust from the oven and pour this mixture over the baked crust. Return the pan to the oven and bake 20 to 25 minutes more, until set. Cool the bars in the pan on a wire rack. Cut them when they have cooled. Garnish with additional confectioners' sugar, if desired.

Kitchen Utensil

If you have a food processor, you can use it to make the crust for these bars. Cut the butter into small pieces and combine the flour, butter, and confectioners' sugar in the bowl of a food processor fitted with a metal blade. Pulse (short on and off bursts) about eight times until the mixture is a bit crumbly and mixed together. Then press the mixture into the pan.

Chapter 25

Quick Breads and Muffins

Quick breads and muffins are great for beginner bakers because they are easy to throw together, don't take very long to bake, and taste so good. They get their leavening from baking soda or baking powder, not from yeast, which makes them "quick" since they need no rising time. Mornings are brighter with hot, homemade muffins, fresh from the oven. Or make a loaf of banana bread for coffee break. These recipes are sure to be a hit and become some of your favorites.

Amish Dutch Applesauce Bread

Prep: 15 minutes
Bake: 50 minutes

Yield: One loaf
Level: Easy

Look for an all-natural or homemade variety of applesauce for this bread. It really makes a difference in taste.

2 cups all-purpose flour

1 teaspoon baking powder

1 teaspoon salt

1 teaspoon baking soda

1 teaspoon ground cinnamon

$^1/_2$ teaspoon ground nutmeg

$^1/_2$ cup (1 stick) butter, softened

$^3/_4$ cup sugar

2 large eggs

1 teaspoon vanilla extract

1 cup applesauce

$^1/_2$ cup walnuts, chopped, if desired

Preheat the oven to 350°F. Grease a 9 × 5 loaf pan.

In a medium-size bowl, sift together the flour, baking powder, salt, baking soda, cinnamon, and nutmeg.

In a separate mixing bowl, cream together the butter and sugar. Beat in the eggs and vanilla. Gradually add the dry ingredients to the creamed butter. Stir in the applesauce and walnuts (if using), mixing just enough to blend all ingredients. Pour the batter into the prepared pan. Let the batter rest for 15 minutes, then bake for 55 minutes to 1 hour, until a toothpick inserted into the center comes out clean. Cool the loaf on a wire rack 10 minutes before removing from the pan to finish cooling.

Banana Bread

Prep: 20 minutes   **Yield:** One loaf

Bake: 55 minutes   **Level:** Easy

This is a great recipe to use when you want to use up over-ripe bananas. Don't use under-ripe bananas for this recipe. The mushier and more ripe the banana, the better, for a great banana flavor.

$1^1/_4$ cups sugar	$^1/_2$ teaspoon salt
$^1/_2$ cup vegetable oil	$^1/_4$ teaspoon baking soda
2 large eggs	3 medium, ripe bananas, mashed
1 teaspoon vanilla extract	$^1/_2$ cup brewed coffee, warm or cold
$2^3/_4$ cups all-purpose flour	$^1/_2$ cup buttermilk
2 teaspoons baking powder	1 cup chopped walnuts

Preheat the oven to 350°F. Grease just the bottom of a 9 × 5-inch loaf pan.

In a large bowl, beat together the sugar, oil, eggs, and vanilla until light and creamy, about 2 minutes. Add the flour, baking powder, salt, and baking soda and stir together just to moisten the flour. Combine the bananas, coffee, and buttermilk together in a separate bowl and stir into the batter. Fold in the nuts.

Pour the batter into the prepared loaf pan. Bake 55 minutes, or until a wooden toothpick inserted into the middle of the loaf comes out clean. Remove from the pan and cool on a wire rack.

Blueberry Muffins

Prep: 15 minutes   **Yield:** 24 muffins
Bake: 20 minutes   **Level:** Easy

This recipe comes from my grandmother's sister, Liz. She used it when she was a pastry chef in a little cafe. I modified it a bit to make these muffins very easy to put together. You only need one bowl and a spoon for mixing. Remember, mix the ingredients until just blended for great-looking muffins.

2 cups all-purpose flour

2 teaspoons baking powder

1 cup sugar

$^1/_2$ cup (1 stick) butter, melted

$^1/_2$ cup milk

1 teaspoon vanilla extract

2 large eggs, lightly beaten

$2^1/_2$ cups blueberries, fresh or frozen (not packed in syrup)

Preheat the oven to 400°F. Grease two 12-cup muffin pans or line them with paper liners.

In a small bowl, combine the flour and baking powder; set aside. In a large mixing bowl, combine the sugar, butter, milk, vanilla, and eggs. Mix to combine. Slowly add the flour mixture to the sugar mixture and stir just to moisten the dry ingredients. Fold in the blueberries just to combine. Do not overmix.

Fill the muffin cups $^3/_4$ full of batter. Bake (both pans side by side is okay) for 20 minutes or until golden brown. A wooden toothpick inserted into the center of the muffins will come out clean. Let the muffins rest 5 minutes on the cooling rack before removing them from the pan.

Kitchen Utensil

If you have greased all of your muffin cups and then find your batter does not fill all of them, pour a few tablespoons of water into the greased empty cups to prevent them from burning while you bake. Just remember, when it's time to remove the muffins from the pan, don't invert the pan to release them or the water will spill out, too!

Lemon Poppyseed Muffins

Prep: 10 minutes   **Yield:** 12 muffins
Bake: 15 minutes   **Level:** Easy

Remember not to overmix the batter. Just make sure the dry and wet ingredients combine and that should do it.

$^1/_3$ cup buttermilk

$^1/_4$ cup vegetable oil

1 large egg, lightly beaten

$^2/_3$ cup sour cream

2 tablespoons fresh lemon juice

1 teaspoon lemon extract

$1^3/_4$ cup all-purpose flour

$^1/_4$ cup poppy seeds

1 tablespoon grated lemon peel

$2^1/_2$ teaspoons baking powder

$^1/_2$ teaspoon baking soda

$^1/_2$ teaspoon salt

Preheat the oven to 400°F. Grease or line 12 muffin cups.

In a large mixing bowl, combine the buttermilk, oil, egg, sour cream, lemon juice, and lemon extract. Add the remaining ingredients and mix with a spoon just until moistened. Fill the muffin cups about $^3/_4$ full. Bake about 15 minutes, or until a toothpick inserted into the center comes out clean. Remove from the pans and cool the muffins on a wire rack.

Kitchen Informant

The *zest* of a lemon is the outer yellow skin. Avoid the bitter white *pith* underneath.

Corn Muffins

Prep: 10 minutes   **Yield:** 12 muffins
Bake: 15 minutes   **Level:** Easy

These are great for a picnic or to serve with a piping hot bowl of chili.

1 cup milk

$^1/_3$ cup vegetable oil

2 large eggs

$1^1/_4$ cup cornmeal

$1^1/_4$ cups all-purpose flour

3 tablespoons brown sugar

$1^1/_2$ teaspoons baking powder

$^3/_4$ teaspoon salt

$1^1/_2$ cups corn kernels, frozen or canned (drain if canned)

Preheat the oven to 400°F. Grease or line 12 muffin cups.

In a large bowl, beat together the milk, oil, and eggs with a wire whisk. Stir in the cornmeal, flour, brown sugar, baking powder, and salt until dry ingredients are just moistened. Fold in the corn kernels. Divide the batter evenly among the muffin cups—they should only be $^3/_4$ of the way full. Bake the muffins 15 to 20 minutes, until a wooden toothpick inserted into the center comes out clean. Remove the muffins from the pan and cool on a wire rack.

Boston Brown Bread

Prep: 15 minutes   **Yield:** Two loaves
Bake: 1 hour   **Level:** Easy

The whole-wheat flour, cornmeal, and dark molasses make this a rich, satisfying bread.
Stir in 1 cup of raisins or walnuts (when you add the flour) to add to its flavor.

$^1/_2$ cup all-purpose flour

$^3/_4$ cup sugar

$1^1/_2$ teaspoons baking soda

$1^1/_2$ teaspoons salt

$^1/_2$ cup cornmeal

2 cups whole-wheat flour

1 cup all-purpose flour

$^3/_4$ cup dark molasses

1 large egg, lightly beaten

2 cups milk

$^1/_2$ cup (1 stick) butter, melted

1 teaspoon vanilla extract

Preheat the oven to 325°F. Grease two 9 × 5-inch loaf pans.

Sift together $^1/_2$ cup all-purpose flour, sugar, baking soda, and salt into a large mixing bowl. Stir in the cornmeal and whole-wheat flour. Add the remaining ingredients, mixing only until all the flour is moistened. Pour into the prepared pans. Bake for 1 hour or until a toothpick inserted in the center of the loaf comes out clean. Remove the bread from pans and cool on a wire rack.

Southern Cornbread

Prep: 10 minutes   **Yield:** One 8- or 9-inch cornbread

Bake: 20 minutes   **Level:** Easy

Down South, they preheat the pan the cornbread goes into. If you have a 8- or 9-inch cast-iron skillet, by all means break it out for this recipe. If you can only find coarsely ground cornmeal, you can use 1 cup of all-purpose flour and 1 cup of cornmeal in place of the finely ground cornmeal.

2 tablespoons butter or vegetable oil	1¹/₂ teaspoons salt
2 cups finely ground cornmeal	1¹/₂ cups buttermilk
4 teaspoons baking powder	1 large egg, lightly beaten

Preheat the oven to 450°F. Place the butter or vegetable oil in the bottom of a 10-inch cast iron skillet or a 8- or 9-inch square baking pan and place it in the oven while it heats for about 3 minutes (if you are using butter, keep an eye on it to make sure it does not burn).

In a large bowl, combine the cornmeal, baking powder, and salt. Mix together the buttermilk and egg and add it to the cornmeal mixture. Stir just to combine; do not overmix.

Pour the batter into the preheated skillet or pan and bake about 20 minutes, until a knife inserted into the center comes out clean. Cool the cornbread in the skillet 20 minutes before serving.

Cranberry-Orange Bread

Prep: 15 minutes   **Yield:** One loaf

Bake: 60 minutes   **Level:** Easy

Fresh cranberries usually appear in our market from late October through December. These tart berries keep very well in the freezer, so stock up when they are in season and you'll always have some on hand to make this moist, tasty bread.

2 cups all-purpose flour	$1/4$ teaspoon salt
1 cup coarsely chopped fresh cranberries	1 large egg
$3/4$ cup sugar	1 teaspoon grated orange zest (peel)
$1/2$ cup coarsely chopped pecans or walnuts	$1/2$ cup orange juice
2 teaspoons baking powder	$1/2$ cup vegetable oil

Preheat the oven to 350°F. Grease and flour a 9 × 5-inch loaf pan.

In a large bowl, mix together the flour, cranberries, sugar, nuts, baking powder, and salt. In a small bowl, mix together the egg, orange zest, orange juice, and oil. Stir the wet ingredients into the dry ingredients and mix until just blended. Pour the batter into the prepared pan and bake for 60 minutes, or until a toothpick inserted into the center of the loaf comes out clean. Cool the loaf for 15 minutes before removing it from the pan, then finish cooling the loaf on a wire rack.

Kitchen Utensil

The easiest way to chop cranberries is to place them in the bowl of a food processor and give them a few pulses, no more than three or four. You can use the same technique for the nuts.

Crumbcake

Prep: 20 minutes

Bake: 45 minutes

Yield: 24 2-inch squares

Level: Easy

Looking for an easy recipe to share with others? This is always a crowd pleaser, especially on Mondays.

For the topping:

1 tablespoon all-purpose flour

$^1/_2$ cup firmly packed brown sugar

2 tablespoons butter, cut into four pieces, softened

$^1/_2$ cup chopped walnuts or pecans

1 teaspoon ground cinnamon

$^1/_2$ teaspoon ground nutmeg

For the cake:

$^1/_2$ cup (1 stick) butter, softened

1 cup sugar

1 teaspoon vanilla extract

3 large eggs

2 cups all-purpose flour

1 teaspoon baking powder

1 teaspoon baking soda

$^1/_2$ teaspoon salt

1 teaspoon ground allspice

1 cup sour cream or plain yogurt

Preheat the oven to 350°F. Grease a 13 × 9-inch baking pan.

Prepare the topping: In a small bowl, combine all of the ingredients. Mix well and set aside.

Prepare the cake: In a large mixing bowl, cream together the butter, sugar, and vanilla until light and fluffy, about 1 minute. Add the eggs, one at a time, and mix well after each addition. Sift together the flour, baking powder, baking soda, salt, and allspice and add to the butter mixture. Mix in the sour cream. Pour the batter into the prepared pan. Sprinkle the top of the batter evenly with the topping. Bake 45 minutes or until a toothpick inserted into the center of the cake comes out clean. Cool in the pan set on a wire rack and then cut into 2-inch squares.

Kitchen Utensil

Try folding 1 cup of fresh blueberries into the batter before you pour it into the pan.

Sweet Chocolate-Chip Pull-Apart Bread

Prep: 20 minutes   **Yield:** 16 balls

Bake: 30 minutes   **Level:** Easy

Some people call this monkey bread. I find it a lot of fun to make and to eat, and who can resist the goodness of chocolate?

2 cups all-purpose flour	1 cup semisweet chocolate chips
$3/4$ cup sugar	$2/3$ cup milk
1 tablespoon baking powder	3 tablespoons melted butter
$1/2$ teaspoon salt	$1^1/_2$ teaspoons ground cinnamon
5 tablespoons cold butter, cut into 5 pieces	

Preheat the oven to 350°F. Grease an 8-inch-square baking pan.

In a mixing bowl or in a food processor, combine the flour, $1/2$ cup of the sugar, baking powder, and salt. Using a pastry blender or a few pulses of the food processor, cut the cold butter into the flour mixture until the mixture resembles coarse meal. Stir in the chocolate chips and milk to combine. Divide the dough into 16 balls and place in the prepared baking pan (the balls will touch). Combine the remaining $1/4$ cup sugar and the cinnamon. Drizzle the balls with the melted butter and sprinkle them with the cinnamon-sugar mixture. Bake for 30 minutes, until light brown and a toothpick inserted into the center comes out clean. Cool in the pan set on a wire rack before removing from the pan.

Jesse's Raisin Buttermilk Scones

Prep: 20 minutes   **Yield:** 6 to 8 servings
Bake: 20 minutes   **Level:** Intermediate

Scones are a cross between a dry, flaky biscuit and a flavorful, moister muffin. They go well with a cup of tea or coffee. Don't worry if the dough seems dry and crumbly. If you have a food processor, by all means use it. Dump all the dry ingredients into the work bowl, then add the cold butter and pulse several times until it looks like coarse meal. Transfer the butter/flour mixture into a bowl and finish as directed.

2 cups all-purpose flour	$3/4$ cup buttermilk
$1/3$ cup granulated sugar	1 large egg, beaten
$1^1/_2$ teaspoons baking powder	$1^1/_2$ teaspoons vanilla extract
$1/2$ teaspoon baking soda	1 teaspoon ground cinnamon
$1/4$ teaspoon salt	$1/2$ teaspoon ground nutmeg
6 tablespoons cold butter, cut into 6 pieces	$2/3$ cup raisins

Preheat the oven to 350°F. Grease a baking sheet.

In a medium-size mixing bowl, mix together the flour, sugar, baking powder, baking soda, and salt. Using a pastry blender or two knives, cut the butter into the flour so it looks like coarse meal or big crumbs.

In a small bowl, mix together the buttermilk, egg, vanilla, cinnamon, and nutmeg. Stir into the flour mixture and mix until just blended. Stir in the raisins. Gather the dough into a ball and transfer the ball to the prepared baking sheet. Pat the dough out into an 8-inch circle, about 1 inch thick. With a knife, cut the circle into 6 to 8 wedges (do not separate the wedges). Bake about 20 minutes, until light brown and a wooden toothpick inserted into the center comes out clean. Cool the scones on the baking sheet set on a wire rack. When they have cooled, re-cut the wedges, if necessary.

Kitchen Utensil

If you want to be fancy, you can soak the raisins in $1/2$ cup brandy, bourbon, or rum, plus additional water to cover, for about 30 minutes. Drain and proceed with the recipe.

Buttermilk Biscuits

Prep: 15 minutes   **Yield:** About 16 biscuits
Bake: 10 minutes   **Level:** Easy

Remember, the secret to good biscuits is to barely handle the dough. Lightly cut in the flour and butter, gently stir in the buttermilk, pat it out, and that should be just about all you need to do. If you can get White Lily brand flour (which is a softer, southern flour), use it instead of all-purpose flour to make super light, flaky biscuits.

2 cups all-purpose flour

$^1/_4$ teaspoon baking soda

1 tablespoon baking powder

1 teaspoon salt

Pinch of sugar

6 tablespoons cold butter, cut into 6 pieces

$^3/_4$ cup buttermilk

Preheat the oven to 425°F.

Sift together the flour, baking soda, baking powder, salt, and sugar into a large mixing bowl. Cut in the butter with a pastry blender until the texture resembles coarse meal. Add the buttermilk and mix until just moistened.

Pat out the dough onto a lightly floured surface until it is about $^1/_2$-inch thick. Cut the dough into 2-inch circles (use a drinking glass or cookie cutter). Gather up the scraps and pat them out again. Bake on an ungreased baking sheet until just barely light brown, 10 to 12 minutes. Serve hot.

Kitchen Informant

Cutting-in is a mixing method in which solid fat is incorporated into dry ingredients, resulting in a coarse texture. You can use a pastry blender, a fork, two butter knives, a few pulses in the food processor, or the very tips of your fingers.

Chapter 26

Yeast Breads

Yeast breads are some of the most satisfying foods you can bake. There are few things so welcoming as a home filled with the aroma of freshly baking bread. Yeast breads do require a time commitment—usually a few hours need to be put aside to allow for the rising and baking.

A few tips for great bread: Don't let the temperature of the water rise above 115°F or it will kill the yeast, knead the bread until it is smooth and elastic (at least 10 minutes), and leave it in a warm place to rise. Try your hand at some of the delicious breads in this section, and you'll find how satisfying and agreeable bread making can be.

Basic White Buttermilk Bread

Prep: 25 minutes

Rise: 1 hour 30 minutes

Bake: 35 minutes

Yield: Two loaves

Level: Intermediate

If you don't have buttermilk on hand, you can substitute whole milk.

$^1/_4$ cup warm water (no hotter than 115°F)

1 package active dry yeast or 1 scant tablespoon

2 tablespoons sugar

$^1/_4$ cup ($^1/_2$ stick) butter, melted, cooled to lukewarm

2 cups buttermilk, at room temperature

5 to 6 cups all-purpose or bread flour

1 teaspoon salt

$^1/_4$ teaspoon baking soda

In a large mixing bowl, combine the warm water, yeast, and sugar. Stir with a whisk to dissolve the yeast. Add the melted butter to the buttermilk and mix it into the yeast mixture. In a large bowl, mix together 5 cups of the flour, the salt, and the baking soda, then mix it into the yeast mixture to form a dough (mix by hand or with an electric stand mixer fitted with a dough hook). Knead the dough on a lightly floured surface until smooth and elastic, about 10 minutes.

Place the dough in a buttered bowl, cover, and set in a warm place to rise until doubled, about 1 hour.

Grease two 9 × 5-inch loaf pans. Punch down the dough and knead it again for about 1 minute. Divide the dough in half and shape it into two loaves. Place the loaves into the prepared pans, cover, and let rise until the dough just barely reaches the edge of the pan, about 30 minutes.

Preheat the oven to 350°F. Bake the bread until it is browned and crusty, about 35 minutes. Cool the bread on wire racks.

Braided Egg Bread

Prep: 30 minutes **Yield:** Two braided loaves
Rise: 1 hour 45 minutes **Level:** Intermediate
Bake: 40 minutes

If you're looking to try just one bread recipe, this should be the one. For a shiny loaf, beat an egg with a little water and brush it over top of the loaves just before they go into the oven.

2^1/$_2$ cups warm water (no hotter than 115°F)

1 package active dry yeast or 1 scant tablespoon

^{1}/$_2$ cup honey or sugar

4 tablespoons butter, melted

2 eggs

1 tablespoon salt

7 to 8 cups all-purpose flour

Place the water in a large bowl and sprinkle in the yeast. Whisk to dissolve. Whisk in the honey, butter, eggs, and salt. Slowly add the 7 cups flour, stirring with the whisk until it gets too thick, then just use your hands, until a kneadable dough is formed. Transfer the dough to a lightly floured surface and knead until the dough is smooth and elastic and you can work with it without it sticking to your hands (add flour when necessary), about 10 minutes.

Place the dough in a buttered bowl, cover, and let it rise in a warm place until it has doubled in bulk, about 1 hour and 15 minutes.

Punch down the dough and knead it for 1 minute more on a lightly floured surface. Divide the dough in half, then divide each half into three equal pieces. Let the dough rest about 5 minutes.

Roll the pieces out into logs about 1^1/$_2$ inches thick and 12 inches long.

Braid three of the logs together and repeat with the remaining three logs, so you have two braids. Tuck the ends under and set the braids on a greased baking sheet. Let rise another 30 to 40 minutes.

Bake the bread about 40 minutes. When you thump it, it should sound hollow. Cool the loaves on wire racks. Let them cool at least 30 minutes before serving.

Kitchen Utensil

If you don't want to braid the bread, when you divide the loaves in half, shape the two pieces into loaves and place them in greased 9 × 5-inch loaf pans. Cover and let rise until the dough just reaches the edge of the pan, about 30 minutes. Bake as directed.

Honey-Oatmeal Bread

Prep: 45 minutes   **Yield:** Two loaves

Rise: 1 hour 30 minutes   **Level:** Intermediate

Bake: 35 minutes

When I worked as a cook during the summers and we served oatmeal for breakfast, we always had a lot left over. To avoid being wasteful we would incorporate it into the bread we made. So, whether you have some leftover oatmeal or want to make some from scratch, be sure to give this bread a try. If you are using leftover oatmeal, use 3 cups instead of making it from scratch.

2 cups simmering water	$^1/_2$ cup warm water (no hotter than 115°F)
1 cup quick-cooking oatmeal (not instant)	$^3/_4$ cup honey or maple syrup
2 tablespoons butter	5 to 7 cups all-purpose flour
1 package active dry yeast or 1 scant tablespoon	2 teaspoons salt

In a medium-size bowl, combine the simmering water, oatmeal, and butter and let stand until it is cool to touch, about 30 minutes.

In a small bowl, combine the yeast, warm water, and honey. Stir to dissolve and let stand about 5 minutes (the water should be foamy).

Measure 5 cups of flour and the salt into a mixing bowl. Add the oatmeal and yeast mixture and stir, adding more flour if necessary, until the mixture forms a kneadable dough.

Knead the dough on a lightly floured surface, adding more flour if the dough gets sticky, until the dough is smooth and elastic and springs back when you touch it, about 10 minutes.

Place the dough in a buttered bowl, cover, and set it in a warm place to rise until doubled, about 1 hour.

Grease two 9 × 5-inch loaf pans. Punch down the dough and knead it again for about 1 minute on a lightly floured surface. Divide the dough in half and shape into two loaves. Place them into the prepared pans, cover, and let rise until the dough just barely reaches the top edge of the pan, about 30 minutes.

Preheat the oven to 375°F. Bake the bread until it is browned and crusty, about 35 minutes. Cool the bread on wire racks.

Jeff's Potato Bread

Prep: 35 minutes

Rise: 1 hour 30 minutes

Bake: 35 minutes

Yield: Two loaves

Level: Intermediate

This bread is wonderful. You can easily shape the dough into large knotted rolls and serve them as hamburger buns.

1 package active dry yeast or 1 scant tablespoon

$^1/_2$ cup lukewarm water (no hotter than 115°F)

$^1/_2$ cup plus 1 teaspoon sugar

1 cup milk, warmed

1 cup warm mashed potatoes (instant is okay)

$^1/_2$ cup shortening, melted and cooled

2 large eggs

2 teaspoon salt

6 to $7^1/_2$ cups all-purpose flour

Dissolve the yeast in the warm water with 1 teaspoon sugar and let stand about 10 minutes.

Meanwhile, in a large mixing bowl, combine the warm milk with the mashed potatoes and shortening. Beat the eggs and add to the potato mixture. Add the yeast mixture and stir to combine. Add the $^1/_2$ cup sugar and the salt to the mixture. Mix in enough flour to make a kneadable dough. Knead the dough on a lightly floured surface until it's smooth and elastic, adding additional flour if the dough gets sticky, about 10 minutes.

Place the dough in a buttered bowl, cover, and set it in a warm place to rise until doubled, about 1 hour.

Grease two 9 × 5-inch loaf pans. Punch down the dough and knead it again for about 1 minute on a lightly floured surface. Divide the dough in half and shape into two loaves. Place the loaves into the prepared pans, cover, and let rise until the dough just barely reaches the edge of the pan, about 30 minutes.

Preheat the oven to 350°F. Bake the bread until it is browned and crusty, about 35 minutes. Remove the loaves from the pan and cool the bread on wire racks.

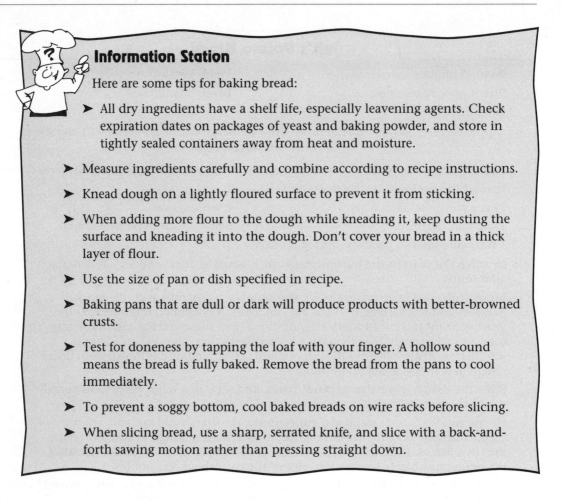

Information Station

Here are some tips for baking bread:

➤ All dry ingredients have a shelf life, especially leavening agents. Check expiration dates on packages of yeast and baking powder, and store in tightly sealed containers away from heat and moisture.

➤ Measure ingredients carefully and combine according to recipe instructions.

➤ Knead dough on a lightly floured surface to prevent it from sticking.

➤ When adding more flour to the dough while kneading it, keep dusting the surface and kneading it into the dough. Don't cover your bread in a thick layer of flour.

➤ Use the size of pan or dish specified in recipe.

➤ Baking pans that are dull or dark will produce products with better-browned crusts.

➤ Test for doneness by tapping the loaf with your finger. A hollow sound means the bread is fully baked. Remove the bread from the pans to cool immediately.

➤ To prevent a soggy bottom, cool baked breads on wire racks before slicing.

➤ When slicing bread, use a sharp, serrated knife, and slice with a back-and-forth sawing motion rather than pressing straight down.

Crescent Rolls

Prep: 30 minutes
Rise: 1 hour 40 minutes
Bake: 12 minutes

Yield: 36 to 48 crescents
Level: Challenging

These rolls are great to make for a party because they look fancy. If you have children, they will love to help you roll the crescents into their shape.

1 package active dry yeast or 1 scant tablespoon
$^1/_4$ cup lukewarm water (no hotter than 115°F)
1 cup milk
$^1/_2$ cup sugar
1 teaspoon salt

$^1/_4$ cup ($^1/_2$ stick) cold butter, cut into 4 pieces
5 to 6 cups all-purpose flour
2 large eggs
Melted butter, for brushing the tops

In a small bowl, dissolve the yeast in warm water with a pinch of sugar. Set aside for 5 to 10 minutes to proof (the surface will become a little foamy).

While the yeast is proofing, warm the milk (do not boil) in a 2-quart saucepan. Remove the pan from the heat and stir in the sugar, salt, and butter. Cool the mixture to lukewarm, about 7 minutes. Add about 1$^1/_2$ cups of the flour to the milk to make a thick batter. Mix well. Add the proofed yeast and eggs to the thick mixture and stir well to combine. Add enough of the remaining flour to make a kneadable dough.

Turn the dough out onto a lightly floured surface or floured pastry cloth; knead until smooth and satiny, about 10 minutes. Place the dough in a buttered bowl, cover, and let it rise in a warm place until doubled in size, about 1 hour.

When the dough has finished rising, punch it down and knead it for about 1 minute more on a lightly floured surface. Turn it out on a lightly floured board. Divide the dough into three equal pieces. Let the dough rest about 10 minutes (this makes it easier to roll the dough out). Roll each piece into a 12-inch circle, about $^1/_4$-inch thick. If you find the dough is shrinking and won't hold the shape you roll it into, just let the dough rest 5 minutes more. Brush the dough lightly with melted butter. Cut into 12 to 16 pie-shaped wedges. Roll up tightly, beginning at wide end. Seal points firmly by pressing them lightly into the bottom. Place the crescents on greased baking sheets, with points underneath, about 2 inches apart. Curve to form a crescent shape; cover. Let rise in a warm place until doubled in bulk, about 30 minutes. Brush lightly with melted butter.

While the rolls are rising, preheat the oven to 400°F. Bake the rolls about 12 minutes. Serve hot.

Fluffy Dinner Rolls

Prep: 30 minutes   **Yield:** About 24 rolls
Rise: 1 hour 30 minutes   **Level:** Intermediate
Bake: 35 to 40 minutes

These are really nice rolls to make. Brush their tops with melted butter before baking them for a very tender crust.

6 to 7 cups all-purpose flour

6 tablespoons sugar

$1^1/_4$ teaspoon salt

2 packages active dry yeast or 2 scant tablespoons

$2^1/_4$ cups warm water (no hotter than 110°F)

3 tablespoons vegetable oil

In a large mixing bowl, combine 6 cups of the flour, 5 tablespoons of the sugar, and the salt.

In a medium-size mixing bowl, dissolve the yeast and the remaining 1 tablespoon sugar in the warm water. Let stand about 5 minutes, until the top gets a bit foamy. Stir in the vegetable oil.

Slowly add the water mixture to the flour mixture and mix until it is thoroughly incorporated. Remove the dough from the bowl and knead on a lightly floured surface, adding the remaining cup as needed if the dough gets sticky, until the dough is smooth and satiny and springs back when you touch it, about 10 minutes.

Place the dough in a large buttered bowl. Cover and let rise in a warm place until the dough has doubled in bulk, about 1 hour.

Punch down the dough and knead it for 1 more minute on a lightly floured surface. Divide the dough into 24 pieces and roll them into balls. Place the balls in a greased 13 × 9-inch baking pan. They can touch each other in the pan and fit snugly against the sides. Cover and let rise until doubled in bulk, about 30 minutes.

Preheat the oven to 350°F. Bake the rolls about 30 minutes, until golden brown and fluffy.

Kitchen Utensil

If you have a stand mixer with a dough hook attachment, by all means use it for this recipe. Mix the dough until it comes off of the side of the bowl. Sprinkle in about 1 cup more of the flour while the dough mixes. Then remove the dough from the bowl and finish kneading by hand on a lightly floured surface.

No-Fail Rolls

Prep: 20 minutes   **Yield:** 24 to 36 rolls

Rise: 1 hour 20 minutes   **Level:** Easy to Intermediate

Bake: 10 minutes

These are very sturdy rolls. They are easy to put together and hard to mess up. If you are looking for a delicious roll recipe but feel intimidated by yeast breads, try these.

1 package dry yeast or 1 scant tablespoon   1 teaspoon salt

1 cup warm water (no hotter than 115°F) $^1/_3$ cup vegetable oil or melted shortening

2 large eggs, lightly beaten $3^1/_2$ to 4 cups all-purpose flour

$^1/_3$ cup sugar

In a large bowl, dissolve the yeast in the warm water. Mix in the eggs, sugar, salt, and oil. Mix in the flour, 1 cup at a time, and stir well until a kneadable dough is formed. Knead the dough on a lightly floured surface, about 10 minutes, until smooth and elastic. Place the dough in a buttered bowl, cover, and let it rise until doubled in size, about 1 hour. Punch the center to let the air out. Form the dough into 24 to 36 rolls by pinching off pieces of dough about the size of a walnut and rolling them on a lightly floured surface. Place them about 2 inches apart on ungreased baking sheets. Cover and let rise until doubled in size, about 20 minutes.

While the rolls are rising, preheat the oven to 400°F.

Bake the rolls until golden brown, about 10 to 15 minutes. Serve warm.

Molly's Sweet Cardamom Rolls

Prep: 45 minutes   **Yield:** 36 rolls
Rise: 2 hours   **Level:** Challenging
Bake: 10 minutes

Cardamom gives this bread such a wonderful taste. This recipe was inspired by the cardamom bread my great-aunt Molly used to make.

2 packages active dry yeast or 2 scant tablespoons

$^1/_4$ cup warm water (no hotter than 115°F)

2 cups granulated sugar

2 cups milk, slightly warmed

$^1/_2$ cup instant potato flakes

5 large eggs, slightly beaten

1 teaspoon salt

1 teaspoon ground cardamom

9 to 10 cups all-purpose flour

1 cup (2 sticks) butter, melted and cooled

$^1/_2$ cup brown sugar, lightly packed

1 tablespoon ground cinnamon

$^1/_4$ teaspoon ground cardamom

Additional melted butter or beaten egg, if desired

In a small mixing bowl, dissolve the yeast in the water with $^1/_4$ cup of the sugar. Let it stand 8 minutes until it's a little foamy. Add the yeast mixture to the warm milk in a large warm bowl. Add the potato flakes, the remaining sugar, eggs, salt, and 1 teaspoon cardamom. Add 5 cups of the flour into the mixture (the dough will be very loose) and mix well. Cover the bowl and let stand in a warm place until doubled, 30 to 45 minutes.

Knead in the remaining flour, 1 cup at a time, and $^1/_2$ cup of the butter.

Knead the dough on a lightly floured surface until it's smooth and elastic, about 10 minutes. Place the dough in a buttered bowl and let rise until doubled in size again, about 1 hour.

Sprinkle a bread board lightly with flour. Preheat the oven to 350°F. Grease a baking sheet.

Mix the brown sugar, cinnamon, and cardamom in a small bowl. Divide the dough into three pieces. Roll the dough $^1/_4$-inch thick. Brush with melted butter; sprinkle with about $2^1/_2$ tablespoons of the brown sugar mixture. Fold dough over; cut into a dozen l-inch strips. Take one end of a strip in each hand and twist the ends in opposite directions. Then take the twisted strip and spiral it around so it looks like a round sticky bun. Repeat with the remaining pieces of dough. Let them rise until doubled, about 20 minutes. Brush the tops of the rolls with any remaining melted butter or beaten egg. Sprinkle with any additional sugar before baking. Bake 10 to 20 minutes until golden brown. Serve warm.

Sesame Seed Rolls

Prep: 30 minutes   **Yield:** 48 rolls
Bake: 20 minutes   **Level:** Challenging
Rise: 1 to 2 hours

You can also top these rolls with poppyseeds, or make an assortment.

1 package active dry yeast or 1 scant tablespoon

1 cup warm water (no hotter than 115°F)

1 cup milk, warm

$5^1/_2$ to $6^1/_2$ cups all-purpose flour

1 tablespoon salt

$^1/_4$ teaspoon ground ginger

2 large eggs, lightly beaten

$^1/_3$ cup sugar

$^1/_3$ cup shortening, at room temperature

Melted butter or beaten egg for brushing

Sesame seeds, for garnish

In a large mixing bowl, dissolve the yeast in the water and warm milk. Let stand 5 minutes. Stir 3 cups of the flour, salt, and ginger into the yeast mixture. Beat well; let stand covered for 20 minutes (it will be foamy). Add the 2 beaten eggs, sugar, shortening, and 5 cups of flour, mixing to make a kneadable dough (the dough will be somewhat soft). Knead the dough on a lightly floured surface, adding a bit more flour if the dough becomes sticky, until it's smooth and elastic, about 10 minutes. Place the dough in a large buttered bowl, cover, and let it rise in a warm place, about 1 hour.

Punch the dough down, turn it out onto a floured board, and knead 1 minute. Put it back into the bowl, cover, and let it rise a second time, about 40 minutes. Punch the dough down again, turn it out onto the floured board and knead again, about 1 minute.

Preheat the oven to 350°F. Grease 2 baking sheets.

Pinch off pieces of dough slightly larger than a walnut. Roll the dough out into a rope, 6 or 7 inches long, and tie it into a loose knot; place them on the prepared baking sheets, about 2 inches apart. Brush the tops of the rolls with melted butter or beaten egg. Sprinkle with the sesame seeds. Cover and let rise until doubled, about 20 minutes. Bake 20 minutes. Serve warm.

Chapter 27

Crisps, Cobblers, Puddings, and Other Delights

One great thing about crisps, cobblers, and other fruity desserts is that they can be thrown together in just a few minutes and they are always a hit. Or if you're in the mood for something creamy and comforting, try a custard or pudding. All the recipes in this chapter are easy, so give them a try!

Apple Crisp

Prep: 10 minutes

Bake: 40 minutes

Yield: 6 servings

Level: Easy

This recipe can be made with fresh apples (try a mix-and-match variety) or with just about any kind of pie filling you like: apple, peach, blueberry, or cherry. Try topping this dish with whipped cream or vanilla ice cream.

4 medium apples (Golden Delicious, Granny Smith, McIntosh, or a mixture) or 1 can (21 ounces) apple pie filling

$1/3$ cup packed light brown sugar

$3/4$ cup all-purpose flour

6 tablespoons cold butter, cut into 6 pieces

$1/4$ teaspoon ground cinnamon

$1/8$ teaspoon ground nutmeg

Pinch of salt

Preheat the oven to 350°F.

Peel and slice the apples (you should have about 4 cups) and arrange them in the bottom of an 8-inch square baking dish, or pour the pie filling into the baking dish.

In a small bowl or the bowl of a food processor, mix together the remaining ingredients with a fork or pulse it a few times until it is crumbly (do not overprocess). Sprinkle the crumbly top over the pie filling. Bake until top is lightly browned, 40 to 45 minutes. Serve warm.

Blueberry Crunch

Prep: 15 minutes

Bake: 30 minutes

Yield: 4 to 6 servings

Level: Easy

The oats and nuts make this topping crunchy. It's great served warm and topped with either whipped cream or ice cream.

3 cups fresh blueberries, rinsed, or 1 package (16 ounces) frozen (not packed in syrup)

2 tablespoons lemon juice

$^2/_3$ cup lightly packed brown sugar

$^1/_2$ cup all-purpose flour

$^1/_2$ cup rolled oats (not instant)

$^1/_3$ cup butter, cut into 6 pieces and softened

$^1/_4$ cup chopped walnuts or pecans

1 teaspoon ground cinnamon

$^1/_2$ teaspoon almond or vanilla extract

$^1/_4$ teaspoon salt

Preheat the oven to 375°F.

Toss the berries with the lemon juice. Pour the blueberries in the bottom of an 8-inch square baking pan.

In a small bowl or in the bowl of a food processor, combine the remaining ingredients and mix just to combine or pulse 5 times in the food processor. Sprinkle the mixture over the blueberries.

Bake until topping is light brown and the blueberries are bubbly, about 30 minutes. Serve warm.

Delicious Baked Apples

Prep: 20 minutes

Bake: 45 minutes

Yield: 4 servings

Level: Easy

These are a great treat to make in the fall when apples are in season and the evenings are getting cooler and you want a hot, satisfying dessert. Look around your local farmers' market for local apple varieties to try out in this recipe.

4 baking apples (McIntosh, Rome Beauty, Golden Delicious, or Granny Smith)

Half of a lemon

$^1/_2$ cup raisins

2 tablespoons honey

$^3/_4$ cup chopped walnuts or pecans

$^1/_2$ cup butterscotch topping

Preheat the oven to 325°F.

Core the apples (do not cut them in half) using an apple corer. Remove the peel from the upper $^1/_3$ of the apple. Rub the peeled part of the apple with the lemon and squeeze a few drops of lemon juice inside each cut apple. In a small bowl, combine the raisins, honey, and 4 tablespoons of the chopped nuts. Stuff each apple with the raisin mixture. Place the apples in a 9-inch-square baking dish. Pour a little bit of water in the bottom of the pan, about $^1/_4$-inch deep.

Bake, uncovered, until the apples are tender (between 45 to 60 minutes, depending on the size of the apples). Let the apples cool for about 10 minutes before serving. Place each apple on a serving plate. Drizzle each apple with some of the juices in the pan, the butterscotch topping, and the remaining nuts.

Peach Cobbler

Prep: 20 minutes

Bake: 30 minutes

Yield: 4 to 6 servings

Level: Easy

A cobbler gets its name from the appearance of the cobbled dough on the top. This is best the day it's made, and it never hurts to have a touch of whipped cream or a bit of peach ice cream on top. Look for freestone peaches in the market. They will separate from the peach pit without any trouble. Clingstone peaches tend to stubbornly hold onto the pit.

For the filling:

1 tablespoon cornstarch

1 tablespoon lemon juice

4 cups sliced, peeled fresh peaches

1 cup sugar

2 tablespoons cold butter, cut into small pieces

$^1/_2$ teaspoon ground nutmeg

$^1/_4$ teaspoon salt

For the topping:

3 tablespoons butter, cut into 3 pieces

1 cup all-purpose flour

1 tablespoon sugar

$1^1/_2$ teaspoons baking powder

$^1/_2$ teaspoon ground cinnamon

$^1/_4$ teaspoon salt

$^1/_3$ cup buttermilk

Preheat the oven to 400°F.

Prepare the filling: Dissolve the cornstarch in the lemon juice then toss all of the filling ingredients together and place in the bottom of a 8-inch-square baking pan.

Prepare the topping: In a mixing bowl or food processor, cut the butter into the flour, sugar, baking powder, cinnamon, and salt (or pulse several times) until the mixture resembles coarse crumbs. Stir in the buttermilk (do not use the food processor for this step.) Transfer the flour mixture into a bowl and proceed. Drop the dough onto the filling by the tablespoonful onto the peaches. (You can leave a little space between the drops, it will spread as it bakes.)

Bake until the top is golden brown and the fruit begins to bubble, 30 minutes. Serve warm.

Kitchen Utensil

To peel peaches, make a small, light X (don't cut through the flesh, only the skin) on the bottom of each peach. Dunk the peach in boiling water for 30 seconds. Remove the peach with a slotted spoon and plunge into ice water. The skin should slip off easily. If some is still resisting, return the peach to the water for 15 more seconds and try again.

Pumpkin Custard

Prep: 15 minutes

Bake: 45 minutes

Yield: 8 servings

Level: Easy

Custard is baked in a water bath. Just fill the baking pan about $1/3$ full of hot water, then add the filled custard cups. The water should come halfway up the sides of the cups. You can also cover the custard cups with aluminum foil to prevent water from sloshing as you carry them to and from the oven, but keep them uncovered while they bake. Top these little beauties with some whipped cream before serving.

1 can (16 ounces) pumpkin purée (not the pie filling)

$1^1/_2$ teaspoons salt

$1^1/_3$ cup evaporated milk

2 large eggs

$2/_3$ cup sugar

2 tablespoons butter, melted

1 teaspoon ground cinnamon

$1/_4$ teaspoon ground ginger

$1/_4$ teaspoon ground nutmeg

$1/_4$ teaspoon ground cloves

Preheat the oven to 350°F.

In a mixing bowl, combine all the ingredients and mix well with a wire whisk to blend thoroughly. Divide the mixture into 8 custard cups or small ramekins. Pour very hot water around the cups to the depth of 1/2 inch. Place the cups in a baking pan to fit. The water should come about half way up the sides of the custard cups; add more water, if necessary.

Bake 45 minutes, or until a knife inserted into the center comes out clean. Cool the custard in the water bath; remove the cups from the water bath when they are cool enough to handle. To serve, invert the custard cups onto a serving plate, loosen and remove the cups.

Kitchen Utensil

If you have a turkey baster, use it to adjust the water level of the water bath. You can add or subtract just the right amount of hot water without burning yourself or spilling any water into the custard cups.

Rich Chocolate Pudding

Prep: 20 minutes   **Yield:** 4 to 6 servings

Bake: 20 minutes   **Level:** Easy

There's nothing like delicious homemade pudding. If you don't have custard cups, you can use any ovenproof material, such as ceramic mugs or small Pyrex bowls. Don't overbake the pudding or it might burn. If you want to make butterscotch pudding, substitute 3/4 cup butterscotch chips for the chocolate.

4 ounces semisweet chocolate or 3/4 cup chocolate chips   2 large eggs

1 cup heavy (whipping) cream   1 tablespoon vanilla extract

3 tablespoons sugar   Boiling water

Preheat the oven to 350°F.

Chop the chocolate into small bits (if using the squares) and melt the chocolate and cream together, stirring often, in the top part of a double boiler placed over simmering water. Once the chocolate has melted, stir in the sugar. Set aside to cool, about 7 minutes.

Beat the eggs and vanilla together. Slowly add the chocolate to the egg mixture, stirring constantly. Carefully pour the chocolate mixture into 4 or 6 small custard cups. Cover each cup with foil. Set the custard cups in a large baking pan and carefully pour the boiling water into the baking pan until the water comes halfway up the side of the cups.

Bake about 20 minutes or until set. Remove from the oven and let cool in the water bath until they are cool enough to handle; remove the puddings from the water bath and serve or refrigerate them until serving.

Kitchen Utensil

If you are afraid to pour the boiling water into the pan, use a ladle to carefully transfer the water from the pot to the baking pan. Don't pour the water on top of the custard cups.

Chapter 28

The Savory Way

Here's a collection of tasty lunch or suppertime dishes that are guaranteed to please. From easy casseroles to the more challenging cheese soufflé, this section has something for everyone.

Cheese Soufflé

Prep: 20 minutes

Bake: 45 minutes to 1 hour

3 tablespoons butter

3 tablespoons all-purpose flour

1 cup milk, at room temperature

5 large eggs, separated

Yield: 3 to 4 servings

Level: Challenging

$^3/_4$ cup grated Swiss cheese, lightly packed

1 teaspoon plus a pinch of salt

$^1/_2$ tablespoon black pepper

$^1/_2$ teaspoon ground nutmeg

Preheat the oven to 350°F. Grease a 2-quart soufflé dish.

In a 2-quart saucepan, melt the butter over medium heat. When the butter has melted, whisk in the flour to absorb the butter. Continue whisking for 1 minute (this will cook out any flour taste). Slowly add the milk in a thin stream, whisking constantly. If the mixture gets lumpy, remove from the heat and keep whisking until smooth and the milk begins to thicken, about 2 minutes. Remove the pan from the heat. Stir in the egg yolks, cheese, 1 teaspoon of the salt, the pepper, and the nutmeg to blend well. Set aside.

In a large bowl, beat the egg whites with the pinch of salt until they hold stiff peaks. Transfer about $^1/_4$ of the egg whites to the cheese mixture and stir it in to lighten up the mixture. Fold the remaining egg whites into the cheese mixture (don't stir or you will deflate the whites) and transfer the mixture to the prepared soufflé dish.

Bake 45 minutes to 1 hour, until the soufflé has risen and a thin straw inserted into the center of the soufflé comes out clean. Serve immediately; the soufflé will deflate soon after it leaves the oven.

Chicken Pot Pie

Prep: 25 minutes   **Yield:** 4 to 6 servings

Bake: 45 minutes   **Level:** Intermediate

Pot pies seem to be back in fashion with the revolution of "comfort foods." This is very easy to make with prepared puff pastry and only using a top crust. If you want it even easier, you can use a 10-ounce package of frozen vegetables instead of the carrots, peas, and corn.

$^1/_2$ cup (1 stick) butter

$^1/_2$ cup all-purpose flour

$1^1/_2$ cups buttermilk

2 cups chicken broth

1 tablespoon olive oil

1 medium onion, diced

1 clove garlic, crushed

3 carrots, peeled and sliced on the diagonal

2 ribs celery, diced

1 small potato, peeled and chopped

2 cups cooked chicken, shredded

$^1/_2$ cup frozen peas

$^1/_2$ cup frozen corn

1 teaspoon chopped fresh rosemary

1 teaspoon black pepper

1 teaspoon salt

$^1/_2$ package ($17^1/_4$ ounce) frozen puff pastry (1 sheet), thawed

Preheat the oven to 375°F.

In a large saucepan, melt the butter over medium heat. Stir in the flour with a whisk and continue whisking for one minute. Turn off the heat. Slowly pour in the buttermilk, then the chicken broth, whisking constantly, until smooth. Cook over medium heat, whisking occasionally (more often as it begins to thicken), until the mixture begins to thicken, about 5 minutes.

While the sauce is thickening, heat the oil in a large skillet over medium heat. Add the onion, garlic, carrots, celery, and potato. Cook, stirring often, until onions are just tender, about 5 minutes (the carrots and potato will still be firm).

In a $2^1/_2$-quart casserole, combine the chicken, peas, corn, rosemary, pepper, and salt with the contents of the skillet. Stir to combine. Pour the thickened sauce over the chicken mixture and stir to combine. Unwrap the puff pastry and roll it out and cut it to fit the casserole, leaving a 1-inch overhang. Cover the casserole top with the puff pastry (the overhang will anchor the top in place). Cut several slits in the top of the pastry for vents. Bake 45 minutes to 1 hour, until pastry is brown and the pot pie is bubbly. Let the pot pie rest 10 minutes before serving.

Potato-Beef Pot Pie

Prep: 30 minutes   **Yield:** 8 servings

Bake: 1 hour 30 minutes   **Level:** Easy

This is like a tender beef stew that you bake. Instead of a pastry crust, this pot pie is topped with slices of potatoes. Slow cooking is the secret to its tenderness.

$1/4$ cup vegetable oil

$1^1/2$ pounds chuck steak, cut into $1/2$-inch pieces

1 medium onion, chopped

$1/2$ cup chopped celery

2 medium carrots, sliced $1/4$-inch thick

1 cup red wine

2 cups beef broth or water

3 tablespoons cornstarch

3 tablespoons cold water

$1/2$ cup frozen peas

$1/2$ cup frozen corn

$1/2$ cup frozen green beans

1 teaspoon black pepper

1 teaspoon salt

2 large baking potatoes, peeled and sliced thick ($1/2$ inch)

Preheat the oven to 300°F.

Heat the oil in a large ovenproof Dutch oven over medium-high heat. Add the steak in batches (do not crowd the pan) and brown the beef, about 1 minute per batch. Transfer the beef to a bowl. Repeat with the remaining beef.

Using the same pot, reduce the heat to medium and cook the onion, celery, and carrots until just tender, 7 minutes. Add the wine and beef broth. Dissolve the cornstarch in the cold water. Slowly add the cornstarch mixture to the broth mixture and bring to a boil. Reduce the heat and stir until thickened, 4 to 5 minutes. Stir in the browned beef, with any accumulated juices and the remaining ingredients except the potatoes. Arrange the potato slices on top of the beef mixture. Cover and bake 45 minutes. Remove the cover and bake 45 minutes longer.

Kitchen Informant

Ovenproof means that the cookware can be used on top of the stove as well as in the oven. If you don't have an ovenproof Dutch oven, prepare the recipe as directed using a large saucepan or Dutch oven and transfer the contents into a $2^1/2$-quart casserole to bake.

Calzones

Prep: 25 minutes   **Yield:** 6 to 8 calzones

Bake: 20 minutes   **Level:** Intermediate

Calzones are like pizza pockets without the sauce. They're fun to make, especially since you can make them as you like them. Serve a flavorful spaghetti sauce alongside for dipping, if desired.

1 cup shredded mozzarella

$^1/_4$ cup grated Parmesan cheese

$^1/_4$ cup pesto

$1^1/_2$ cups ricotta (or a mix of cottage cheese and ricotta cheese)

1 clove garlic, diced

1 teaspoon black pepper

1 teaspoon salt

Make-Your-Own-Pizza Dough (see recipe that follows)

Preheat the oven to 425°F.

In a mixing bowl, combine all the ingredients except the pizza dough. Set aside.

Divide the pizza dough into 6 to 8 pieces. Roll each piece out on a lightly floured surface to about $^1/_4$-inch thick. Divide the filling evenly among the dough circles. Fold in half by stretching the dough across the top of the filling and pinch the edges closed to seal (they will be half-circles). Place the calzone on a baking sheet and bake 20 to 30 minutes, until golden brown. Let rest about 5 to 10 minutes before serving. The filling will be hot.

Try adding other fillings to the cheese mixture (you can omit the pesto, too). Use about 1 cup, total, of the filling of your choice:

Sautéed broccoli, mushrooms, garlic, and onions

Steamed spinach

Salami, cut into thin strips

Italian sausage, cooked

Cooked chicken, shredded

Make-Your-Own Pizza Dough

Prep: 50 minutes

Rise: 45 minutes

Bake: 15 minutes

Yield: One 16-inch pizza

Level: Intermediate

Everyone loves pizza. And what could be better than custom-making your own pizza? The dough is easy to put together. You just have to plan accordingly because it needs some time to rise.

1^1/$_2$ cup warm water (not over 115°F)

1 package active dry yeast

1 teaspoon honey

4 cups all-purpose flour

^{1}/$_2$ teaspoon salt

In a large bowl, combine the water, yeast, honey, and ^{1}/$_4$ cup of the flour. Stir to combine. Cover the bowl and let stand in a warm place 30 minutes or until foamy. Add the remaining flour and salt and knead for 10 minutes, adding small amounts of flour if sticky, until the dough is smooth and elastic. Transfer the dough to a large buttered bowl, cover, and let rise in a warm place until doubled in size, about 45 minutes.

Punch the dough down, knead it again for about 1 minute, then roll it out to fit a greased 16-inch pizza pan or a large baking sheet.

For the basic cheese pizza:

1 cup pizza or marinara sauce

2 cups shredded mozzarella cheese

^{1}/$_4$ cup grated Parmesan cheese

Preheat the oven to 400°F. Spread the sauce over the dough, leaving a ^{1}/$_4$-inch border. Sprinkle both cheeses on top. Bake until the cheese melts, about 15 minutes.

Try these add-ons (about 2 cups, total):

Sautéed mushrooms, bell peppers, onions, broccoli, zucchini, or eggplant

Black and green olives

Diced cooked ham

Feta cheese

Steamed spinach

Fresh tomato slices

Sun-dried tomatoes packed in oil

Marinated artichoke hearts

Pepperoni

Cooked ground beef

Gorgonzola cheese

Broccoli and Cheese Quiche
With Potato Crust

Prep: 25 minutes

Bake: 1 hour

Yield: 8 to 10 servings

Level: Intermediate

3 medium-size russet potatoes, peeled if desired, and cut into 1-inch cubes

2 tablespoons butter

1 large onion, chopped

2 cups chopped broccoli

1 cup shredded cheddar cheese, firmly packed

4 large eggs

$1/4$ cup sour cream

$1/4$ cup plain yogurt

$1/2$ cup milk or buttermilk

$1^1/2$ teaspoons salt

$1^1/2$ teaspoons pepper

Preheat the oven to 350°F. Grease a 9-inch pie plate.

Place the potatoes in a large saucepan and cover with water. Bring to a boil over medium-high heat and cook until tender, about 15 minutes. Drain the potatoes and set aside to cool.

While the potatoes are cooking, melt 1 tablespoon of the butter in a medium-size skillet over medium heat. Add the chopped onion and cook, stirring occasionally, until softened but not browned, 5 to 7 minutes. Remove half of the onions from the pan and set aside.

Add the broccoli to the remaining onions in the skillet, return to the heat and continue cooking over medium heat until the broccoli changes color to a bright green and is tender-crisp, 3 to 5 minutes (don't overcook the broccoli; it will cook in the oven).

When the potatoes are cool enough to handle, combine the remaining 1 tablespoon butter and the reserved onion and mash to combine (you don't have to make the mixture perfectly smooth). Press the potato mixture evenly into the bottom and sides of the prepared pie plate.

Pat the cheese on top of the potatoes. Sprinkle the broccoli and onions on top of the cheese.

In a mixing bowl, combine the eggs, sour cream, yogurt, milk, and salt and pepper and beat well. Pour on top of the broccoli. Place the pie plate on a baking sheet and transfer to the oven. Bake the quiche for 1 hour, or until the quiche is set and no longer moist or jiggly in the center. Let the quiche cool 10 minutes before serving.

Kitchen Utensil

You can fill a quiche with just about anything you like. Try cooked ham, sautéed mushrooms and red onions, shredded zucchini, bell peppers, cooked spinach, crumbled feta cheese, or blanched asparagus.

Index

When You're Smart Enough to Know
That You Don't Know It All

**For all the ups and downs you're sure to encounter in life,
The Complete Idiot's Guides give you down-to-earth answers
and practical solutions.**

You can handle it!

The Complete Idiot's Guide to Learning French on Your Own
ISBN: 0-02-861043-1 ▪ $16.95

The Complete Idiot's Guide to Dating
ISBN: 0-02-861052-0 ▪ $14.95

The Complete Idiot's Guide to Hiking and Camping
ISBN: 0-02-861100-4 ▪ $16.95

The Complete Idiot's Guide to Cooking Basics, 2E
ISBN: 0-02-861974-9 ▪ $16.95
Available November 1997!

The Complete Idiot's Guide to Learning Spanish on Your Own
ISBN: 0-02-861040-7 ▪ $16.95

The Complete Idiot's Guide to Gambling Like a Pro
ISBN: 0-02-861102-0 ▪ $16.95

The Complete Idiot's Guide to Choosing, Training, and Raising a Dog
ISBN: 0-02-861098-9 ▪ $16.95

Y o u   c a n   h a n d l e   i t !

The Complete Idiot's Guide to Trouble-Free Car Care
ISBN: 0-02-861041-5 ▪ $16.95

The Complete Idiot's Guide to the Perfect Wedding, 2E
ISBN: 0-02-861963-3 ▪ $17.99

The Complete Idiot's Guide to Trouble-Free Home Repair
ISBN: 0-02-861042-3 ▪ $16.95

The Complete Idiot's Guide to Getting into College
ISBN: 1-56761-508-2 ▪ $14.95

The Complete Idiot's Guide to the Perfect Vacation
ISBN: 1-56761-531-7 ▪ $14.99

The Complete Idiot's Guide to First Aid Basics
ISBN: 0-02-861099-7 ▪ $16.95

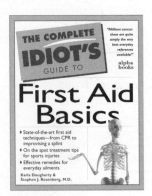